Shade Gardening

Created and designed by
the editorial staff of
ORTHO BOOKS

Editor
Jennifer Bennett

Writer
A. Cort Sinnes

Designer
Gary Hespenheide

Ortho Books

Publisher
Robert B. Loperena

Editorial Director
Christine Jordan

Manufacturing Director
Ernie S. Tasaki

Managing Editor
Sally W. Smith

Editors
Robert J. Beckstrom
Michael D. Smith

Prepress Supervisor
Linda M. Bouchard

Sales & Marketing Manager
David C. Jose

Graphics Coordinator
Sally J. French

Publisher's Assistant
Joni Christiansen

Acknowledgments

Editorial Coordinator
Cass Dempsey

Illustrator
Ron Hildebrand

Copyeditor
Barbara Feller-Roth

Proofreader
David Sweet

Indexer
Elinor Lindheimer

Special Thanks to
Deborah Cowder
David Van Ness

Color Separations by
Color Tech. Corp.

Printed in the USA by
Banta Book Group

ORTHENE® is a registered trademark of Monsanto Company.

Photographers
Names of photographers are followed by the page numbers on which their work appears.
R = right, C = center, L = left, T = top, B = bottom.

William Aplin: 65L, 78L, 91R
Liz Ball: Photo/Nats: 73L
Laurie A. Black: 7B, 17, 18, 22B, back cover TL and BR
Gay Bumgarner: Photo/Nats: 73R
Kristie L. Callan: 6L, 7T, 32R
Josephine Coatsworth: 42R, 55R, 68L, 72R, 88L
R. Todd Davis: 50L, 66L, 72L, 92L
Alan and Linda Detrick: 62L, 65R
Derek Fell: 40L, 41R, 47L, 48R, 54L, 54R, 57L, 59L, 60L, 62R, 63L, 66R, 67L, 67R, 68R, 69L, 71L, 74R, 75R, 77R, 78R, 79R, 86R, 87L, 87R, 88R
Pamela Harper: 64R, 76R
Margaret Hensel/Positive Images: 27B, 31T
Saxon Holt: 16, 83R, 84L, 84R, 85L
Jerry Howard/Positive Images: 24
Susan Lammers: 81L, 81R
Michael Landis: 46R, 50R, 51R, 52L, 60R, 77L, 86L
Janet Loughrey/American Landscapes: 41L, 74L, 82L, 82R
Michael McKinley: 1, 3T, 3CB, 3B, 4–5, 8T, 8B, 14, 15T, 19, 20, 25, 27T, 28–29, 30, 31B, 36, 38–39, 40R, 42L, 43L, 44L, 44R, 45L, 45R, 48L, 49R, 52R, 53R, 55L, 56L, 56R, 57R, 58L, 59R, 61L, 63R, 69R, 70R, 75L, 79L, 80L, 80R, 83L, 89L, 89R, 90L, 90R, 91L, back cover TR and BL
J. Paul Moore: Photo/Nats: 64L
Jack Napton: 46L, 71R, 92R
Ortho Photo Library: front cover, 37T, 43R, 47R, 49L, 58L, 61R
Pam Peirce: 53L, 76L
Ben Phillips: Photo/Nats: 51L, 85R
Charles C. Powell: 32L
Tom Tracy: 3CT, 12–13, 22T
Virginia Twinam-Smith: Photo/Nats: 70L
Wolf von dem Bussche: 15B

Front Cover
This garden path wanders through a burst of color despite its shady location. With the proper plant selection, this scene is easy to recreate.

Title Page
In dense shade, gravel can be a real problem solver. Plantings include Japanese maple, mahonia, liriope, and aucuba.

Back Cover
This book shows you how to plan and install many different garden styles in the shade, including woodland, oriental, formal, and intimate.

Address all inquiries to
Ortho Books
Box 5006
San Ramon, CA 94583-0906

1 2 3 4 5 6 7 8 9
96 97 98 99 2000 01

ISBN 0-89721-288-6
Library of Congress Catalog Card
Number 95-74576

THE SOLARIS GROUP

2527 Camino Ramon
San Ramon, CA 94583-0906

Shade Gardening

Many Shades of Success

A shady spot in the garden can be a challenge and an asset. By learning the special needs of shade-loving plants, you can create a cool, attractive, refreshing haven to enjoy on a summer day.

The cooling effect of a shade garden in midsummer is one of life's refreshing pleasures. Dappled sunlight and shadow act as magnets, drawing those nearby to stop and rest for a moment. Shade in the yard need not be a deterrent to gardening. By considering shade an asset, rather than a problem to overcome, you can create a pleasing, attractive outdoor environment.

To help you garden most effectively in the shade, this book assesses all the aspects of growing plants in low light. It suggests ways to capitalize on the best aspects and minimize the problems. Here is all the information you need, whether gardening in open shade with dappled sunlight under tall trees or in an area of dense shade created by walls and overhangs. You'll learn how to identify the types of shade in your garden, as well as shade plants' basic needs and how to meet them.

The photographs and detailed care information in the "Plant Selection Guide" (beginning on page 39) introduce you to the long and varied list of shade plants, including shrubs, trees, ground covers, and annual and perennial flowers. As you will see, gardening in the shade can be as interesting and rewarding as it is in the sun.

Shade is the magic ingredient that lends this woodland scene its special charm.

HOW PLANTS USE LIGHT

Even a cursory understanding of how a plant works can greatly increase your competence as a gardener—especially when it comes to gardening in the shade.

Plants use the energy from sunlight to produce the food they need in order to grow. In this sense, all plants need some light to survive. But don't confuse *light* with *direct sunlight;* many plants can exist on relatively small amounts of reflected light.

As light falls on a plant's leaves, the chlorophyll (green pigment) inside the leaf uses the energy contained in the light to convert water and carbon dioxide into oxygen and sugar, which, in turn, power the plant's growth process. The plant receives most of its water from beneath the surface of the soil; the carbon dioxide is taken from the air surrounding the plant and is then processed through the pores of the leaves. This miraculous process is known as photosynthesis, which to this day is not completely understood. The accompanying illustration shows how this complex system works.

Knowing the amount of sun or shade required by a plant is a key element in growing it successfully. Even when you narrow your selection of plants to those that prefer shade, it is important to determine the degree of shade required. This applies also to plants that may not actually prefer shade but will tolerate it. Here is why the amount of light received is so important.

Most plants need more sunlight than shade for normal, healthy growth. When a sun-loving plant is placed in a spot with a minimum acceptable level of light, it merely maintains itself and seldom flowers or sets fruit. It

This chrysanthemum is a sun-loving plant. Planted in the shade, it has grown leggy and become weak in its effort to reach the light.

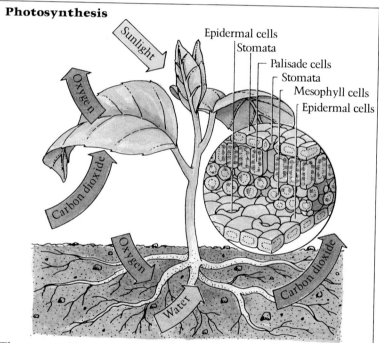

Photosynthesis

Sunlight

Oxygen

Carbon dioxide

Epidermal cells
Stomata
Palisade cells
Stomata
Mesophyll cells
Epidermal cells

Oxygen

Water

Carbon dioxide

The upper and lower surfaces of a leaf are protected by epidermal cells, which are covered with a waterproof cuticle to limit the loss of water from the plant.

Water vapor, oxygen, and carbon dioxide enter and exit the leaf through apertures called stomata. The stomata are flanked by guard cells that normally open in the presence of light to permit photosynthesis and close in darkness to limit the loss of moisture.

Just beneath the upper surface is a layer of cylindrical palisade cells. This is where most of the photosynthesis takes place. In this complex process the energy of sunlight converts water and carbon dioxide into sugars. These sugars are transported throughout the plant and combined with nutrients from the soil to form the chemicals needed by the plant.

Under the palisade cells is a layer of mesophyll cells where the sugars produced by photosynthesis are stored until they are needed in other parts of the plant.

produces less foliage and long, weak stems and leaves as it reaches toward the light it needs.

The stress produced by insufficient light often weakens the plant to the point where it may die. A plant in this state may appear healthy for some months, but in fact it is utilizing stored carbohydrates and is slowly declining. If left in this declining state for too long, the plant may not regain its vigor even when transplanted to a spot with adequate light.

ADAPTATIONS TO SHADE

Some plants are adapted to growing in dense shade. Others can tolerate the filtered shade under leafy trees. The top layer of leaves in the canopy intercepts about 90 percent of the light that falls on it, leaving only a small amount for plants underneath. It is understandable, then, that many of the best shade plants are natives of the forest floor. Good examples include the houseplants that originate in tropical rain forests.

Compared to sun-loving plants, shade-loving plants are more sensitive to light and better able to make use of small amounts of it. They have more chlorophyll than do plants adapted to the sun. They may also be variegated with additional pigments—such as patches or stripes of white or cream—that take advantage of a wide range of light frequencies.

The price they pay for this sensitivity is that they cannot tolerate direct sun for long. Direct sunlight destroys the chlorophyll in their leaves, resulting in a yellow or gray color. On warm days, the leaves overheat and die, either by becoming scorched at the edges or by developing burned spots on the surfaces that face the sun.

TYPES OF SHADE

A noted horticulturist recalls a college professor asking his students to list modifiers for the word *shade* with regard to growing plants. They came up with more than 200 words, including *light, deep, partial, dry,* and *dappled.*

Although a list of 200 types of shade would be overwhelming for any practical purpose, this does serve to illustrate that the word *shade* should not stand alone when used in reference to gardening. By itself, it means only the relative absence of light. To help the gardener determine the best spot to position a shade-loving plant, a descriptive adjective

Top: When exposed to direct sunlight for too long, shade-loving plants such as clivia develop sunburn and may die.
Bottom: Dappled shade is often found in woodland settings. The relatively open canopy of trees in this garden allows direct sunlight to reach the ground, but breaks it up and keeps it moving around.

should accompany the word *shade.* Definitions of the four categories of shade most useful to understand—dappled, open, medium, and dense—follow. The plants discussed in the "Plant Selection Guide" (beginning on page 39) all carry a recommendation keyed to these categories.

Dappled Shade

The intermittent shade produced by open shrubs, or trees such as birch, is characterized by a moving pattern of sunlight and shadow

Top: The medium shade produced by the combination of a northern exposure and mature trees does limit the number of plants that can be grown satisfactorily—but that's no reason to have a boring garden. A combination of clipped boxwood, rhododendrons, and multicolored impatiens enlivens this area considerably.

Bottom: A pale shade of paint on a north-facing wall reflects light into this small garden, which would otherwise be very dark.

across the ground. This is the lightest type of shade, in which direct sun on any given area is minimal for any length of time. Dappled shade occurs in front of east-facing walls, where there is some direct sun early in the day—not long enough for sun-loving plants. This type of shade provides the widest range of gardening possibilities because it is hospitable to many plants.

Open Shade

This is the shade created on the north side of a building, wall, or fence where there is good reflected light but no direct sunlight. Fiberglass-roofed patios and whitewashed greenhouses under direct sun can also be considered open shade situations. Proximity to a south-facing wall that reflects light will greatly increase brightness in an open-shade location.

Medium Shade

An open shade location in which light is further diminished by an overhanging tree or structure characterizes medium shade. Often the difference between open and medium shade is due to the amount of sky reflecting light into the shade. To judge this, crouch down where the plants will be and find out how much sky they can "see." If a large area of sky is visible, it is open shade; if only a small amount of sky is visible, it is medium shade. Medium shade also occurs under decks and in stairwells.

Dense Shade

This is the deepest shade, found in narrow, north-facing side yards and directly under evergreen trees. Tall walls and fences block all but the narrowest strips of light, although there will be some reflected light. Plant selection is quite limited; it should be based on how the area will be used. Ferns, or something as simple as moss, stones, and gravel, may be the most visually pleasing and effective.

Any description of a particular type of shade is open to many interpretations. The only truly scientific measurement of light, or relative lack of light, is accomplished with a light meter. But most gardeners and horticulturists agree that determining exact footcandle measurements with a light meter to describe different types of shade would make shade gardening more complex than necessary.

LATITUDE AND CLIMATE

If you've ever moved from one part of the country to another, particularly from north to south or vice versa, you may have been surprised at the differences in gardening between the two. For instance, the azalea that took almost full sun in Oyster Bay, Long Island, needs protection from the elements in Louisville, Kentucky.

One reason for such differences is that the intensity of the sun increases as you get closer to the equator. Add to that basic fact the multitude of climatic influences—such as clouds, fog, rain, and wind—and you quickly realize the difficulty in making blanket statements concerning the type of exposure to give a plant.

Experience and a little common sense are your best guides in interpreting planting instructions. The instructions in this book may, for example, say to provide medium to open

Plants for Deep Shade

Consult this list for the plants that interest you, then read all about them in the "Plant Selection Guide" beginning on page 39.

Plant	Flower/Foliage Color	Type of Plant	Coldest Zone
Asarum species, Wild ginger	Deep green/brown	Ground cover	Varies
Athyrium nipponicum 'Pictum', Japanese painted fern	Gray-green, with red stems	Fern	7
Aucuba japonica, Japanese aucuba	Variegated, with red berries	Shrub	7
Bergenia cordifolia, Bergenia	Light green/pink	Ground cover	2
Carex species, Sedge	Yellow-green, variegated	Sedge	4
Clivia miniata, Kaffir-lily	Medium green/orange	Perennial	9
Dennstaedtia punctilobula, Hay-scented fern	Yellow-green	Fern	4
Digitalis purpurea and hybrid, Foxglove	Medium green/yellow, buff, purple, white, pink	Perennial	4
Dryopieris species, Wood fern, shield fern	Medium green	Fern	3
Fatsia japonica, Japanese aralia	Green/white	Shrub	7
Gaultheria procumbens, Wintergreen	Deep green/white, with red berries	Ground cover	3
Hedera species, English ivy	Light–deep green, yellow, white	Ground cover	5
Hosta species, Hosta, plantain lily	All shades of green, variegated/blue, white	Perennial	3
Hydrangea quercifolia, Oakleaf hydrangea	Medium green/white	Shrub	6
Impatiens wallerana, Impatiens, busy-lizzie	Medium green/mauve, pink, orange, white, red, rose, salmon, magenta	Annual	
Kerria japonica, Japanese kerria	Light green/yellow	Shrub	5
Leucothoe fontanesiana, Drooping leucothoe	Bronze new growth, variegated/white	Shrub	5
Lysimachia nummularia, Creeping-jenny	Medium green/yellow	Ground cover	4
Osmunda cinnamonea, Cinnamon fern	Yellow-green	Fern	4
Pachysandra terminalis, Pachysandra	Light–medium green/white	Ground cover	4
Pittosporum tobira, Tobira	Dark green/white	Shrub	8
Polygonatum species, Solomon's-seal	Medium green/white	Perennial	4
Polystichum species, Sword fern	Medium green	Fern	4
Sarcococca ruscifolia, Fragrant sarcococca	Medium green/white, with blue berries	Shrub	7
Soleirolia soleirolii, Baby's tears	Light green	Ground cover	10
Taxus species, Yew	Deep blue-green needles, with red berries	Shrub	4
Tiarella cordifolia, Foamflower	Green, bronze/white	Ground cover	5

shade for tuberous begonias. If you live in an area that has a distinct marine influence, with frequent fog, moderate temperatures, and high humidity, you could conclude that the begonias can stand a great deal more sun than they could if you were living in Lubbock, Texas.

Once you get to know your own climate, and the many little climates that surround your house, the process of providing the right conditions for each plant becomes much easier.

CONSIDERING YOUR MICROCLIMATE

The gardener who has a shaded location can take some practical steps to match plants with the conditions.

First, when you are at the nursery or garden center, it's best to confine your initial selection to those plants already growing in shaded conditions. Almost every good-sized nursery or garden center has a special place set apart for shade-loving plants.

Prepare for talking with nursery staff by checking what grows in other shady gardens in your area, and by studying the various microclimates and conditions in your garden. The staff may ask you specific questions, such as, "Is the area under large trees?" "Are the trees deciduous or evergreen?" "Is the shade dense or dappled with sunlight?" "Does the area receive sunlight during any part of the day?" By doing a little investigative work in your garden and in neighboring gardens, and comparing your notes with the descriptions of shade beginning on page 7, you should be able to provide the right information to nursery staff.

If your planting area is under a large tree, the type of tree makes a difference in the plants you can grow there. If the tree has a mass of surface roots, which is characteristic of a sycamore, a maple, or an elm, or drops leaves that are toxic to most plants, such as a eucalyptus or walnut, you may be advised against planting anything under the tree, or to limit the plants to containers. If the tree is deep rooted, as are oaks and most conifers, but produces deep shade, you may be advised to do some selective thinning (see page 34) to allow more light into the area.

If the shade in your planting area is produced by a structure, such as a house or fence, the light is different from the play of sunlight and shadow produced by a canopy of leaves.

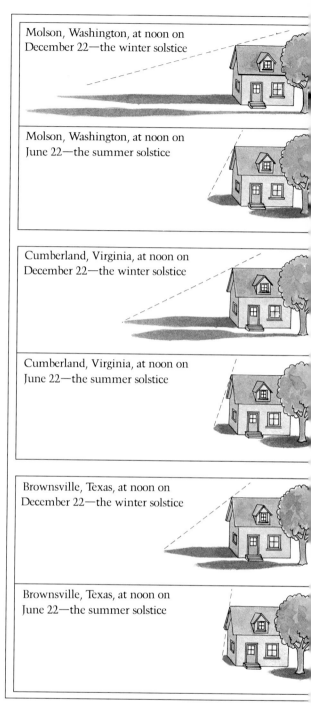

Molson, Washington, at noon on December 22—the winter solstice

Molson, Washington, at noon on June 22—the summer solstice

Cumberland, Virginia, at noon on December 22—the winter solstice

Cumberland, Virginia, at noon on June 22—the summer solstice

Brownsville, Texas, at noon on December 22—the winter solstice

Brownsville, Texas, at noon on June 22—the summer solstice

Depending on the way your house is set on the land and how far you are from the equator (see illustration above), the amount of morning sun the planting area receives can vary. For shade-loving plants, the difference between the intensity of the sun at 10 o'clock in the morning and at noon is significant, especially when light and heat are increased by a wall or fence in the background.

The old rule of thumb is that most shade-loving plants will tolerate the morning sun until noon, but after that success is variable.

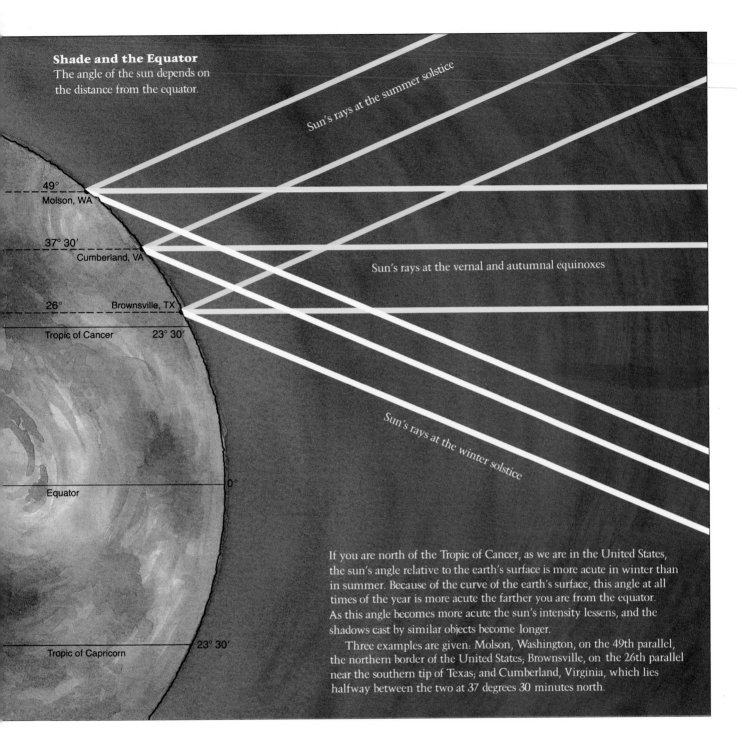

Shade and the Equator
The angle of the sun depends on
the distance from the equator.

Sun's rays at the summer solstice

49°
Molson, WA

37° 30'
Cumberland, VA

Sun's rays at the vernal and autumnal equinoxes

26°   Brownsville, TX

Tropic of Cancer   23° 30'

Sun's rays at the winter solstice

Equator   0°

Tropic of Capricorn   23° 30'

If you are north of the Tropic of Cancer, as we are in the United States,
the sun's angle relative to the earth's surface is more acute in winter than
in summer. Because of the curve of the earth's surface, this angle at all
times of the year is more acute the farther you are from the equator.
As this angle becomes more acute the sun's intensity lessens, and the
shadows cast by similar objects become longer.

Three examples are given: Molson, Washington, on the 49th parallel,
the northern border of the United States; Brownsville, on the 26th parallel
near the southern tip of Texas; and Cumberland, Virginia, which lies
halfway between the two at 37 degrees 30 minutes north.

There are certainly many exceptions to the
rule, but in general it is sound advice. Keep in
mind, too, that as the sun changes its course
during the year, the amount of light an area receives can change dramatically. North of the
equator, the amount of sun an eastern exposure receives tends to increase as the sun ap-
proaches its peak at the summer solstice on
June 22. In other words, a planting area may
have the right conditions of light for shade
lovers in spring, only to have the light increase
unbearably by the middle of summer.

In assessing the amount of light an area receives, you may discover that you can plant
part of the area with true shade-loving plants
and another part with sun-loving plants that
tolerate some shade. Most sun-loving plants
will accept some degree of shade during part of
the day, as long as they receive the overall
amount of sun they need. Shade-loving plants,
on the other hand, will rapidly show signs of
distress from too much direct sun (especially
the hot, late-afternoon sun) even though they
receive adequate shade for the rest of the day.

Creating Gardens in the Shade

Do you want a subtle, sophisticated shade garden? A cool retreat? A cheerful, colorful corner to glimpse from the kitchen window? Do you prefer a formal or a natural style? Here is the information to help you decide.

All successful gardens, no matter what their location or exposure, are a combination of three things: the sensitive placement of plants for color, texture, and foliage; a well thought out plan or design; and, more often than not, a style to pull it all together. This chapter takes a look at these three areas and pays special attention to the process of selecting and combining plants in the shade garden.

People with shaded garden areas often feel that their selection of plants is so limited that only the most predictable sort of garden can be created. Although gardeners do have fewer plant choices for shade than for sunny conditions—and the deeper the shade, the more limited the selection—the list of exciting possibilities is extensive enough to create a sophisticated and interesting garden. Some of the most beautiful plants can be grown only in shade. Foliage plants alone provide a fascinating variety of textures, shapes, and colors.

Impatiens and ferns thrive in the filtered light produced by this towering tree.

COLOR AND TEXTURAL INTEREST

When considering color in a shade garden as compared to a sunny garden, bear in mind that fewer plants produce bright color, and colors appear more muted in shade. Shade gardeners have to make the material available to them mean more than it normally does in other gardens, where the focus may be on splashy, sun-loving plants. In short, shade gardeners have to create more with less.

Gardeners used to the dramatic seasonal displays of sun-loving marigolds, zinnias, celosia, and other popular annuals may at first find it hard to adjust to the more demure, less powerful blossoms of most shade-loving plants. Orange and yellow flowers are somewhat more scarce; whites, pinks, blues, and of course greens are more predominant. Flowers are often small and delicate. Many of the best shade plants depend on foliage for impact rather than on flowers.

Good shade gardeners are both smart and sensitive. They have found out by experimentation and observation that there are many attractive ways around the most perplexing limitations. When you begin to appreciate the colors, shapes, and textures that foliage can

For a splash of color around the base of a tree, try primulas.

provide, for instance, you will see that shade gardening presents a new world of possibilities: the purples and pinks of coleus, the brightly banded yellows, greens, and whites of hostas, the glossy blue-green needles of yews, and many, many more.

PLANNING AND DESIGNING A GARDEN

Most gardeners are faced with one of two situations: renovating an existing garden planted by a former owner, or creating from scratch a new garden. In either case, you will create a more beautiful garden if you take the time to draw up an overall plan.

Chances are that any garden that catches your eye had the benefit of a carefully designed plan early in its life. The shape and size of the lawn, the paths and walkways, shade trees, shrub borders, hedges, garden structures, decks, patios, and other sitting areas were probably all considered both individually and in light of how each contributed to the total effect.

By the time your garden matures, the underlying structure or design may not be as apparent as when the plants were still young, but the organization that the design gives the garden will still be strongly felt. The sense of order a plan provides is important, particularly in gardens where a wide variety of plant material is used.

If you are timid about designing your own garden, this is the time to hire a professional landscape architect or designer. The relatively small fee charged to draw up a plan will be more than paid back during the life of the garden in terms of beauty, the lack of costly mistakes, and the ease of maintenance.

Once the plan has been drawn up, you can request suggestions for plant material or make up your own list. You can do the actual construction and planting yourself or put it out to bid by landscape contracting companies.

The first and most important step in designing any garden is to determine what purposes the garden will serve. Would you like it to be an outdoor living and entertaining area for adults? A playground for children? A space to house a particular plant collection? An area for retreat and meditation? Once the purpose is decided, the next step is to determine what will be needed to make the garden fulfill that function.

A formal garden need not be large. An attractive planting of dwarf boxwood provides a peaceful scene.

There are four basic considerations in designing an attractive garden.

•Consider the size, shape, and topography of your yard, and determine which plants or other objects are presently in place that you cannot move or that you want to keep.

•Determine the point or points from which the garden will most often be seen.

•Decide whether you want a formal or an informal design.

•Choose the garden style that you want to predominate.

Size and Shape

Think about the size and shape of your yard, the slope of the ground, and the areas of sun and shade at various times of the year. Are there large trees that you will have to work around? Are they deciduous or evergreen? How about garden furniture—is it movable or stationary? Are there any garden structures, existing or projected? If you take all of these factors into account from the beginning, your garden more likely will fit your needs and tastes.

Viewing Point

From what angle or location will the garden most often be viewed? If it will be seen primarily from inside the house, make sure that the view of the garden through your favorite window is the one you want to see. If you spend a lot of time on the deck or patio, lay out your garden with that spot in mind.

This formal garden relies heavily on symmetry and a geometric division of space.

Formal and Informal Gardens

Do you prefer a garden that is laid out along formal, straight lines or according to a less formal, naturalistic design of random curves?

A formal design is the easiest type of garden to lay out. Because of its visual simplicity, it is often the best choice for a small lot. A formal garden is composed primarily of straight lines and classical symmetry—that is, what appears on the right side of the garden is matched, sometimes nearly perfectly, on the left side. The outermost dimension of the garden is frequently rectangular, a shape that is repeated in other parts of the plan—in pools, patios, and flower beds and borders.

Informal gardens provide an opportunity to mix colors and foliage textures in exciting ways.

Often a single element, such as a statue, pool, or sundial, is chosen as the center of interest. For optimum effect, it is usually placed toward the rear of the garden, directly in the line of sight from your favorite viewing spot.

An informal garden features a predominance of curved, flowing lines and a seeming disregard for symmetry. The curves of lawn areas, patios, walkways, flower beds, and borders are usually gentle, wide arcs that frequently follow the natural terrain. One curve should lead to another, creating a feeling of natural harmony.

The decision to plan a formal or an informal garden may be influenced as much by the existing conditions of your land as by your aesthetic preferences. A formal design is difficult to achieve on an irregular lot—with slopes, hills, or rock outcroppings—or on land with a number of mature trees that you wish to leave standing. Such a site lends itself naturally to an informal plan. On the other hand, if your yard is relatively flat, with no outstanding natural features, you'll be free to choose whatever style you wish.

Flowering Shrubs for Shade

Consult this list for the plants that interest you, then read all about them in the "Plant Selection Guide" beginning on page 39.

Shrub	Color	Shade Tolerance*	Coldest Zone
Aesculus parviflora, Bottlebrush buckeye	White	1–3	5
Aesculus pavia, Red buckeye	Red (deep rose)	1–3	6
Amelanchier canadensis, Serviceberry	White	1–3	4
Camellia japonica, Camellia	White, pink, red	1–3	8
Camellia sasanqua, Sasanqua camellia	White, pink, red	1, 2	8
Clethra alnifolia, Sweet pepperbush	White	1, 2	5
Enkianthus campanulatus, Enkianthus	Yellow to bronze	1–3	5
Fothergilla species, Fothergilla	White	1–3	6
Fuchsia species and hybrids, Fuchsia	Red, pink, white, blue, purple	1–3	9
Halesia species, Silverbell	White	1, 2	6
Hamamalis × *intermedia,* Witch hazel	Yellow	1, 2	6
Hydrangea macrophylla, Common hydrangea	White, pink, red, violet, blue	1–4	6
Hydrangea paniculata 'Grandiflora', Peegee hydrangea	White, pink	1–3	4
Kalmia latifolia, Mountain laurel	Pink, white	1, 2	5
Kerria japonica, Japanese kerria	Yellow	1–4	5
Mahonia species, Mahonia, Oregon grape	Yellow, with blue berries	1–3	5
Pieris japonica, Japanese pieris	White, pink, with red new growth	1–3	6
Rhododendron species and hybrids, Rhododendron	All colors	1–3	Varies
Sarcococca ruscifolia, Fragrant sarcococca	White, with blue berries	1–4	7

*Each plant is given a shade tolerance rating between 1 and 4. These numbers refer to degree of shade: 1 and 2 are types of open shade, 3 is medium shade, and 4 is dense shade. For definitions of these categories, see page 7.

Garden Styles

Styles of gardening are slow to develop. Generations of gardeners have experimented with plants and their cultural requirements and growing conditions, and with garden designs. Handed down from one gardener to the next are the successes—the "styles" of gardening—which succeed for two important reasons: they are aesthetically pleasing, and they permit the desired plants not just to grow but to flourish. A shade garden in the Japanese style, for example, is not only beautiful to look at, but if properly pulled together it provides an ideal environment for ferns, mosses, azaleas, and other suitable plants.

On pages 17 to 26, four distinct styles of gardens are examined. The first two styles—woodland and oriental gardens—are particularly well suited to shade-loving plants. The remaining two styles—perennial borders and lawns—have been adapted here to shady conditions.

Select a style that appeals to you, or adapt a style to suit your taste. Style is, after all, a personal statement. The stronger the sense of style you can project onto the garden, the more distinctively yours the design will be.

The woodland garden Woodland gardens evoke the magic of a path through the woods, making the most of the play of dappled sunlight and shade on the forest floor. The woodland garden is one of the most informal of garden styles. As with any garden design, careful planning enhances the effect.

Because the eye can't penetrate very far into a forest or grove of trees, woodland gardens are usually viewed from a path that meanders through the grove. Although a bench or rustic shelter may invite the viewer to linger awhile, much of the view is an ever-changing vista that unrolls as the path is traversed. When viewed from a distance, only the edge of the woodland garden can be seen, and much of the charm of that view may be derived from the veiled path that disappears into the woods.

Begin designing your woodland garden by laying out the path from which it will be viewed. If the path will have an end point rather than simply wandering through the woodland and returning to its origin, place a focal point at the end as a destination for the walker. This may be a small pool, a bench, or a piece of garden statuary.

As you lay out the path, think of the effect that each point along it will have on the viewer. A constricted place between tall shrubs may open suddenly into a small glade. A sharp turn in the path may reveal a view of a distant mountain or a fallen log covered with lichens and mosses. Think of each spot along the path as a separate "room," each with its own "theme" and each holding its own delight for the viewer.

Once the path is laid out and the theme for each room is determined, think about the light in different parts of the garden. In areas where you would like to have flowers that need more light, thin out the tree canopy as described on page 34. Because it is the play of light and shade on the forest floor that contributes to this garden's charm, controlling the light is perhaps more critical in the woodland garden than in any other style of garden. Sunny glades

Although carefully planned, this garden calls to mind the wild beauty of an untouched woodland.

Understory Trees

Consult this list for the plants that interest you, then read all about them in the "Plant Selection Guide" beginning on page 39.

Plant	Flower Color	Shade Tolerance*	Coldest Zone
Acer palmatum, Japanese maple	Green	1, 2	6
Aesculus species, Buckeye	White, deep rose	1–3	5
Amelanchier canadensis, Serviceberry	White	1–3	4
Cercis species, Redbud	Pink	1, 2	5
Cornus florida, Dogwood	White, pink	1	7
Halesia tetraptera, Carolina silverbell	White	1, 2	6
Hamamelis × intermedia, Witch hazel	Yellow	1, 2	6
Ligustrum species, Privet	White	1–3	Varies
Tsuga canadensis 'Pendula', Sargent's weeping hemlock	Brown cones	1	4

*Each plant is given a shade tolerance rating between 1 and 4. These numbers refer to degree of shade: 1 and 2 are types of open shade, 3 is medium shade, and 4 is dense shade. For definitions of these categories, see page 7.

The path through a woodland garden can be covered with mulch, or, as in this garden, planted with grass for a quiet, soft walking surface.

or spots of open shade should contrast with deeper shade, which should convey a feeling of stillness and protection.

Shrubs and understory trees to a large extent define the garden "rooms" in a woodland garden. Plan your rooms and the effect each has by selecting shrubs that will form the "walls." Rhododendron and andromeda (*Pieris*) are perfect woodland candidates. Consider also aucuba, boxwood (*Buxus*), hydrangea, and mountain laurel (*Kalmia*).

Understory trees are usually more open and spreading than shrubs. They fill the space over your head but below the tree canopy. Some of

the most beautiful understory trees are Japanese maple (*Acer palmatum*), dogwood (*Cornus florida*), and witch hazel (*Hamamelis*).

Finally, select the plants that will carpet the floor of the woodland garden. Some of these will be ground covers—plants that spread over fairly large areas of ground. Others will be flowers or ornamentals that are most attractive as individuals or in small groupings. One of the special properties of a woodland is the long dormancy of most deciduous trees in its high canopy. This period of leaflessness allows late-winter and early-spring bloomers to flourish in the weak sun of the early season, then lie protected or dormant in shade through the hot months.

The edge of a woodland is a perfect place for naturalizing bulbs, perhaps in grass unclipped except when the bulb foliage has died back.

Bulbs are attractive in clumps, or "drifts." In nature, a flower in a favorable location divides and seeds for many years, slowly spreading its progeny. In the garden, this natural effect is often achieved by broadcasting an armful of bulbs over an area, then planting each where it falls.

Many bulbs will naturalize in woodland gardens, including snowflakes (*Leucojum* species) and squill (*Scilla* species); see the list on page 19 for more suggestions.

Spring flowers other than bulbs that naturalize easily and beautifully include columbine (*Aquilegia*), lily-of-the-valley (*Convallaria*), bleeding-heart (*Dicentra*), Solomon's-seal

Bulbs and Bulblike Plants for Shade

Consult this list for the plants that interest you, then read all about them in the "Plant Selection Guide" beginning on page 39.

Plant	Flower/Foliage Color	Shade Tolerance*
Begonia tuberhybrida, Tuberous begonia	White, yellow, bronze, pink, orange	1–3
Caladium hybrids, Caladium	Red, pink, white foliage	1–3
Clivia miniata, Kaffir-lily	Red, orange, yellow, white	1–4
Convallaria majalis, Lily-of-the-valley	White, pink	1–3
Cyclamen species, Hardy cyclamen	White, pink	1, 2
Erythronium californicum, Fawn lily	Yellow, pink, white	1–3
Fritillaria meleagris, Snake's-head lily	Cream, maroon	1, 2
Scilla species, Bluebells, squill	Blue, purple, pink, white	1, 2
Tiarella cordifolia, Foamflower	White, pink	1–3

*Each plant is given a shade tolerance rating between 1 and 4. These numbers refer to degree of shade: 1 and 2 are types of open shade, 3 is medium shade, and 4 is dense shade. For definitions of these categories, see page 7.

(*Polygonatum*), and violets (*Viola*). Read about these in the "Plant Selection Guide" beginning on page 39.

The shaded bog garden is a specialized woodland garden. A wet spot in your shade garden can be an asset. Here is your chance to use such bold-textured plants as wild ginger (*Asarum*), caltha, rodgersia, and trillium, as well as the water-loving maidenhair fern (*Adiantum*) and cinnamon fern (*Osmunda cinnamonea*). Other especially beautiful bog plants for shade are summersweet (*Clethra alnifolia*) and Japanese iris (*Iris ensata*).

If your garden lacks a boggy spot or pond, you can create one. A tiny pool or a short stream, perhaps with one or two large rocks and a recirculating pump, can create a focal point of great beauty with very little water. Fiberglass pool liners can be purchased at garden centers and sunk in the ground very simply. To keep mosquitoes from breeding in the pool, stock it with some mosquito-eating fish such as goldfish.

If you encounter matted tree roots when making a garden in an existing woodland, you can either thin the roots, removing the weakest and some of the most crowded, or you can select plants that compete successfully with tree roots—for example, lily-of-the-Nile (*Agapanthus*), ajuga, bergenia, lily-of-the-valley (*Convallaria*), English ivy (*Hedera*), epimedium, and periwinkle (*Vinca*).

Another option is to grow plants in large containers so they have their own soil supply.

A small waterfall made from several large rocks adds the music of water to the garden.

Houseplants grow well in shady situations. They can be moved outdoors in summer and indoors for winter.

Because of its natural style, a woodland garden is easily tended. Leaves and twigs allowed to lie where they fall will soon decompose into a deep layer of humus that conserves moisture, admits air to the roots, and forms a fertile growing medium that provides nutrients for the plants.

For optimum growth, a granular fertilizer should be spread over the entire woodland garden when growth is most vigorous in spring, and the garden should be watered every couple of weeks during dry periods. It's best to control the growth on any shrubs or trees that threaten to overwhelm their neighbors, or who cast too dense a shade.

Weeds in woodland gardens, as in all shady gardens, seldom gain a foothold. Because of the informal character of the woodland garden, accidental plants can often be considered casual visitors rather than weeds.

The oriental garden   Gardens in the oriental style are to many people the subtlest and most beautiful. Because of the simplicity of this style, it lends itself to nearly every garden space, including the shadiest; in fact, shade has traditionally been part of the style. The thoughtful selection and arrangement of just a few simple materials can transform your large, shaded area or tiny nook into a special place for serenity and contemplation.

If you walk into an oriental garden in the United States, you might automatically think of it as Japanese. It might be—or it might be Chinese. A true Chinese garden has precise, traditional combinations of rocks, water, and plants. A true Japanese garden has these combina-

tions too, but it also has an intricacy of arrangement and symbolism that is obscure to most westerners.

The Chinese character representing garden is composed of two words: *land* and *water.* Interpreting *land* to include plants, rocks, and mountains, and interpreting *water* to include streams and lakes gives you the basics of the traditional Chinese garden.

The old Taoist concept of a garden was a country retreat among trees in the mountains, with streams and waterfalls. Taoists believed that even an in-town garden should mirror nature, having within its walls a stream (if only a dry stream bed of rocks, gravel, and sand); flowers; a carefully planned, curving path, creating illusions of space and distance and leading to new perspectives; and a mound, giving the illusion of a mountain. This illusion could be further refined through the use of rocks on the mound. Rocks themselves were used as miniature mountains. The garden walls also provided a certain amount of shade.

Historically, a Chinese garden, large or small, was intimate. It was laid out so that it showed itself little by little rather than all at

The center of this Japanese-style garden is a large pond and some severely pruned trees and shrubs. The Japanese maple has been pruned to grow skyward, admitting light and allowing a more complete view of the garden.

Foliage Shrubs for Shade

Consult this list for the plants that interest you, then read all about them in the "Plant Selection Guide" beginning on page 39.

Plant	Height/ Point of Interest	Shade Tolerance*	Coldest Zone
Aucuba japonica, Japanese aucuba	To 6'/brilliant variegation, red berries	1–4	7
Buxus sempervirens, Common boxwood	To 10'/excellent for formal training	1–3	6
Calycanthus floridus, Carolina allspice	To 10'/fragrant maroon flowers	1, 2	5
Chamaecyparis species, False-cypress	To 5'/elegant habit	1, 2	Varies
Euonymus fortunei, Wintercreeper	To 2'/some have variegated foliage	1–3	5
Fatsia japonica, Japanese aralia	To 15'/tropical appearance	1–4	7
Gaultheria shallon, Salal	To 5'/red berries, white flowers	1–4	6
Ilex species, Holly	To 20'/red berries	1–3	Varies
Leucothoe fontanesiana, Drooping leucothoe	To 5'/bronze new growth, variegated foliage	1–4	5
Ligustrum species, Privet	To 25'/white flowers if unpruned	1–3	Varies
Nandina domestica, Heavenly-bamboo	To 8'/red-bronze foliage	1–3	7
Osmanthus species, Sweet olive	To 10'/insignificant but fragrant flowers	1–3	7
Pittosporum tobira, Tobira	To 10'/white flowers, orange berries	1–4	8
Prunus laurocerasus, Cherry-laurel	To 30'/shiny evergreen	1, 2	7
Taxus species, Yew	To 50'/deep blue-green needles, red berries	1–4	4

*Each plant is given a shade tolerance rating between 1 and 4. These numbers refer to degree of shade: 1 and 2 are types of open shade, 3 is medium shade, and 4 is dense shade. For definitions of these categories, see page 7.

once. Pavilion doors and vantage points along the path framed particularly fine views and focused attention on beautiful details. Bending forward to draw water from a drinking basin might suddenly reveal an otherwise hidden wonder, perhaps a splendid rock or a peephole view to a mountain peak.

The influence of Chinese garden design eventually spread to Korea, then to Japan, where it was adopted and made essentially Japanese. The two main types of Japanese garden style are "level gardens" and "gardens of artificial mountains." The "dry," or Zen, garden, which may contain no plants at all, is only one form of the level garden.

A more recent development is the tea garden. It is far less austere than the level garden but nevertheless restrained. There are evergreen trees but few flowering plants. The flowers might serve only to mark the seasons. The evergreen trees are often pruned to accentuate their individual characteristics. The function of the tea garden is to serve as a path to and away from the teahouse. Invariably the garden includes a stone lantern, stone basin, and well. The experience of moving through the garden is meant to be an exercise in detachment and meditation.

Much that is Far Eastern can be adapted to current American gardening tastes. Japanese and Chinese gardens can still be beautiful to lovers of gardens and nature, even if the layers of elaborate symbolism and subtle meaning are perhaps inaccessible.

Maybe you have only a dark, rather dank spot where you want a simple oriental garden. If you live in an area where mosses grow on trees and rocks, you might make a garden with a stone lantern (or a concrete facsimile); white river rocks, which will brighten the area and gather moss; some larger rocks; and a few ferns that thrive in deep shade, such as *Adiantum* and *Polystichum* ferns.

Various dwarf ornamental conifers are naturals for an oriental garden in open shade. You might work *Chamaecyparis* species and *Cryptomeria* species into whatever plan you develop.

Azaleas and camellias are oriental. In traditional Japanese gardens azaleas are used very sparingly for color. In fact, they are often kept sheared and compact, so that there are few if any blossoms, although a fully blossoming plant or cluster of plants may be used as an accent. As long as you don't use too many colors, you can use azaleas as part of your design without compromising the traditional oriental feeling. If your climate is warm enough, you can use camellias too, for larger, bolder-textured effects. They are best used conservatively, though, to not stray too far from traditional

Top: A weathered stone lantern tucked among the greenery provides a subtle accent to an oriental garden. Bottom: The profusion of flowers in perennial borders brings color into the shady garden.

style. Remember that both plants like deep, well-drained, acid soil, and that they should not be allowed to dry out.

If you wish to depart from the traditional style, which dictates that plants never decorate walls, *Camellia sasanqua* makes an especially effective espalier, although *C. japonica* and *C. reticulata* can also be used.

Suitable trees for the oriental garden include pine, flowering plum, cherry, crabapple, beech, the larger Japanese maples, ginkgo, and saucer magnolia.

Among the many plants suited to shaded areas of oriental gardens are *Buxus, Liriope,* and *Ophiopogon.*

Whatever combinations you choose, remember to utilize oriental restraint and understatement. A Japanese maple, a few small evergreens, some tufts of dwarf bamboo, one flowering plant, pebbles, a lantern, and a flat, weathered bench might fill a large space adequately and beautifully. A tiny pool (perhaps a birdbath top) sunk among rocks and ferns, and a beautifully shaped, subtly pruned dwarf andromeda (*Pieris*) can create a magical world in a tiny, shaded courtyard.

The shady border   Perfected in England, the perennial border is a romantic gardening style suitable to many shaded places, especially along a pathway or beside a wall or fence. This means that you can turn to the old English gardening texts, such as those by Gertrude Jekyll or Vita Sackville-West, for many ideas about suitable plants.

The weather in England is relatively cloudy and wet, and the angle of the sun is lower than in the continental United States, so that many plants that thrive in exposed perennial borders in England require shade here, especially in the southern states. Many favorite border perennials, such as *Aconitum, Astilbe, Heuchera, Hydrangea,* and *Primula,* also happen to be shade lovers.

Certain rules for creating perennial borders apply in all situations, sunny or shady. There should be no large, empty spaces at any time during the season. Of course, it will take at least two to three years for your perennials to reach full size, so plan to fill empty spaces with shade-tolerant annuals as the perennials grow. Make sure that there is always something interesting in the garden, spring to fall.

Vines and Perennials for Shade

Consult these lists for the plants that interest you, then read all about them in the "Plant Selection Guide" beginning on page 39.

VINES

Plant	Flower or Fruit	Shade Tolerance*
Actinidia species, Kiwifruit		1–2
Aristolochia macrophylla, Dutchman's-pipe	Dense green foliage	1–4
Clematis species and hybrids, Clematis	White, blue, pink	1–2
Euonymus fortunei, Wintercreeper	Variegated and colored foliage	1–3
Gelsemium sempervirens, Carolina jessamine	Yellow flowers	1–2
Hedera helix, English ivy	Bright green foliage	1–4
Jasminum polyanthum, Bridal jasmine	Fragrant white flowers	1–2
Lonicera species, Honeysuckle	Fragrant, mostly white flowers	1–2
Parthenocissus species, Virginia creeper	Deciduous red fall foliage	1–3

PERENNIALS

Plant	Flower Color	Shade Tolerance*	Coldest Zone
Acanthus mollis, Bear's-breech	White	1–3	8
Aconitum species, Monkshood	Blue, purple, white, yellow	1, 2	5
Agapanthus species, Lily-of-the-Nile	White, blue	1–3	8
Anemone species, Japanese anemone	White, pink, red, purple, blue	1, 2	6
Aquilegia species and cultivars, Columbine	All colors and combinations	1, 2	3
Aruncus species, Goatsbeard	Ivory white	1, 2	4
Astilbe hybrids, Astilbe, false-spirea	White, pink, red	1–3	4
Brunnera macrophylla, Siberian bugloss	Sky blue	1, 2	3
Caltha palustris, Marshmarigold	Yellow	1, 2	3
Campanula persicifolia, Peachleaf bellflower	Blue, white	1, 2	3
Chrysogonum virginianum, Goldenstar	Yellow	1, 2	5
Cimicifuga racemosa, Black snakeroot	White	1	3
Clivia miniata, Kaffir-lily	Orange	1–3	9
Dicentra spectabilis, Bleeding-heart	Rose pink	1–3	3
Digitalis species and hybrids, Foxglove	Yellow, buff, purple, white, pink	1–3	4
Doronicum orientale, Leopard's-bane	Yellow	1, 2	4
Helleborus niger, Christmas-rose	White	1, 2	3
Heuchera species, Coralbells	White, coral, pink, crimson	1, 2	4
Hosta species, Hosta, plantain lily	Blue, white	1–4	3
Iris ensata, Japanese iris	Blue, violet, white	1, 2	4
Ligularia dentata, Golden groundsel	Yellow	1, 2	4
Lilium species, Lily	White, yellow, orange, pink, scarlet	1, 2	4
Liriope species, Lilyturf	Blue, white	1–3	6
Lobelia cardinalis, Cardinal flower	Crimson	1, 2	2
Mertensia virginica, Virginia bluebells	Violet/blue	1–3	3
Ophiopogon japonicus, Mondograss	Blue	1–3	7
Polygonatum species, Solomon's-seal	White	1–3	4
Primula species, Primrose	All colors, some bicolor	1–3	5
Pulmonaria saccharata, Bethlehem-sage	Violet, white	1–3	4
Rehmannia elata, Rehmannia	Rose violet, spotted	1, 2	9
Rodgersia species, Rodgersia	White, pink	1, 2	6
Tradescantia virginiana, Spiderwort	White, pink, magenta, purple, blue	1–3	4
Trillium species, Trillium	White, pink, maroon	1–3	Varies
Trollius europaeus, Common globeflower	Yellow	1–3	3

*Each plant is given a shade tolerance rating between 1 and 4. These numbers refer to degree of shade: 1 and 2 are types of open shade, 3 is medium shade, and 4 is dense shade. For definitions of these categories, see page 7.

Lily-of-the-valley makes a delightful ground cover when planted in large swaths.

Ground Covers for Shade

Consult this list for the plants that interest you, then read all about them in the "Plant Selection Guide" beginning on page 39.

Plant	Foliage/Flower Color	Shade Tolerance*	Coldest Zone
Ajuga reptans, Ajuga, carpet-bugle	Variegated, green, bronze/blue	1–3	6
Alchemilla mollis, Lady's-mantle	Gray green/yellow	1, 2	4
Asarum caudatum, Wild ginger	Deep green/brown	1–4	6
Bergenia cordifolia, Bergenia	Light green/pink	1–4	2
Convallaria majalis, Lily-of-the-valley	Deep green/white	1–3	1
Cornus canadensis, Bunchberry	Deep green/white, with red berries	1, 2	2
Duchesnea indica, Indian-strawberry	Medium green/yellow, with red berries	1–3	4
Epimedium species, Barrenwort	Medium green/white, pink, yellow	1–3	3
Euonymus fortunei, Wintercreeper	Deep green, variegated	1–3	5
Fragaria chiloensis, Wild strawberry	Deep green/white	1, 2	5
Galax urceolata, Galax	Deep green/white	1–3	6
Galium odoratum, Sweet woodruff	Deep green/white	1–3	4
Gaultheria procumbens, Wintergreen	Deep green/white, with red berries	1–4	3
Geranium macrorrhizum, True geranium	Green/pink, magenta	1–3	3
Hakonechloa macra, Forestgrass	Variegated creamy white	1, 2	4
Hedera species, English ivy	Light–deep green, yellow, white	1–4	5
Hosta species, Hosta, plantain lily	All shades, variegated/blue, white	1–4	3
Lamium galeobdolon, Golden deadnettle	Green/yellow	1, 1	5
Lamium maculatum, Spotted deadnettle	Green, silver/purple, pink	1–4	5
Liriope species, Lilyturf	Yellow or white variegation/blue, white	1–3	6
Lysimachia nummularia, Creeping-jenny	Green, gold, variegated/yellow	1–4	4
Mahonia repens, Creeping mahonia	Deep green, bronze/yellow	1–3	3
Mentha requienii, Corsican mint	Light green/pink	1, 2	7
Ophiopogon japonicus, Mondograss	Deep green/blue	1–3	7
Pachysandra terminalis, Pachysandra	Light–medium green/white	1–4	4
Pratia angulata, Pratia	Medium green/white, with violet berries	1–3	7
Sagina subulata, Irish-moss	Light or dark green/white	1, 2	5
Saxifraga stolonifera, Strawberry-geranium	Green or variegated/pink	1–4	7
Soleirolia soleirolii, Baby's tears	Light green	1–4	10
Tiarella cordifolia, Foamflower	Medium green/white	1–3	5
Vaccinium vitus-idaea var. *minus*, Mountain cranberry	Dark green/white	1, 2	1
Vancouveria hexandra, American barrenwort	Medium green/white	1–3	6
Vinca minor, Periwinkle	Deep green/blue	1–3	4

*Each plant is given a shade tolerance rating between 1 and 4. These numbers refer to degree of shade: 1 and 2 are types of open shade, 3 is medium shade, and 4 is dense shade. For definitions of these categories, see page 7.

Taller plants, including shrubs, go at the back of the border (closest to the wall, if you have one), with shorter plants in front. Ground covers go in the foreground, often coming right up to meet a walkway or patio. If the border is next to a lawn, make a sharp crease on the lawn with an edging tool or a spade, and cut this edge again every spring to keep the grass from moving into the border. This front edge can be straight or undulating. If there is a wall behind the border, it may support climbers or vines. English borders are traditionally informal, with interwoven drifts of different types of plants and a curved front edge, but you can also use a formal approach, with plants in neat, parallel rows.

The wider the border, the more plants it will be able to support. Many established English borders are more than twelve feet wide; in a city garden, three to four feet may be a more appropriate width.

To start a new border, remove any weeds and sod. Dig organic matter into the soil before planting. You may also need to add topsoil, because the soil level in the border should be several inches higher than the level of the pathway or lawn, curving down gently along the front edge. This encourages soil drainage, and helps keep background plants higher than foreground ones.

If the border is against a house wall, be aware that the area under the roof overhang does not benefit from rainfall. It is best to avoid planting in this dry strip. If you do choose to plant there, be prepared to water regularly.

The shady lawn An expanse of lawn is often considered part of the garden, whichever style you choose. Lawn is most suitable where there are young children who need a place to play, or where there are elderly people who want a quiet area with comfortable lawn furniture.

Having a lawn in the shade is possible if you choose a variety of grass developed for shady conditions.

Annual Color for Shade

Consult this list for the plants that interest you, then read all about them in the "Plant Selection Guide" beginning on page 39.

Plant	Flower/Foliage Color	Shade Tolerance*
Begonia Semperflorens-Cultorum, Fibrous-rooted begonia	White, pink, rose, red	1–3
Browallia speciosa, Sapphireflower	Blue, white	1–3
Campanula medium, Canterbury bells	Blue, pink, white	1, 2
Clarkia species, Godetia	Pink, salmon, red, white	1, 2
Impatiens wallerana, Impatiens, busy-lizzie	Mauve, pink, orange, white, red, rose, salmon, magenta	1–3
Lobelia erinus, Lobelia	Blue, pink, magenta, violet, lilac, white	1–3
Mimulus species, Monkeyflower	Yellow, maroon	1–3
Myosotis sylvatica, Forget-me-not	Sky blue	1–3
Nicotiana alata, Nicotiana, flowering tobacco	White, lime, pink, deep rose	1–3
Nierembergia hippomanica, Cupflower	Blue, white	1, 2
Solenostemon scutellaroides, Coleus	Blue/red, purple, yellow, green	1–3
Torenia fournieri, Wishbone flower	Blue, violet, yellow	1–4
Viola species, Violet, pansy, viola	All colors	1–3

*Each plant is given a shade tolerance rating between 1 and 4. These numbers refer to degree of shade: 1 and 2 are types of open shade, 3 is medium shade, and 4 is dense shade. For definitions of these categories, see page 7.

Although most lawn grasses thrive in sun, certain types tolerate some shade, especially dappled shade under trees. Buy a good-quality, shade-tolerant grass seed blend, which will likely contain at last one type of fine fescue.

Even shade-tolerant grasses are not as tough as grasses grown in sun, however. If you want to put outdoor furniture on a shady lawn, it should be set on an area of paving or gravel. Make sure there are pathways, too, to save the lawn from wear and tear. A children's play area should be in the sunniest part of the yard.

To keep a shady lawn in good condition, water it only when it looks dry, and use only about half as much fertilizer as you would in a full-sun area. Set the lawn mower at about two inches, and never mow when the grass is wet. Rake leaves soon after they fall to allow more air and light to reach the grass.

Damp, shady lawns often harbor moss. In the oriental gardening tradition, moss is a valued ground cover, but the American preference is for grass without moss. Chemical moss removers offer only temporary help; the moss will return unless you change the conditions that fostered its growth. This may mean pruning overhanging tree branches, raking away existing moss, and liming the ground to make it less acid. It would be easier to cultivate an oriental-style garden, complete with moss, or to choose an alternative ground cover that tolerates shade but will crowd out the moss. See the list on page 24.

CREATING THE PICTURE

Planting a garden is much like painting a picture. Like the artist, the gardener uses color, texture, form, and line to create a picture that is visually pleasing.

When it comes to choosing a color scheme, you should look for plants that suit your preferences and harmonize with the exterior of your house and other nearby structures.

You might try using tints and shades of only one color—for example, scarlet, various tints of pink, and a deep shade of red or maroon. The various shades of "leaf" green will be a pleasant complement to these colors. Or use plants whose colors are related—red-violet, violet, and blue-violet, or yellow-orange, orange, and red-orange.

Some gardeners prefer using plants whose colors complement each other—orange and blue, yellow and violet, red and green. Although these combinations are very bold, they may be ideal in a deeply shaded garden. Another color scheme is to plant a random sampling of any and every color available. This light-hearted approach to gardening with color can be most attractive.

If you long for summer warmth in your cool, shady yard, try using plants such as lilies with warm colors ranging from yellow to red. The colors will brighten the area and make it feel intimate and welcoming, partly because massed warm-color flowers make a space appear smaller than it actually is. Colors ranging from green to violet will give the impression of coolness highlighted with subtle hues. Cool-color plants are good for close viewing and help make an area appear larger.

Use blooming plants to highlight areas that would otherwise be unnoticeable or unappealing. Along walkways or beside doorways, give visitors a cheery welcome with colorful plants such as primulas. If you enjoy relaxing and entertaining on your patio, decorate it with potted plants, and landscape the surrounding garden areas that can be viewed from the patio.

The area under a tall shade tree need not lay fallow just because grass won't grow there. That area might be fairly sunny in early spring before the tree leafs out. Plant some woodland bulbs for early color before the shade develops. Select later-blooming shade-loving plants for color after the tree is in leaf.

When selecting flowering plants, note which are early-, mid-, and late-season bloomers so that you can plan and plant your garden for a sequence of bloom. For the greatest impact, mass or group the plants together rather than planting them individually or in straight rows.

Plan to get the most from your garden by selecting some plants that are also good cut flowers, including some that are fragrant.

Top: Color in the shade can come from interesting foliage. Dozens of varieties of caladiums are available with a seemingly endless choice of leaf color, pattern, and shape. Bottom: Many bulbs naturalize in woodland conditions, providing a burst of color in the spring.

Shade Gardening Practices

Shade gardens are beautiful when suitable plants and gardening methods are used. Here's all the information you need to assess your garden space and match its quirks and characteristics with the growth needs of a wide selection of shade-loving plants.

Gardening in the shade is different from gardening in the sun. Although the good garden practices of adequate soil preparation, proper watering and fertilizing, and keeping the garden clean apply to all kinds of gardening, the emphasis on some of these areas changes in the shade.

This chapter covers the basics and explains how some of the practices you may have grown accustomed to in the sun must be modified for shade gardening. Matching the right plant with the right location—particularly important when growing plants in the shade—requires that you know the various conditions in your yard as well as the needs of the plants. The following pages give you the information you need to assess the microclimates in your garden. Then you can match this information with that given in the "Plant Selection Guide" (beginning on page 39), where the requirements of each plant are noted. This puts you well on your way to creating a successful shade garden.

This formalized treatment of the woodland theme features a select plant list and mass plantings, proving once again that you don't need a great diversity of plants to make an impact. Kurume azaleas, boxwood, and flowering dogwood create a springtime sight few can forget.

PREPARING THE SOIL

Most shade plants are natives of the world's forests, places where leaf litter naturally collects on the ground and where the environment is often damp and shady. Any garden soil, from the heaviest clay to the most porous sand, benefits from regular additions of organic matter—compost, well-rotted manure, peat moss, chopped leaves, grass clippings, or any of the other widely available organic soil amendments. In a shade garden, a high level of organic matter is especially important.

When gardening in the shade, the extra time taken to prepare the soil will pay off handsomely in healthier plants. For all but the very best loamy soils, you should add plenty of organic matter before planting anything. If your soil is a rich loam, the addition of organic matter will improve its quality even more.

To enrich the soil and improve its aeration and drainage, spread a 2- to 4-inch layer of organic matter on the soil surface. Dig the material into the soil to a depth of 6 inches. If the soil is particularly heavy or you are planting a large shrub, work the soil several inches deeper. Plants with roots growing in deep, rich soil will have better overall growth than plants that are forced to compete for water and nutrients in shallow, poor soil.

Soil in a shade garden requires ample amounts of organic material to keep the plants healthy and free from disease.

Providing Organic Matter

The incorporation of quantities of organic matter into the soil results in the superior growth of plants. This is true for several reasons, the most important of which is the effect that organic matter has on soil structure. The word *structure,* as it applies to soil, refers to the way the particles of soil adhere to each other. Soil with good structure has the right amount of air space to promote both good drainage and adequate water retention. Good drainage is especially important in all shaded gardens except bog gardens. Because of the absence of direct, intense sunlight, soil in shade tends to stay damp much longer than it would in a sunny location. Without excellent drainage, the shady garden will likely have water-related growing problems, such as stunted, weak plants and the presence of fungus diseases.

How can you tell if your soil has good structure? The following characteristics are typical indications.

•The soil doesn't compact after a watering or rain, and doesn't crack or leave a hard crust on the surface as it dries.

•The soil is easy to work using a hand spade or cultivating fork.

•The soil is friable—it has a loose, almost fluffy texture.

Mulching

One of the easiest ways to add organic matter to the soil is by mulching. Many of the organic materials used as soil amendments can also be used as mulches. The difference is in the way you apply them. Mulch is intended to lie on top of the soil, whereas a soil amendment is meant to be incorporated or mixed into the soil. Leaves and leaf mold are natural mulches under trees. Pine needles and pinecones are also natural. Straw, compost, and grass clippings untreated with herbicides all improve the soil as they decompose. Peat moss, although an excellent soil amendment, is best avoided as a mulch because it blows away when dry and is difficult to re-wet.

Mulches help keep the soil cool in summer and warm in winter, reduce water evaporation, deter weeds, and aid in the long-term improvement of the soil. A layer of material 2 to 3 inches deep is usually recommended; it should be applied in spring before weed growth begins. Simply tuck the mulch around the plants and spread it evenly among them. For winter protection in cold-winter areas, replenish the mulch soon after the ground freezes, so that subsequent freezing and thawing do not "heave" the plants out of the ground and damage their roots.

Top: Shredded bark is a widely available mulch that stays in place once it is spread and decomposes slowly. Bottom: A soil-improving mulch of pine needles looks natural in a woodland garden.

Fertilizing

Organic matter supplies some nutrients to plants but not necessarily enough. Even though the metabolism of plants growing in the shade is slower than that of those growing in the sun, they still need a steady supply of nutrients. In spring and early summer, monthly applications of a comparatively mild complete fertilizer help nourish plants during their periods of strongest growth.

Acid-loving plants can be given special fertilizers that have an acid reaction in the soil. These fertilizers are often labeled "azalea and camellia food," or something similar.

WATERING

The most important things to remember about watering are to water thoroughly and to let the soil dry out slightly between waterings. Deep soakings help plants develop deep, strong root systems, able to withstand some neglect during dry periods. Frequent light waterings result in shallow root systems susceptible to disease and unable to cope with drought and weeds.

It is important to avoid overwatering, however. It's easier to overwater a shade garden than it is a garden in the sun, because the lack of direct sunlight reduces the amount of evaporation. If too much water stays in a plant's root zone for too long, root growth stops and the roots die from lack of air. The longer that air is cut off, the greater the damage to the roots. Damaged roots have little defense against the entrance of rot-causing organisms, and the plant can succumb to root rot.

Monitor the watering of a shade garden by inspecting the soil after a typical irrigation. Using a shovel, check to see that the water has penetrated to a depth of 4 to 5 inches. Then allow the soil to dry out somewhat before watering again.

There are several ways to water the garden. Sprinklers are popular, but they can waste water by evaporation, and they wet the foliage, which may foster plant diseases. If you use automatic sprinklers on a lawn adjacent to a shade garden, be especially careful to adjust the sprinklers to avoid watering the garden when watering the lawn. The lawn may need three or four waterings a week, but if the sprinklers also water the shade garden, it's probably receiving too much moisture.

Powdery mildew (left) and root rot (right) are hazards of improper watering.

Watering by hand is one alternative for a small garden. You may be able to set a barrel under a downspout to gather rainwater for hand watering. This is not only a good water conservation policy, it also provides water at air temperature, which is best for plants.

Another water conservation method is a trickle irrigation system, which uses perforated or permeable hoses to apply water directly to the soil. As with a sprinkler system, an automatic timer can ensure that watering takes place on schedule, even when you are away.

Most overwatering problems can be avoided by making sure that your soil is high in organic matter. Such soil has good structure and porosity, so that even large amounts of water will drain through, leaving the all-important air in the soil.

Too little water can also be a problem in shade gardens. A canopy of leaves can prevent rain from reaching the soil, or competition from shallow-rooted trees, such as willows or pines, can prevent enough water from reaching the desired plants. A more common situation occurs next to a house where rain does not fall on a planting bed because of wide eaves or

Drip Irrigation Parts

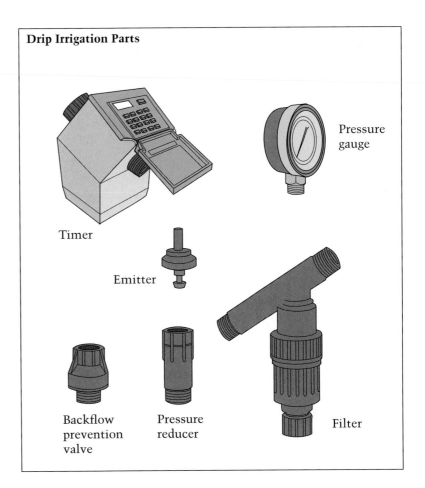

Timer

Pressure gauge

Emitter

Backflow prevention valve

Pressure reducer

Filter

Plants for Dry Spots

Consult this list for the plants that interest you, then read all about them in the "Plant Selection Guide" beginning on page 39.

Plant	Type	Shade Tolerance*	Coldest Zone
Acanthus mollis, Bear's-breech	Perennial	1–3	8
Aucuba japonica, Japanese aucuba	Shrub	1–4	7
Bergenia cordifolia, Bergenia	Ground cover	1–4	2
Cercis canadensis, Eastern redbud	Tree	1, 2	5
Cornus canadensis, Bunchberry	Ground cover	1, 2	2
Duchesnea indica, Indian-strawberry	Ground cover	1–3	4
Epimedium species, Barrenwort	Ground cover	1–4	3
Euonymus fortunei, Wintercreeper	Vine or shrub	1–3	5
Geranium species, Cranesbill	Perennial	1–3	Varies
Kerria japonica, Japanese kerria	Shrub	1–4	5
Ligustrum species, Privet	Shrub	1–3	Varies
Mahonia species, Mahonia, Oregon grape	Shrub or ground cover	1–3	Varies
Nierembergia hippomanica, Cupflower	Annual	1, 2	Varies
Polygonatum biflorum, Great Solomon's-seal	Perennial	1–4	4
Pratia angulata, Pratia	Ground cover	1–3	7
Sarcococca ruscifolia, Fragrant sarcococca	Shrub	1–4	7
Tradescantia virginiana, Spiderwort	Perennial	1–4	4
Vinca minor, Periwinkle	Ground cover	1–3	4

*Each plant is given a shade tolerance rating between 1 and 4. These numbers refer to degree of shade: 1 and 2 are types of open shade, 3 is medium shade, and 4 is dense shade. For definitions of these categories, see page 7.

overhangs. Being aware of these potential problems allows you to remedy them by watering by hand or another method of your choice.

PROVIDING ENOUGH LIGHT

In some situations, the amount of shade in a garden can be modified. If your garden feels dark and dank because it is too heavily shaded by overgrown trees in your own yard, you may choose to remove some trees entirely or prune them back. Dealing with large trees is best done by a professional. The cost of extensive work is usually considerable, but the results can be worth the expense.

If you have only a few problem trees or shrubs, however, and want to do the pruning job yourself, the information in this section will help you do the job correctly. You'll need a good

pruning saw—the type with a curved blade on the end of an extension pole—a wide-bladed saw similar to a carpenter's saw, and a pair of hand pruners.

Pruning Trees

There are two basic methods of pruning: thinning and heading back. Removing the ends of branches is called *heading back.* This type of pruning results in smaller but denser trees. Hedges are created by extreme heading back. Removing entire branches is called *thinning;* it produces a more open, graceful tree. Thinning is the most important type of pruning you can do if your objectives are to permit more light to reach the ground and to increase air circulation.

Before pruning any branches, examine the tree and the shade pattern it casts at various times throughout the day. Make sure that you prune in a balanced way, so that the tree continues to look natural and attractive.

When thinning a shade tree, first remove any branches that rub against each other or that grow toward the center of the tree rather than outward. If less shade is desired after these branches are removed, selectively prune away additional small branches before removing any major limb. Continue pruning one branch at a time until the desired amount of shade is achieved.

No matter what size branch you are pruning, always prune at a junction of two branches, and cut just outside the fleshy collar at the base of the branch. Avoid leaving a stub or cutting into the collar, and avoid removing more than a third of the branches per year. Trees respond to severe pruning done early in the season with a rush of vigorous growth, which can choke the tree and make it more dense than ever. If you wish to prune heavily, do so in late June or July, when the response will be less vigorous.

Removing Trees

The complete removal of a large shrub or tree is recommended for gardens in which the plants were placed too close at the outset. When deciding which plant has to go, spend some time imagining what the area will look like without it. If possible, have someone pull the plant as far to one side as it can go while you stand back and make a choice. This is a

---

Increasing Light

A mature tree casts dense shade, limiting the selection of plants that will grow beneath it.

Selective thinning creates dappled shade and permits a wider selection.

cautious first step that can take some worry out of an irrevocable decision.

You may want to remove shrubs yourself, but tree removal should be handled by experts; the job is dangerous and requires heavy equipment. It also generates considerable debris, which most professionals either haul away as part of the total cost, or chip on the site, leaving the material for use as a mulch or for compost.

You may choose to replace overly large or competitive trees with other types, such as leguminous trees—locust, laburnum, and acacia—which have feathery leaves that allow the passage of light to the plants beneath. They are also capable of producing their own nitrogen in the soil.

Painting Walls

If the shade in your yard is produced by neighboring structures such as house walls, you can paint the walls a light color to reflect whatever available light there is. This can often make a significant difference in the mood of the garden.

PROVIDING ENOUGH SPACE

Gardeners often place plants closer together than is recommended. Although you can sometimes get away with close planting in the sun, it is not recommended in the shade.

Increasing Air Circulation

The combination of soil that stays damp for comparatively long periods of time and the reduced air circulation typical against walls or under canopies of large trees increases the possibility of disease. For this reason it is always best to err on the side of placing shade plants too far apart. The extra space allows for good air circulation (a deterrent to disease) and gives each plant the opportunity to receive its fair share of light and nutrients.

As a general rule, the greater the size of the mature plant, the more space the young plant should be allowed. You can remove perennials if they become crowded as they grow, but you should space shrubs and trees properly at the outset. Space all plants so that leaf tips will just touch when the plants are fully grown. Most trees, then, should be planted at least 20 feet apart, shrubs about 4 feet apart, and perennials about 2 feet apart. The area between widely spaced young plants can be filled with annuals or planted containers.

Avoiding Diseases

Soil that is covered with decaying leaf litter and other garden debris invites fungus diseases. In the shaded garden, this situation spells double trouble. The cool, damp conditions are the perfect environment for the growth of many common fungus diseases.

In any garden where disease might be a problem, air circulation should be maximized. Farmers are well aware of the wind-reduction properties of trees. For countless generations they have planted rows of towering trees to act as windbreaks, protecting valuable crops. In smaller gardens, however, a tree's ability to reduce wind and air circulation can have a harmful effect, especially in humid climates. A large tree, dense with foliage, not only limits air circulation but also increases the humidity

Increasing Air Circulation

An overgrown and neglected shrub limits air circulation to the surrounding plants.

Pruning to raise the canopy and eliminate tangled branches not only permits more air and light but also usually makes the shrub more attractive.

When planting shrubs, careful attention to spacing will minimize the opportunity for disease.

of the garden by decreasing the amount of available sunlight. The lower a leafy canopy is to the ground, the more it contributes to stagnant air. For maximum air circulation, trees should be pruned as high off the ground as possible without detracting from the aesthetics of the garden.

Limiting the number of plants in the garden and giving them plenty of space to grow will help minimize disease problems. If, in spite of these efforts, diseases such as powdery mildew, rust, and mold are still a yearly occurrence, you should use a commercial fungicide. Fungicides are best used as a deterrent to disease rather than as a cure. For this reason, they should be applied before the problem occurs in any given

year, or at the very first sign of attack, to limit the damage. Consult a nursery for product names and best times for application. Read and follow the label directions carefully.

You can avoid problems such as mildew, petal blight on camellias, and botrytis on azaleas by maintaining an even mulch layer and removing all other garden debris. If you still have problems, it might help to remove the mulch each year and replace it with fresh material.

Damp, cool locations are also the preferred home of snails and slugs. To keep these pests under control, minimize places where they can hide, and use high-quality snail and slug bait whenever an outbreak occurs.

Proper pruning and maintenance of trees prevent the shade garden from becoming too dark and damp.

Minimizing Root Competition

The soil directly around some types of mature trees is often congested with roots, leaving little space, water, and nutrients for other plants. Often the competition for nutrients and water is so rigorous that the smaller plant beneath the tree either dies or simply never grows. Here are some ways to ensure success when planting under mature trees.

•Choose plants that compete well with tree roots. Some are listed on page 18. Local nursery staff can advise you on more choices.

•Employ a watering and feeding system that provides the water and nutrients directly to the desired plants; see the watering information on page 32.

•Root-prune outside the tree's drip line. This is done by digging a 16- to 18-inch-deep trench, then cutting and clearing out the tree roots in it. As a further deterrent to invading roots, position a sheet of black plastic against the tree side of the trench, then refill the trench with soil, covering the plastic entirely.

If all you desire is a little color under an aging shade tree, you can simply build a portable deck and place containers of colorful, shade-loving annuals or perennials on it. This can be especially useful under oak trees susceptible to oak root fungus. A major deterrent to this disease is keeping the surface soil as dry as possible. With a portable deck and a few containers, you can have your flowers and oaks too.

Decreasing Root Competition

Plastic or metal root barrier

New shrubs

Root pruning and the addition of a barrier to hold new root growth back will help keep competition under control.

Plant Selection Guide

Delight in the diversity of plants suitable for shade gardens. After perusing the wide selection in this illustrated guide, you may be eager to turn a little-used corner of your garden into an attractive, restful glade.

Selecting the right plant for the right situation is the secret to successful shade gardening. To help you in your selection, this chapter lists a wide range of appropriate plants. Each listing includes a description of the plant's shade tolerance (the four types of shade are defined on pages 7 to 9), cultural requirements, special features such as fragrance and blossom color, and the plant's zones of adaptation (particularly important in areas with cold winters). These zones are shown on the map on page 93. The zone number listed in the following guide is the coldest one for which the plant is recommended.

The plants in the selection guide are listed alphabetically by genus. If a particular species within the genus is recommended, then that species name follows. Otherwise, if all species in the genus are recommended, then just the word species is given. A subgrouping within a particular species is the cultivar, or horticultural variety. A cultivar is very similar to other members of the species, but a minor characteristic such as leaf color or size sets it apart from the other members of the species, and it is given a separate name. The cultivar's name is denoted by single quotation marks.

This naturalistic garden features native stone and an abundant planting of azaleas, ferns, baby's-tears, and aspidistra.

Acanthus mollis

Acer palmatum

Acanthus mollis
Bear's-breech, acanthus

Perennial
Medium shade to full sun
Hardy to Zone 8

Bear's-breech is grown for its clumps of immense, coarse, glossy leaves and tall flower spikes. It is usually considered a landscape plant rather than a border perennial.

The deeply lobed, dark green leaves, up to 2 feet long, grow in basal clusters often 2 feet high and 4 feet wide. The foliage is imposing and effective from March to October. The flowers are creamy white, lavender, or rose, with greenish or purplish bracts, and appear along upright stems 2 to 3 feet tall. They bloom in late spring and early summer.

Bear's-breech does best in moist, rich loam with good drainage, but it performs reasonably well in dry, sandy soil. It prefers filtered shade but tolerates full sun in cool climates. It withstands drought, but the foliage will be more lush with adequate moisture. In the northern limits of its range, it should be planted in a warm, protected location and mulched in winter. Plants should be spaced 3 to 4 feet apart.

Care is easy. Remove spent flower stalks. To grow for foliage alone, remove stalks as they appear. Bear's-breech is a very invasive plant. The roots spread a considerable distance underground and the plant forms spreading clumps, like bamboo, so confine the roots unless you want a large stand. Snails and slugs can be a problem. The plant rarely requires division for rejuvenation but is easily propagated by that method. Divide anytime from October to March.

Acer palmatum
Japanese maple

Deciduous tree
Open shade to full sun
Hardy to Zone 6

Japanese maple is the aristocrat of small trees for open shade. Even in old age, the smallest Japanese maples remain low mounds or miniatures of great character and grace. The taller forms become small trees, no higher than 20 feet. A grafted specimen of a given variety in most cases remains smaller than a seedling specimen.

Japanese maple flowers are small, delicate, and inconspicuous, appearing in spring before the leaves. The pendulous clusters of winged seeds are showier than the flowers.

All forms are deciduous, but in size, habit, color, and texture there is enormous variation. Some varieties, if given enough light, have foliage that is deep red until autumn, when the color changes; some have red foliage only in spring; others have bright green, deep green, bronze-tinged, or variegated foliage. Some have simply lobed leaves, others have leaves cut as elaborately as lacy snowflakes.

The taller forms are useful for creating an understory beneath a high, thin tree canopy or for planting on the north or east sides of buildings. Smaller types, the dwarfs, make dramatic accents in oriental gardens, in planters (sometimes as bonsai), and in various focal points. It's best to select a site that is sheltered from hot, drying summer winds; cold, drying winter winds; and late frosts—all of which burn and curl the leaf tips. The laceleaf types are most vulnerable. Well-drained, acid soil, moist and rich in organic matter, is important.

In the coldest zones the roots of container plants need extra winter protection. You can use heavy mulch, insulate around the container, or sink the container into the ground. In hot weather frequent watering is advised.

There are hundreds of varieties of Japanese maple. 'Aconitifolium', a dwarf, has deeply cut green leaves.

'Atropurpureum' is especially hardy and is similar to the species in its relatively uncut leaves and its size (up to 20 feet but usually smaller). 'Atropurpureum' leaves are purple or purple-bronze.

'Bloodgood', which is similar to 'Atropurpureum', is the deepest red of all the Japanese maples.

'Burgundy Lace' is smaller than 'Atropurpureum', and its leaves are far more deeply cut. It is very hardy.

Aconitum species

Actinidia species

A. palmatum var. *dissectum* (laceleaf or threadleaf maple) is a gracefully spreading weeping dwarf with very finely cut leaves. It seldom reaches 8 feet in height. There are many forms. 'Crimson Queen' has especially deep red leaves. 'Flavescens' has bright yellowish green leaves. 'Ever Red' is purplish red and mounding; 'Garnet' is similar but slightly more vigorous. 'Ornatum' is bright red and has especially bright autumn foliage; it is very hardy. 'Oshu Beni' is very like 'Atropurpureum' but has longer branches. 'Dissectum Roseomarginatum', 'Tricolor', and 'Versicolor' have variegated foliage, respectively pink edged; spotted with red, pink, and white; and variegated white, pink, and light green. 'Butterfly' has creamy variegations against bluish to pale green.

'Senaki', a bright-green-leafed variety, makes a spectacular winter display of coral red branches. It grows upright to about 10 feet, taller when it is raised from a seedling.

A. circinatum (vine maple), a deciduous shrub or a small multistemmed tree native to the West Coast, is similar to *A. palmatum* and has similar uses in the garden. Like other species of Japanese maple, it grows best in some shade except in the gentlest climates. It is also rather small, 6 to 8 feet as a shrub, 20 feet or taller as a tree. It likes rich soil and moisture and will tolerate wetness. In a moist, sheltered spot with medium shade, it may sprawl and vine a bit. This form can be particularly attractive against a shaded wall or as an understory tree in a woodland garden.

Aconitum species and hybrids Monkshood, wolfsbane

Perennial
Open shade to partial sun
Hardy to Zone 5

In informal gardens, these tall perennials, most with 4- to 6-foot spires of blue or purple flowers, can take the place of their more sophisticated relatives the delphiniums. There are also bicolored, white, and yellow forms and several hybrids. The foliage is elegantly indented. Monkshood is best planted in groups, with individual plants 6 inches apart, in soil rich in organic matter. If the soil dries out, the plants are likely to lose their lower leaves. Monkshood can be easily divided in spring. It is poisonous.

A. carmichaelii provides purple-blue flowers in late summer.

A. napellus is the common European monkshood. 'Carneum' is a pink form best suited to cool shade. 'Album' is a white form. The variety *bicolor* is variegated purple and white.

A. lycoctonum vulparia (wolfsbane) has yellow flowers.

Actinidia species Kiwifruit, silver vine

Deciduous vine
Open shade to sun
Hardiness varies according to species

All of these vines appreciate rich soil and will not tolerate wet feet. They form woody stems and climb by twining but need some help, so they should be tied to a structure. The 2-inch creamy flowers, which appear in early summer, are fragrant and moderately showy. Both a female and a male vine are necessary for production of the fruit, which is edible on all species although flavor, size, and quality vary. Vines grown in shade produce less fruit than those grown in sun. The vines should be sheltered from strong winds and from cats, who are almost as attracted to these plants as they are to catnip. *Actinidia* bears on new wood, so leave plenty of it when you prune in early spring.

A. deliciosa (*A. chinensis*, kiwifruit; hardy to Zone 8) grows rapidly to 30 feet. It is not the most decorative member of the genus and is the least hardy, but its fruit is the largest. The leaves are dark green on top, whitish beneath.

A. kolomikta is hardy to Zone 5 and produces foliage variegated white, dark green, and pink, with colors brighter in sun. The fruit is small and edible but tends to drop when almost ripe.

A. polygama (silver vine; hardy to Zone 6) is named for the silver cast to the heart-shaped leaves. It grows fairly slowly to 15 feet. The white flowers are fragrant; the fruit is edible but less tasty than that of the other species.

Adiantum pedatum

Agapanthus africanus

Adiantum pedatum
Maidenhair fern

Fern
Medium shade to medium sun
Hardy to Zone 4

This hardy maidenhair fern is native throughout most of North America. The fronds are delicate in appearance but are wiry, growing to 2 feet high. The plant spreads by creeping rhizomes, resulting in a beautiful, fine-textured ground cover. Moist, cool soil with a leaf mold mulch is necessary to keep the delicate, fibrous roots from drying out. Medium shade is best, although some sun is tolerated. This fern will naturalize well with wildflowers in a native garden. It also thrives in the shade of taller-growing rhododendrons and similar shrubs or tucked into the pockets of a stone wall.

Aesculus species
Buckeye

Deciduous shrub
Medium shade to full sun
Zones 5 to 8

Spectacular late-season flowers, trouble-free foliage (unusual for the buckeyes), and adaptability to shade make these shrubs excellent subjects for specimens, or for massing and clumping in problem shady areas, such as under large shade trees. Not shrubs for small areas, buckeyes have an open, wide-spreading (8 to 15 feet), suckering habit that can be troublesome if the shrubs are not given enough room to grow.

A. *parviflora* (bottlebrush buckeye) has profuse, large, erect clusters of flowers that grow 8 to 12 inches long, are white with red anthers, and bloom from early to late July. Bottlebrush buckeye prefers moist, well-drained soil that is high in organic matter.

'Roger's' is a superior cultivar that is worth seeking. It produces huge flower clusters, 18 to 30 inches long, 2 weeks later than the species and does not exhibit the suckering habit.

A. *pavia* (red buckeye; Zones 6 to 8), like bottlebrush buckeye, is relatively resistant to most of the leaf diseases that plague the buckeyes. Mildew can be a problem; however, it will not affect this shrub's long-term vigor. Red buckeye differs from bottlebrush buckeye by having bright red flowers in early spring. It is also less hardy. In size and form it is much the same. The cultivar 'Atrosanguinea' has darker red flowers; 'Humilis' is a low, often prostrate form.

Agapanthus species
Lily-of-the-Nile

Perennial
Medium shade to full sun
Hardy to Zone 8

Agapanthus is a genus of summer-flowering perennials native to South Africa. It does best in good garden soil but accepts heavy soil. Medium shade is tolerated; it will flower more in open shade to full sun. Ample water is recommended, particularly when the plant is in bloom. Flower stalks should be removed after bloom. Clumps should be divided every 5 to 6 years. Agapanthus is easy to grow in mild-winter climates (it is hardy to 15° F) and is seldom bothered by pests. There are both evergreen and deciduous varieties; all have varying size and flower color, fleshy roots, and leathery, straplike leaves.

A. *praecox orientalis* is the form most commonly cultivated. Its leaves are evergreen, approximately 2 feet long and 2 inches wide. Flower stalks (to 4 to 5 feet) bear many separate flowers; white, double blue, and giant blue varieties are available. This tall species is often mistakenly sold as A. *africanus* or A. *umbellatus*.

A. *africanus* is a smaller version of A. *praecox orientalis*. The leaves are narrow (½ inch), and the flower stalks reach to 1½ feet.

A. *inapertus* is deciduous, with dark blue flowers that hang from 4- to 5-foot flower stalks. Leaves are 2 inches wide and 2½ feet long.

'Dwarf White' is evergreen, 1½ feet tall, and bears white flowers on 2-foot stalks.

'Peter Pan' is also evergreen and very dwarf, 8 to 12 inches tall. Blue flowers are clustered atop 15-inch stalks.

Ajuga reptans

Anemone × hybrida

Ajuga reptans
Ajuga, carpet-bugle, bugleweed

Ground cover
Medium to open shade
Hardy to Zone 6

Lushness, brief but showy flowering, and rapidly spreading tight growth make ajuga one of the most useful ground covers for medium to open shade. This evergreen perennial is sometimes used as a grass substitute in small to medium-sized areas, especially on slopes. Because it is shallow rooted, it makes a satisfactory cover for small bulbs. It is also useful around shrubs, in shaded parking strips, in moist rock gardens, and in the front of mixed borders.

From spring to early summer, bright blue or blue-purple flowers appear on spikes usually 4 to 6 inches above the foliage. Individual flowers are small, but the mass of spikes is striking. Foliage of smaller varieties is about 2 inches tall; foliage of larger varieties is 3 to 4 inches tall. Bronze or variegated leaves of some varieties contrast interestingly with other foliage in the garden. Green ajugas redden at first frost.

Moist, rich soil and good drainage are necessary for healthy, long-lived ajuga. It can be invasive if conditions suit it. The plants should be spaced 6 to 12 inches apart, a bit farther for the big varieties. Stepping-stones aid in maintenance, as ajuga will tolerate little or no foot traffic. Care is moderately easy. Brightness, air circulation, and good drainage minimize the likelihood of root rot, powdery mildew, and root-knot nematodes. Spikes may be clipped after flowering.

A. reptans 'Atropurpurea' has purple-tinged foliage. So does 'Giant Bronze', whose leaves are larger and somewhat metallic. 'Giant Green', also large, has clear green leaves. 'Jungle Bronze' and 'Jungle Green' are both large, particularly the latter, with 8- to 10-inch flower spikes. *A. reptans rubra* has dark purplish foliage but needs sun to color. The leaves of *A. reptans* 'Variegata' are edged and dappled with creamy yellow. *A. pyramidalis* has blue flowers on 6-inch stems.

Alchemilla mollis
Lady's-mantle

Ground cover or perennial
Medium shade to full sun
Hardy to Zone 4

Distinctive, pleated gray-green leaves that catch and hold drops of dew are among the features that have made this deciduous plant a treasure since antiquity. Sprays of tiny, greenish yellow flowers that appear on stems 18 inches tall in early summer are much less showy. Lady's-mantle grows best in moist, well-drained soil, where it looks tidy all season. It does best in medium to open shade and will tolerate full sun only where summers are cool. In sun, it grows tall and loose, and may be better treated as a clump-forming perennial than a ground cover. It self-seeds freely, but seedlings are easy to remove, so it is not considered overly invasive.

Amelanchier species
Serviceberry, shadbush

Deciduous shrub or small tree
Open shade to full sun
Hardy to Zone 4

These extremely hardy shrubs are native to woodland edges, where their white blossoms are often the first to appear in spring. All bear edible purplish fruit, though fruit production is best in sun.

A. canadensis is 20 feet tall. The autumn color is brilliant yellow to red. Plants sold as shadblows are often *A. laevis*, which is about 5 feet taller and has flowers in drooping clusters.

A. × grandiflora is a hybrid of *A. canadensis* and *A. laevis*. It grows 20 feet tall and has especially large flowers followed by pink berries that attract birds.

Anemone × hybrida
Japanese anemone

Perennial
Open shade to full sun
Hardy to Zone 6

Attractive foliage and loose, open clusters of white or pink flowers are especially valuable for providing fall color in open shade.

The flowers are 1½ to 3 inches across, depending on variety and conditions of growth. The leaves are dark to light green, large, deeply lobed, and

Aquilegia species

Aruncus dioicus

pleasantly coarse in texture. Reminiscent of maple leaves, they cover the plant densely at the bottom and become smaller and more scarce toward the top, leaving the upper 1 to 2 feet of stem bare. The plant grows 2 to 5 feet tall.

Japanese anemone increases slowly in size and number of flowering stems. It is well behaved, long lived in favorable locations, and resents disturbance once established. It needs rich, moist soil that is high in humus and very well drained; it usually does not survive wet soil in winter. The plant prefers open shade but tolerates full sun, especially in cool climates. The plants should be spaced 18 inches apart.

Care is moderately easy. Water during dry spells in summer. In the northern limits of its hardiness range, protect the plants with a loose mulch, such as evergreen boughs. Do not apply this protection until the ground is frozen, however, or trapped moisture will kill the plants. The black blister beetle can quickly defoliate established plants. Clumps rarely require division; if necessary, divide in early spring. Propagate by root cuttings.

Aquilegia species and cultivars
Columbine

Perennial
Open shade to full sun
Hardy to Zone 3

Columbine is a delicate, airy plant with curiously spurred, showy flowers in a wide range of colors and forms. It is useful in borders and in "wild" gardens. This ideal woodland plant needs cool, moist soil that is rich in organic matter. It prefers filtered, open shade but will take full sun in moderate climates. The long-spurred modern hybrids, such as *A. canadensis, A. alpina,* and *A. vulgaris,* need more sun than the species.

The flowers, which appear in May and June, come in shades of white, blue, purple, red, pink, yellow, orange, reddish brown, and nearly black, in solids or bicolors. Each bloom consists of 5 sepals and 5 tubular petals that extend into spurs beyond the rear of the blossom. Hybridizers have developed a huge array not only of colors but of flower sizes, from 1½ to 4 inches across and up to 6 inches long. The flowers nod gracefully at the ends of

long, slender stems that grow 18 to 36 inches tall.

The foliage is light green, often with a slight silvery, dusty cast. Notched compound leaves, which catch and hold dewdrops, give it an open, finely textured appearance somewhat like that of maidenhair fern. The foliage can be effective into August if not attacked by leafminers.

Columbine is usually short lived, especially if the soil does not have perfect drainage. It self-sows in favorable environments, but the offspring differ, often radically, from hybrid parents.

Aristolochia macrophylla
Dutchman's-pipe

Deciduous vine
Dense shade to full sun
Hardy to Zone 4

Well known to the Victorians, this North American climber is now difficult to find, but for anyone who wants a dense screen of leaves to cover an unattractive wall or other eyesore in shade, this may fit the bill. The vigor, hardiness, and foot-wide, heart-shaped, bright green leaves of Dutchman's-pipe recommend it. The leaves are milky

white underneath, which is noticeable only if they are growing against a porch or over an arbor.

The brownish flowers that give the plant its common name are pipe shaped. Dutchman's-pipe may take a year or two to become established, but it then twines rapidly to 20 to 30 feet, producing a dense screen that requires a strong trellis for support. It will grow on even a north-facing wall. Its chief requirement is well-drained soil. Pinching stems encourages branching. A vine that becomes too large can be cut to the ground in late winter and will regrow strongly in spring.

Aruncus dioicus
Goatsbeard

Perennial
Open shade to full sun
Hardy to Zone 4

Goatsbeard, formerly listed as *A. sylvester,* is a large, shrublike perennial that produces showy, silky white plumes, similar to those of astilbe, in midsummer. The plant is excellent in partial shade in the rear of the border or as a shrub accent, particularly if grown in combination with astilbe.

Asarum europeaum

Astilbe

The plant's gracefully relaxed plumes, which are composed of minute flowers, are often as long as 16 inches. The large, boldly textured, compound leaves are medium green. Goatsbeard is effective all season long. It grows 5 to 7 feet tall, spreading 3 to 5 feet across. It is long lived and, despite its large size, restrained in growth and not invasive.

Goatsbeard needs moist, preferably rich soil that is high in organic matter. It grows best in open shade, such as under a high canopy of trees or on the east side of a building, but with sufficient moisture it tolerates full sun. The plants should be spaced 3 to 5 feet apart.

Care is easy. Water goatsbeard generously and deeply. Fertilize regularly during the growing season. Despite its height, it never needs staking. It has no serious pests and can go many years before needing division for rejuvenation. Division for increase is difficult and rarely successful.

The cultivar 'Kneiffii', which is much smaller than the species, has finely divided foliage. *A. aethusifolius* is less than half the size of the species.

Asarum species
Wild ginger

Ground cover
Dense to open shade
Hardiness varies according to species

Wild ginger is an incomparable ground cover for the heavily shaded, woodland soils to which it is native. It is especially attractive combined with evergreen shrubs or wildflowers in a natural setting. Although not related to culinary ginger, wild ginger has creeping rhizomes and pungent leaves that have a gingerlike fragrance. The roots of *A. canadense* can be dried and used as a ginger substitute. The 2- to 7-inch, heart-shaped leaves grow on 7- to 10-inch stalks. Flowers are small and appear early in spring.

Wild ginger does best in either native or generously amended soil, although it will grow in heavy soil if well watered. A location protected from drying wind is best. It is propagated by division of the creeping rhizomes.

There are several species, both deciduous and evergreen, with variations in leaf size and color.

A. caudatum (British Columbia wild ginger) is evergreen. *A. europeaum* (European wild ginger) is similar to *A. caudatum* but has glossier leaves. Both are hardy to Zone 5. Other evergreens are *A. arifolium* and *A. virginicum.* Hardy to Zone 6, they are similar to *A. caudatum* and *A. europeaum* except for reduced cold tolerance.

Deciduous types are native over much of the eastern United States. *A. canadense* (Canadian wild ginger) is one of the most hardy, to Zone 4. *A. shuttleworthii* is similar but has thinner, mottled, usually larger leaves and is hardy only to Zone 7. The deciduous forms are not cultivated as frequently as the evergreen forms because of the lack of winter effect.

Astilbe hybrids
Astilbe, false-spirea

Perennial
Medium shade to partial sun
Hardy to Zone 4

Astilbe is a favorite perennial for late-summer color in cool, moist locations with medium to open shade, and with deep, rich soil that is high in organic matter. It does not tolerate wet winters well without adequate drainage, and it will not take summer drought. It performs

well in dense shade but accepts part sun if watered deeply and often.

Astilbe has glossy, dark green foliage—sometimes tinged with bronze—and fluffy plumes of white, pink, lavender, or red flowers on erect or arching stems. The tiny flowers are produced in great quantities from June to September, and the effect is delicate and feathery.

The leaves resemble ferns and are always lush and refined. The foliage forms bushy mounds rarely exceeding 2 feet tall; the flowers often reach another 12 to 18 inches. Most flower heads are erect and pyramidal; others arch gracefully.

Plants should be spaced 1 to 2 feet apart; astilbe gradually spreads as clumps expand. A heavy feeder, it depletes the soil, and will flower less as the years go by; but division every 3 to 4 years rejuvenates the flowering. The plant is restrained in growth, not invasive, and long lived.

Aucuba japonica var. *variegata*

Begonia 'Glamour Picotee'

Athyrium nipponicum 'Pictum' Japanese painted fern

Fern
Dense to open shade
Hardy to Zone 7

This is the only variegated fern that is readily available in nurseries. It is a stunning plant that lights up shady areas with dark pink stems, softly silver young fronds, and mature fronds that are about 2 feet tall with a silver stripe in the center. Japanese painted fern is sometimes listed as cultivar 'Metallicum' or as *A. goeringianum.*

To thrive, the plant requires moist, peaty soil and shelter from dry winds. In sun, the fronds become grayish and stunted.

Aucuba japonica Japanese aucuba

Evergreen shrub
Dense to open shade
Hardy to Zone 7

A female Japanese aucuba was introduced to England in 1783; but not until nearly a century later, after a male plant had been imported, were the English able to see Japanese aucuba's scarlet berries. Beautiful though the berries are, it is probably the bold, varied, evergreen foliage and the plant's suitability for dense shade that have made it one of the most popular candidates for shady gardens. The foliage of variegated forms adds brightness to spots so dark that little else grows well.

If unpruned, Japanese aucuba grows at a moderate rate to 6 to 10 feet high but becomes leggy and open. Therefore, it is usually seen as a shrub pruned to a dense, rounded form. Instead of being sheared, it should be pruned to leaf nodes in winter. It is often used as a large container plant.

The tiny mahogany flowers are very inconspicuous, but the ¾-inch berries are showy. The glossy, serrated leaves are 4 to 7 inches long and 2 to 3 inches wide.

Japanese aucuba usually fares well against competing tree roots and is drought tolerant once established. It will accept nearly any soil but grows best in rich, moist, well-drained soil. It is susceptible to spider mites and mealybugs.

Here are some of the most popular, commonly available varieties.

A. japonica crassifolia is a male with thick green leaves.

A. japonica 'Crotonifolia' is a male with white-spotted green leaves.

A. japonica 'Dentata' is a female with small, coarsely serrated green leaves.

A. japonica 'Gold Dust', available in both sexes, has gold-flecked green leaves.

A. japonica longifolia is a free-fruiting female with long leaves.

A. japonica 'Nana' is green leaved and smaller than the species.

A. japonica 'Picturata' is a female with a large yellow blotch in the center of a spotted green leaf.

Azalea

For information on *Azalea,* see *Rhododendron* species.

Begonia semperflorens-cultorum hybrids Fibrous-rooted begonia, wax begonia

Perennial used as annual
Medium to open shade

Fibrous-rooted begonias are popular annuals that grow well in medium to open shade. They need rich, well-drained soil and plenty of fertilizer, applied regularly. The soil should be allowed to dry out between waterings. Flowers are pink, white, or red. Foliage is green, bronze, mahogany with a reddish tint, or variegated green and white. Most begonias grow to 6 to 12 inches; a few varieties reach 16 inches. Cuttings can be rooted in water.

Begonias call to mind the lavishness of Victorian estate gardens, which, at the turn of the century, were marked by the exotic and curious, by hothouses, and by the newfound glory of scientific hybridization. All three seemed to be epitomized in the begonia, and the fibrous-rooted annuals of this genus quickly became some of

Begonia tuberhybrida

Bergenia cordifolia

the most important plants for bedding and edging, particularly in the shade.

Unlike many other annuals of that era, however, begonias increased in popularity and are one of the most popular bedding plants in America. Among their many attributes are an easy nature tolerant of abuse, a compact floriferous habit, wide variety in form and flower shape, long-season effectiveness, and the dual attraction of both colorful foliage and flowers.

Hybridizers have had a field day with begonias, and a profuse array of new varieties appears yearly. All bear glossy, waxy leaves and flowers from May until frost.

Begonia tuberhybrida hybrids
Tuberous begonia, begonia

Perennial used as annual
Medium to open shade

Few bulbous flowering plants are as spectacular as the tuberous begonia. It grows best in open shade. Vibrant single or double flowers appear all summer until frost in a variety of colors ranging from vivid red, fluorescent orange, and bright yellow to pastel apricot, pink, and pure white. The flowers

enhance and brighten any shade garden, whether in a shrub border, flower bed, windowbox, or flowerpot on the patio.

Tuberous begonias are available in numerous forms: upright plants that grow 12 to 18 inches tall; bushy, multiflora varieties with small flowers; and the pendula, or hanging, varieties with stems trailing to 18 inches. The pendulas are effective in moss-lined hanging baskets in a cool, shady spot.

Not winter hardy, tuberous begonias should be dug up each fall and replanted in spring. The tubers should be planted outdoors after the last spring frost in well-drained soil that is kept evenly moist. They should be fertilized with a complete fertilizer twice a month. To encourage continual blooms, each fading blossom should be removed, and the stem tips should be pinched back if the plants become too leggy.

Tuberous begonias make good cut flowers. They should be snipped when they are fully open and floated in a shallow bowl. Gently sprinkling the petals with water makes them last longer. The stems are very brittle, so they should be handled carefully.

Bergenia cordifolia
Bergenia, heartleaf bergenia

Ground cover
Dense to open shade
Hardy to Zone 2

Because of its bold, evergreen foliage, its toughness, and its ability to grow happily in almost any exposure, even dense shade, bergenia is a basic plant for the shade garden. Its most common uses are as drifts of ground cover for small to medium-sized areas, as a rock garden subject, as edging, and as a clumping accent in any shaded area.

Its ¾-inch spring flowers, white to rose-pink, appear in tight nosegaylike clusters atop stems 6 to 12 inches above the foliage.

Their cabbagelike leaves, 12 to 16 inches high and up to 10 inches wide, create useful contrasts with smaller-textured ground covers, taller bedding plants, and shrubs. The leaves are waxy edged and more or less heart shaped at the base.

Any but very light soil suits this adaptable plant, although excessively moist, fertile soil necessitates frequent division. Bergenia is quite drought tolerant once established (although it is unsuited to dry desert climates). Fair to good drainage,

some shade, and protection from heavy winds are its only requirements. Plants should be spaced 10 to 18 inches apart.

In most respects bergenia can be neglected with impunity, although it needs protection from snails and slugs, which it harbors. If clumps become crowded or rhizomes leggy, they should be divided in fall or early spring,

'Perfect', a new cultivar, is tall and robust. It produces rosy red flowers on strong stems. The foliage of *B. cordifolia* 'Purpurea' changes color dramatically in fall, to purple with crimson highlights.

B. crassifolia (winter-blooming bergenia) grows slightly taller than *B. cordifolia*, to about 20 inches. Leaves are slightly smaller, and in autumn they color more vividly. Lilac, reddish pink, or purple flowers appear in dense clusters in January and February.

Browallia 'Heavenly Bells'

Buxus sempervirens

Browallia speciosa
Sapphireflower

Annual

Dense to open shade

Sapphireflower is a member of the exclusive club of shade-tolerant annuals. Still relatively undiscovered by gardeners, this low-growing jewel deserves wider use. Most varieties trail, but some are dwarf and compact. There are white cultivars available, but the usual flower color is blue. It forms a carpet in the filtered shade of trees or on the sunny east side of the house, or it can be planted to cascade over a wall or from baskets under the eaves or lathes.

It should be planted in rich, well-drained soil. Shade is best, since the flowers will fade in full sun. The soil should be kept evenly moist, and a light fertilizer should be applied frequently. The plants should be cut back in fall and brought indoors, where they will bloom all winter long.

Brunnera macrophylla
Siberian bugloss

Perennial

Open shade to full sun

Hardy to Zone 3

The tiny, sky blue flowers of Siberian bugloss, produced in delicate clusters, resemble those of Italian bugloss, or for-get-me-not (*Anchusa azurea*). Siberian bugloss, however, has the advantage of large, heart-shaped leaves that remain attractive all season long. This very adaptable plant performs well in any soil and in sun or shade, although open shade is best. Like most garden plants, however, it responds best to moist soil that is high in organic matter.

Flowers bloom generously in April and May in branching, open clusters atop stems 12 to 15 inches tall. The dark green leaves are clean, lush, and pest free. They reach 6 to 8 inches long in July and grow in basal clumps about 12 inches high. The foliage is attractive until the first frost.

The plants should be spaced 12 to 18 inches apart; they expand outward gradually. Siberian bugloss is well behaved, not invasive, and lives quite a long time without requiring division.

Buxus sempervirens
Common boxwood

Broadleaf evergreen shrub

Medium shade to full sun

Hardy to Zone 6

This is the plant most often used in formal gardens to be sheared into whimsical shapes. Besides topiary and trimmed hedges, common boxwood also makes an uncommonly beautiful specimen in old age, since it grows quite slowly into a gnarled, spreading, and open treelike shrub, 10 to 20 feet in height and width. Most gardeners know it as a young plant, however, when it is a dainty, rounded, compact shrub.

Common boxwood requires well-drained, moist soil that has been generously amended with organic matter, then mulched heavily to provide a cool, moist root run. Since its roots are close to the surface, cultivating around them should be avoided. The plant's inner dead twigs should be pruned annually, and the fallen leaves that accumulate in the branch crotches should be removed. This will help prevent twig canker disease, which is common in the East.

Common boxwood is subject to a wide variety of insects and diseases. It does not tolerate drought. It should be protected from drying winds and extreme temperatures, and given medium shade in hot climates, medium shade to full sun elsewhere. Many cultivars are available for increased hardiness and in different forms and sizes. 'Northern Find' and 'Vadar Valley' are two of the hardiest (to Zone 5).

B. microphylla (littleleaf boxwood) is similar to common boxwood except that it is slightly hardier and more finely textured, and its foliage usually turns yellow-brown in cold weather. However, 'Tide Hill', and 'Winter Green' and other cultivars of *B. microphylla* var. *koreana* (Korean boxwood) are the hardiest and retain their excellent green foliage all winter long. They can survive temperatures of -30° F, although they may be damaged by winter sun and wind if not protected with burlap. Cultural instructions and landscape uses are the same as for common boxwood.

Caladium

Caltha palustris

Caladium bicolor
Caladium

Tender perennial
Dense to open shade

Although this South American tuber produces small pink flowers, it is grown not for its blooms but for its striking leaves. The arrow- or heart-shaped leaves are veined, edged, or mottled in numerous variations of pink, red, green, silver, and white. The plants grow about 12 inches tall. They enhance any shrub border or flower bed, make good container plants for adding color on porches and patios, and are often kept indoors over winter as houseplants.

Caladium is hardy outdoors only in Zone 10. In other zones it is grown as an annual that is dug up just before the fall frost and brought indoors for the winter. In spring, about 2 months before the air temperature will remain above 70° F, the tubers can be planted 1 to 2 inches deep in moist vermiculite or peat moss. When small leaves appear, the young plants should be transplanted to 4- to 7-inch-diameter containers. Move them outdoors when the weather is reliably warm (above 70° F).

Caladium grows equally well in open or dense shade and prefers a well-drained soil that is kept evenly moist. To maintain attractive plants and to encourage new, colorful leaves, the dead leaves should be cut from the base of the leafstalk.

Caltha palustris
Marshmarigold

Perennial
Open shade to full sun
Hardy to Zone 3

Marshmarigold is a cheerful little plant for wet, soggy soil or standing water. It has bright golden yellow flowers about 1 inch across borne singly above the foliage. The round, bright green leaves are held horizontally on tall, juicy stems. A spring bloomer (May), the plant disappears entirely by mid-summer.

The plant is fairly low growing, from 12 to 18 inches high. The plants should be spaced 12 to 24 inches apart. Although not considered invasive, it expands to form loose clumps and mats. It reseeds if conditions are favorable. Plants bloom the third year from seed.

Marshmarigold needs rich soil that is high in organic matter and is constantly moist. It requires open shade to full sun.

Care is moderately easy to moderately difficult. Water abundantly and fertilize regularly. Mulch well if the plant is in an exposed, dry location. There are no serious pests. Divide to increase just after blooming. The plant can go for years without needing division.

Calycanthus floridus
Carolina allspice, strawberry shrub

Deciduous shrub
Open shade to medium sun
Hardy to Zone 5

For fragrant blooms and easy care, this native of the southeastern United States is hard to beat. It should be planted wherever you can enjoy the fragrance—near outdoor living areas, under windows, beside screen doors, in the shrub border. The 2-inch, dull reddish brown flowers gloriously permeate the garden with a sweet strawberry scent in mid-May, and often sporadically into July.

The shrub grows slowly to a neat, rounded outline, 6 to 9 feet high and 6 to 12 feet wide. It grows in any soil but performs best in deep, moist loam. It

prefers open shade and will not grow as tall in full sun. The shrub transplants readily and is highly resistant to pests. It should be pruned immediately after flowering.

C. fertilis (pale sweetshrub; hardy to Zone 6) and *C. occidentalis* (California sweetshrub; hardy to Zone 7) are similar species that are occasionally mistaken for Carolina allspice, but they do not have the latter's pleasing floral fragrance. Since fragrance is the chief motive for acquiring *C. floridus*, it should be purchased while in flower to ensure positive identification.

Camellia japonica
Camellia

Evergreen shrub
Open to dappled shade
Hardy to Zone 8

Beloved by southern and western gardeners, the camellia has attractive, dense, shiny, dark green foliage that sets off the blossoms beautifully. The camellia is very effective standing alone or planted in groups. It blends nicely with other broadleaf evergreens and is frequently mixed in shrub borders. The

Campanula persicifolia

Campanula carpatica

camellia commonly grows 6 to 12 feet tall but may reach 20 feet in old age. It sometimes has a single trunk, and branches well up from the ground, but the effect is usually a roundish mass of dense foliage that is nearly as broad as it is tall. From October to May, depending on the cultivar, the plant is a mass of color, ranging from white through every shade of pink to red. Individual blossoms measure from 2½ to 5 inches in diameter and may be single, semidouble, or double. They are especially attractive cut and floated in a shallow bowl.

Camellia transplants easily into any type of soil that is high in organic matter and slightly acid. The plant should be watered when the soil is dry 3 to 4 inches deep. Camellia is shallow rooted, so cultivating around the roots should be avoided. Camellia can also be grown in tubs that can be moved indoors in winter.

C. sasanqua (sasanqua camellia; hardy to Zone 8) blooms earlier, from autumn to early winter, than does the common camellia. This camellia is very versatile, with flowers ranging from white to pink to scarlet. Available as a low-growing, sprawling shrub that is useful as a ground cover and espalier, it

also comes as an upright shrub ideal for hedges or screens.

Campanula medium
Canterbury bells

Biennial grown as annual
Open shade to full sun
Hardy to Zone 4

Dangling its loose, open clusters of bell-shaped flowers atop waving, leafy stems, Canterbury bells is perfect for the informal garden where a soft, natural look is desired. It can be planted about the rock garden in small groups or across a sunny meadow in a broad swath. It can be mixed into the cottage garden or massed in waves in the border. It behaves best when planted in dense groups that help to support each other's 12- to 36-inch flexible stems. (It may still have to be staked in windy spots.) It blooms from June through July, in white and shades of blue, lavender, and pink.

Canterbury bells needs rich, evenly moist, well-drained soil. It will accept open shade to full sun. Plants should be spaced

4 to 12 inches apart. Several forms of this biennial are offered as "annual" strains, but even these should be started well in advance to ensure flowering the first year. Many nurseries offer young plants for sale. Canterbury bells is very likely to reseed, which increases its desirability in naturalized gardens.

Campanula persicifolia
Peachleaf bellflower

Perennial
Medium shade to full sun
Hardy to Zone 3

The blue or white blossoms of peachleaf bellflower are a charming addition to any wild garden or informal border. The flowers are bell shaped and single or double; they appear in July on long, slender, flexible stems and spread open to 1½ inches in diameter. The leaves are medium green and straplike; as indicated by the common name, they are similar to those of the peach tree.

The plants should be spaced 12 to 18 inches apart; they spread outward gradually although the plant is restrained in growth and not invasive. It can be quite long lived. Native to mountainous meadows and open woods, this bellflower

requires soil that is well drained and high in organic matter and of average fertility. It does best in areas with cool summers and does not perform well in the South.

Care is easy. Water regularly, as bellflowers do not tolerate prolonged drought. Feed lightly and infrequently. The tallest varieties may require staking, although this is unusual. Crown rot can be a serious problem if water stands around the roots for any length of time. Regular applications of insecticide may be beneficial in protecting the plants from aphids and thrips.

When the clumps begin to decline, usually not before the third or fourth year, they should be divided to rejuvenate them. Division in early spring is an excellent means of increase.

C. carpatica (Carpathian harebell; hardy to Zone 3) is a low, 6- to 12-inch-tall perennial with large blue, purple, or white blossoms from June to August. It is neat, compact, and long blooming and is useful in rock gardens, in front of borders, or as an edging. Slugs are often a problem.

Cercis canadensis

Chamaecyparis obtusa 'Spiralis'

Carex species
Sedge

Sedge
Dense to open shade
Hardy to Zone 4

True grasses are mostly sun lovers, but certain sedges will bring into shady areas the chief asset of the grasses: narrow, vertical, gracefully arching foliage that contrasts well with the rounder leaves of most shade plants. Sedges grow best in moist soils rich in organic matter but will tolerate fairly dry conditions in cool shade.

C. morrowii is a Japanese native whose variegated forms provide gold-striped or white-striped leaves 1 foot high. It complements small spring bulbs.

C. plantaginea is a North American species that looks green and neat all season long. It is softer than *C. morrowii* and about the same height.

C. pendula (great drooping sedge, pendulous sedge) produces 2-foot clumps of wider, bright green leaves as tall as 3 feet. The drooping, russet-colored flower spikes resemble a cat's tail.

Cercis canadensis
Eastern redbud

Deciduous tree
Open shade to full sun
Zones 5 to 8

Best known for its pea-shaped, pinkish red flowers that grace bare branches in spring, eastern redbud blooms at about the same time as the dogwood; together, they make an attractive combination.

Eastern redbud is a year-round performer, with its heart-shaped green leaves, yellow fall color, interesting seedpods, and reddish brown bark in winter. It grows rapidly to 25 to 35 feet in height and an equal width, with an irregular, round head and attractive, horizontally tiered branches.

Eastern redbud will grow in open shade or sun and in acid or alkaline soil. It is an excellent tree for a large container on a patio or anywhere that space is limited.

'Forest Pansy' has red branches and beautiful purple foliage that is best viewed where the light can shine through. 'Oklahoma', with its dark red flowers and shiny foliage, is the best redbud for high heat and alkaline soils. 'Alba' has white flowers and is susceptible to fire blight as well as borers.

Chamaecyparis species
False-cypress

Coniferous shrub
Open shade to full sun
Hardiness varies according to species

Although the species are all large trees, each is available in a variety of dwarf cultivars that can be used as coniferous evergreen shrubs. Many species of false-cypress are primarily adapted to moderate and moist coastal climates, although a few perform well in the harsher conditions of the Midwest. Care should be taken to match the selection to the climate.

The evergreen foliage of false-cypress is similar to the young leaves of junipers. Cultivars vary in color—bright yellows, deep greens, grays, and blues—and habit—from tiny, inches-high tufts to open, picturesque, small trees.

False-cypress should be transplanted into rich, well-drained soil in spring, then given full sun in moist, mild climates and open shade elsewhere. Pruning to control form is best accomplished just before the new foliage emerges in spring. Most forms have a tendency to die out in the center and lose their lower branches with age. A strong jet of water is the easiest way to remove this foliage. Protect all *Chamaecyparis* from hot, drying winds.

C. lawsoniana (Lawson false-cypress; Zones 6 to 8) is best adapted to coastal, moist climates; it is not suitable for midwestern conditions. Root rot is a significant problem on the West Coast. Yellow-leaved varieties are particularly susceptible to burn by hot sun and winds.

C. obtusa (Hinoki false-cypress; Zones 5 to 8) tolerates neutral soils somewhat better than other false cypresses and is probably the best choice for midwestern conditions. It is available in a wide variety of dwarf forms.

C. pisifera (Japanese false-cypress; Zones 4 to 8) is the hardiest of the false cypresses, but it is notorious for losing its inner and lower foliage with age. It prefers acid soil.

Chrysogonum virginianum

Cimicifuga racemosa

Chrysogonum virginianum Goldenstar

Perennial
Open shade to full sun
Hardy to Zone 5

Goldenstar is a low, trailing plant with small, daisylike, bright yellow flowers and vivid green or gray-green leaves. It is useful either in sun or shade. It is particularly delightful when grown against rocks. Goldenstar must have excellent drainage and prefers a sandy soil high in organic matter. The soil should be fairly dry and of only average fertility.

The flowers, which appear from mid-June until frost, are produced along the joints of the trailing, leafy stems. The leaves are small and round, about an inch across, and are densely produced.

The plant has a loose, open habit that follows the contour of the ground and rocks. It usually grows 2 to 4 inches high and rarely exceeds 8 inches. It often spreads into a loose mat with stems rooting where they touch the soil. The plants should be spaced 8 to 12 inches apart. Goldenstar is always restrained in growth and never intrusive, seldom exceeding a spread of 12 to 20 inches.

Cimicifuga racemosa Black snakeroot, bugbane

Perennial
Open shade
Hardy to Zone 3

Black snakeroot produces tall, thin, graceful spires of fluffy white flowers, sometimes reaching 8 feet above the clumps of foliage. It is excellent in the rear of a perennial border.

Open and airy in bloom, the wandlike flower stalks sway with each breeze. The flowers, which are small and exude a cloyingly sweet fragrance, are produced densely along the upper part of the stalks in clusters up to 3 feet long. The peak bloom occurs in late June and July, but small lateral branches bear flowers into August.

The glistening, dark green leaves are compound, divided into 3-toothed leaflets. The foliage forms dense clumps 2 to 3 feet high and provides good color until frost. Since the plant is native to the deep, rich, moist soils of open woodlands and the forest edge, it does best in moist, well-drained soil high in organic matter. It grows tallest in deep soil and open shade and ideally should not have more than 4 hours of direct sun each day. In dense shade, however, it will not flower well.

Black snakeroot does not self-sow freely or spread about the garden. The rhizomes expand slowly to increase the clump. The plant is long lived.

Clarkia species Godetia, Rocky Mountain garlandflower, farewell-to-spring

Annual
Open shade to full sun

In most catalogs the gardener will find listed as separate flowers *Clarkia unguiculata* (Rocky Mountain garlandflower, farewell-to-spring) and *Godetia* (sometimes also called farewell-to-spring). Indeed, they bear little resemblance to each other—*Godetia* was formerly a distinct genus—but both are now considered hybrids of species from the same genus, *Clarkia*.

Godetia produces clusters of upward-facing cup- or funnel-shaped blossoms with contrasting margins and centers. The flowers, 1 to 3 inches wide, resemble azalea blossoms; they appear on strong stems ideal for cutting. Godetia is widely grown commercially for cut flowers.

The flowers usually referred to as clarkia concentrate their showy blossoms in the axils, where branches join the main stem. The blossoms can be either single or double; they look like many tiny ribbons that have been fancifully cut and gathered.

Both clarkia and godetia perform best, and flower the longest, in regions where summers are dry and cool. They bloom, in shades of pink, purple, red, and white, from summer until frost in optimum climates, and for a shorter time where summers are hot and wet. Both species reach 18 to 24 inches in height. In their native habitat they complete their life cycle on the gradually decreasing moisture from stored winter rain or snow melt. In the South and hot-summer regions of the East and Midwest, the protection of open shade and successive plantings 30 days apart may help to achieve a longer blooming season.

Clarkia 'Royal Banquet'

Clethra alnifolia

Clarkia and godetia are musts for any cutting garden, but they are also excellent choices for large beds, mixed borders, and planter boxes. Their requirement for perfectly drained soil makes them natural plants for the rock garden. The soil should also be light, sandy, and of low fertility.

These plants require open shade to full sun. Clarkia grows well in coastal and high-altitude areas where the nights are cool. Good success, although a shorter season, can also be enjoyed from spring sowing in the plains states. The plants should be allowed to dry out between waterings.

Clematis species and hybrids
Clematis

Climber
Open to dappled shade
Hardiness varies according to species

Clematis is among the best of the flowering climbers for a wall, fence, or trellis, or even a deciduous shrub or tree whose base, at least, is in shade. The roots require cool, rich, well-drained soil, but the tops of the plants need exposure to some direct sun.

There are hundreds of species and hybrids in great variety, from small perennials to climbers with spectacular flowers 6 inches wide. Flower color is most commonly in the white, blue, pink, and purple range, but there are also yellow forms, notably *C. tangutica*.

Most clematis begins to flower the second year after planting, and eventually grows to a height of about 15 feet. The leaf petioles twine around a slender support, but the stems often need training and tying. Most hybrids bloom on the current season's growth, so they should be pruned in early spring. Species that flower in early spring should be pruned after they bloom, if at all. With the exception of *C. armandii* (evergreen clematis; hardy to Zone 8), clematis often looks twiggy, spindly, and dead in winter, so it is not a good flowering vine to cover large areas. Where winters are cold, however, it may be the only choice. There are small-flowering species hardy to Zone 3.

Clethra alnifolia
Summersweet, sweet pepperbush

Deciduous shrub
Open shade
Hardy to Zone 5

The extremely fragrant, cool white flower spikes of summersweet make a welcome addition to the garden in July and August, when flowers are scarce. Summersweet is particularly useful in those difficult wet, shady areas of the garden. Once established, it grows slowly to a broad, oval mass 3 to 8 feet high and 4 to 8 feet wide. It is cloaked in handsome, pest-free, dark green foliage that inconsistently turns a clear yellow in fall before dropping. The plant will attract great quantities of bees while it is in flower. 'Rosea' has clear pink buds that open into flowers of white tinged with pink.

Although summersweet is quite tolerant of salty, sandy coastal conditions, its best garden performance is in moist, acid soil that is heavily supplemented with organic matter. The plant is reputedly difficult to establish. The best chance of success is with balled-and-burlapped or container-grown plants set out in early spring and watered profusely. Although native to swamps, summersweet is usually grown in the nursery in well-drained soil, so that its roots are no longer adapted to swampy soil conditions. When transplanting into wet soils, you can ease the transition by planting 3 to 4 inches higher than the soil level and mulching heavily. Summersweet is very intolerant of drought.

This shrub should be left to attain its naturally clean, dense, oval shape. Although pruning is rarely necessary, it is best done in early spring.

Clivia miniata
Kaffir-lily

Bulb
Dense to open shade
Zones 9 and 10

Kaffir-lily foliage is impressive the year around, but its spring flowers are showstoppers. Individual flowers are 2 to 3 inches wide. Umbels of up to 20 flowers atop 12- to 18-inch stems appear in spring, or earlier if the plant is grown indoors. The flowers of some modern hybrids are white or shades of red, salmon, and yellow, although the orange-red,

Clivia miniata

Convallaria majalis

yellowish centered Victorian favorites are still the most common. Kaffir-lily blooms brilliantly in dense shade and even more brilliantly in medium shade. Blooms are sometimes followed by 1-inch bright red berries.

Straplike, dark green leaves grow to 20 inches long and 3 inches wide in balanced pairs from the center of the plant. The foliage is substantial and among the most graceful of any in the garden.

Kaffir-lily can be set in the ground, but it usually does better in a container for two reasons. Its large, fleshy roots need to be crowded to induce heavy blooming, and it prefers nighttime temperatures no lower than 50° F, so it is best moved indoors during cool weather. The tuber should barely show above the soil surface, and the plant should be left undisturbed for as many years as possible. The soil should be kept moist except when growth slows in fall, when it should be allowed to dry just slightly but not so much that the leaves begin to wilt. Regular light feeding is beneficial, winter through summer.

Convallaria majalis
Lily-of-the-valley

Ground cover
Medium shade to medium sun
Zones 1 to 7

The heady fragrance and pristine, delicate beauty of the flowers of lily-of-the-valley account for their popularity in bridal bouquets and their traditional use as a May Day love gift in France. This deciduous perennial ground cover, 6 to 8 inches high, is effective alone or with ferns, beneath trees, among shade-loving shrubs, and against the north or east sides of walls or buildings. A tough, tenacious plant, lily-of-the-valley is a useful soil binder. It thrives in all but the mildest climates in a wide range of exposures, including medium shade. Plantings enlarge rapidly. From spring until frost it makes a dense, bold-textured carpet.

In midspring, just before its foliage has completely unfurled, it produces delicate stems of ¼-inch, bell-shaped, pure white flowers whose sweet fragrance ranks with that of gardenia, jasmine, and violet. Small fruits may form but most drop before the mature red stage.

Because lily-of-the-valley requires chilling, it does not thrive in Zones 8 to 10. It is hardy in all

other zones. Its exposure and soil requirements are compatible with but not limited to those of most rhododendrons and camellias. Ideally it should have a deep, sandy humus, but ordinary garden soil will do as long as drainage is good. In dense shade blooms are sparse. When conditions are suitable, it can become invasive.

For the most pleasing effect, lily-of-the-valley should be planted in drifts, with the pips (divisions with upright tips) spaced from 2 to 8 inches apart. Planting is best done in autumn after dormancy; for the best foliage and blooms, well-rotted manure should be applied liberally. The soil should be kept moist throughout the growing season. Plants may be thinned every few years.

Aside from the species, two varieties are sometimes available. 'Fortin's Giant' (often sold as 'Fortune's Giant') is a more robust plant with larger flowers and leaves. *C. majalis* var. *rosea* is like the species except for its pink flowers.

Cornus species
Dogwood, cornel,
bunchberry

Deciduous tree, shrub, ground cover
Open shade
Hardy to Zone 4

Dogwood is appreciated for its mass effect of flowers, usually white, which consist of bracts encircling a darker center. Glossy scarlet berries in sparse clusters last into winter or until birds have stripped them, and several species have colorful leaves in fall and brightly colored twigs in winter. Well-drained, acid soil is necessary. Roots need moisture and protection from extreme heat. Mulch helps to provide both and maintains soil acidity as it decays. Branches may be selectively thinned to emphasize structure. All species will grow in open shade unless another exposure is specified.

In open shade *C. florida* (flowering dogwood; hardy to Zone 7) is a small (about 20 foot), deciduous tree that creates a beautiful understory. It is brilliant with blossoms in spring, lush through summer, ablaze with autumn color, and striking when its layered structure is revealed in winter. The growth rate is slow to moderate.

Cornus florida

Cyclamen

Several cultivars and related species offer variety in size, form, color, and adaptation. It is susceptible to disease in the East. A nursery can advise you on local hardiness of the different varieties and species. 'Cherokee Chief' has rich rose-red flowers and a fairly upright habit. 'Cherokee Princess' has an abundance of white flowers. 'Cloud 9' produces white flowers early and very profusely; it accepts temperature extremes better than the species. *C. florida* 'Pendula' is a weeping form. *C. florida plena* has double white flowers. 'Rainbow' has white flowers and yellow-and-green leaves that color brilliantly in late summer and early fall. *C. florida* 'Welchii' has variegated grayish green leaves with irregular pink-and-white margins.

C. alba 'Sibirica' (Siberian dogwood; hardy to Zone 2) is a 6- to 7-foot shrub with clusters of tiny white flowers and startling coral red branches. Two variegated species grow to about 6 feet and are not as hardy as 'Sibirica', but both are very effective in shade. *C. alba* 'Argenteomarginata', often listed as 'Elegantissima', is variegated green and white. *C. alba* 'Spaethii' has yellow-variegated foliage and vivid red bark.

C. canadensis (bunchberry;

hardy to Zone 2) is a deciduous ground cover 5 to 9 inches high. It grows best in shaded, moist, woodland settings, though it will tolerate full sun in a cool place. It spreads by rhizomes and is easily propagated by division. Flowers appear in spring or summer, followed by edible bright red berries.

C. kousa (Kousa dogwood, Japanese dogwood; hardy to Zone 6) is sometimes multi-stemmed, has 2- to 3-inch white flowers with pointed petals, and bears edible fruit. The Galaxy series are hybrids of *C. florida* ×*C. kousa. C. kousa* var. *chinensis* (Chinese dogwood) also has larger flowers.

C. mas (Cornelian cherry; hardy to Zone 5) is a slow-growing shrub or small tree as tall as 24 feet that bears small yellow flowers on bare branches in late winter and early spring. The fruit is edible. Its flowering branches will extend from a partially shaded spot into a deeply shaded one.

C. stolonifera (*C. sericea*) (redosier dogwood; hardy to Zone 1) is a shrub that can form a thicket about 7 feet tall. It accepts constant moisture. The flowers are white, in small clusters, followed by berries that are white or bluish. The twigs are brilliant red in winter. *C. stolonifera* 'Flaviramea' has yellow twigs.

Cyclamen species and cultivars
Hardy cyclamen

Perennial
Open shade
Zones 5 to 9

Both the familiar florist's cyclamen and the smaller, less well known hardy species are native to Mediterranean regions. Florist's cyclamen is generally grown indoors; it will grow outdoors only in Zones 9 and 10. For the shade garden, only the hardy cyclamen is appropriate.

Cyclamen's attractive, heart-shaped leaves are often marked in pale green, white, or silver. The teardrop-shaped buds blossom into butterfly-like blooms with reflexed petals that turn backward like wings; they hover over the plants on slender, brownish red stems.

Hardy cyclamen is especially attractive in woodland settings. It grows to 4 to 5 inches tall, with ¾- to 1-inch flowers. Although it does best in Zones 5 through 9, it can tolerate colder climates if adequately mulched in winter. Tubers should be planted in midsummer in open shade and rich soil.

Species bloom in fall or spring. *C. cilicium* (Sicily cyclamen) bears pale pink flowers against silver-traced leaves in fall. *C. coum* is a spring bloomer with white, pink, or red flowers. Fall blossoms of the European cyclamen (*C. purpurascens*) are rose-red and very fragrant; the foliage is mottled in silver and white. Marbled foliage is also characteristic of late-summer–blooming *C. hederifolium* (Neapolitan cyclamen), the hardiest of the cyclamens. The rose-pink or white flowers of this fragrant plant bloom before its foliage appears.

Dennstaedtia punctilobula

Dicentra eximia, Polystichum acrostichoides

Dennstaedtia punctilobula
Hay-scented fern

Fern
Dense shade to full sun
Hardy to Zone 4

Hay-scented fern is native to the eastern United States and Canada. The finely cut pinnacles form fronds with a pyramidal outline. These feathery fronds are yellow-green and grow 20 to 32 inches long and 11 inches wide. When broken they smell of freshly cut hay, hence the common name. The fronds are deciduous, turning brown in early fall.

This fern adapts to a wide range of growing conditions, from dense shade to full sun, and alternately wet and dry seasons. It prefers a slightly acid (pH 5.5 to 6.5), damp soil with a woodland mulch but will grow in most types of soil. The rhizomes spread rapidly, forming a dense mat just below the soil surface. Hay-scented fern is an excellent ground cover, but it should be planted only where it can be allowed to spread freely. If it becomes too invasive, the excess rhizomes can simply be pulled out, then planted to establish the fern in another area. Hay-scented fern is especially effective for erosion control on slopes. Snails and slugs, which feed on the tender, young foliage, can be controlled with bait commercially available in nurseries.

Dicentra spectabilis
Bleeding-heart

Perennial
Medium shade to medium sun
Hardy to Zone 3

The flowers of bleeding-heart are aptly named. They are puffy and suggest a heart with two "drops of blood" flaring up and out from the base, resulting in an overall lyre shape. The blossoms, which are pink, rose-pink with white tips, or occasionally white, hang pendulously from horizontally arching and drooping stems. The flower clusters, up to 9 inches long, are produced within and on top of the foliage.

The foliage is medium green, often with a slightly gray cast, with deeply cut leaves that give the plant a fine-textured appearance. Dense clumps send arching sprays of foliage 30 inches high and up to 36 inches wide. Because of its relatively large size and a tendency to die down after blooming, it is best used as a specimen rather than massed, and accompanied by plants that will succeed it later in the season.

Bleeding-heart prefers rich, moist, well-drained soil that is high in organic matter. It is best kept out of drying winds. It will tolerate medium to full sun; however, in full sun the foliage will burn and die back quickly after flowering. If not grown as single specimens, the plants should be spaced 2 feet apart.

D. eximia (fringed bleeding-heart) is notable for its beautiful, finely dissected gray-green foliage, which contrasts effectively with its deep rose to white flowers. It also has a longer blooming season than the species. Several hybrid forms of this plant (probably crosses with *D. formosa,* among others) will bloom intermittently all summer long if faded blossoms are removed regularly. One example is the beautiful hybrid *D. exima* 'Bountiful', with intense, deep red flowers off and on from June until frost.

An aggressive spreader, *D. formosa* (western bleeding-heart) has flower stems about 1 foot tall and rose-purple to white blossoms.

Digitalis purpurea
Foxglove

Biennial
Dense to open shade
Hardy to Zone 4

Flowering spikes of foxglove, ranging from purple to white, glow in the darkest hollow of a woodland garden and shine in the back of a shaded bed. Because of its scale (up to 5 feet, sometimes higher) and its innate beauty, foxglove is an imposing flower, and one of the few that will bloom freely in dense shade. It is a biennial, establishing itself the first year and blooming in late spring and summer of the second. Because it self-sows freely in a suitable spot, it may be considered a perennial—and by some gardeners a pretty pest.

The flowers are tubular, to 3 inches long, usually with spotted throats. Flowers of the species are pendulous and grow on only one side of the stem. Flowers of one group of hybrids are dense, evenly distributed around the stem, and held straight outward.

Digitalis species

Dryopteris species

The evergreen leaves are large, rough-textured ovals, dark green above, light green and fuzzy beneath. They are largest and most concentrated at the base of the plant. The leaves are poisonous to humans and animals if eaten. Digitalis, a medicinal drug, is derived from them.

Foxglove requires moisture, good drainage, some degree of shade, shelter from strong wind, and rich, acid soil. Hybrids often adapt to less favorable soils. Plants should be spaced 12 to 24 inches apart and staked if necessary. Cutting spikes severely after about half the flowers have finished blooming will spur development of new spikes; cutting them later may encourage second-year bloom. Snail bait, fungicide for powdery mildew, and insecticides for aphids, mealybugs, and Japanese beetles may be needed.

Hybrids of *D. purpurea:* Excelsior hybrids produce dense, undrooping flowers all around the stems. Colors are white and shades of mauve, pink, yellow, and rose. Height is 5 feet or more. Peak bloom is in June. Some gardeners consider this the choicest group of hybrids.

The slightly pendulous flowers of 'Foxy', the first annual cultivar, begin at 18 inches and continue until the plants reach their full height of 3 feet.

Hyacinth hybrids have 3-foot flower spikes. The flowers are large and are mottled with red or brown.

Shirley hybrids also have 3-foot flower spikes. The flowers are large and crowded; many of them are dotted.

Related species and hybrids: *D. grandiflora* (*D. ambigua;* yellow foxglove, or perennial foxglove) has 3-foot spikes that bear 2-inch, pale yellow flowers with blotched throats in July. *D. ×mertonensis* (Merton's foxglove) bears large, showy, strawberry-colored flowers on 3- to 3½-foot spikes in June and July; it is short lived in cold climates.

Doronicum orientale
Leopard's-bane

Perennial
Open shade
Hardy to Zone 4

The spring-blooming, daisy-like, bright yellow flowers of leopard's-bane appear in great quantities above clusters of large, heart-shaped leaves. Each blossom is 2 to 3 inches across and appears on its own 9- to 15-inch stem. The plant blooms in May. The foliage declines and often dies down after blooming is complete. The 3- to 5-inch leaves are green, medium to coarse in texture, and are produced in low basal clumps. The clumps grow 8 to 12 inches high; with flowers the plant can reach 2 to 3 feet in height, spreading nearly as wide.

Leopard's-bane produces shallow, dense, fibrous roots. The clumps expand rapidly and start dying out in the center unless divided. Because foliage dies out early in the season, the plant is best used as a specimen rather than massed, and should be combined with other plants that will fill in the empty space. In warm climates with long, mild autumns, the foliage may come back and there may be more blooms.

The plant needs rich, moist soil that is high in organic matter. It prefers open shade, especially in hot climates. The plants should be spaced 12 to 15 inches apart and watered moderately during the growing season. There are no serious pests. Division for rejuvenation is usually required every 2 to 4 years and is best done during dormancy in August or in very early spring. Division is an excellent means of increase.

Dryopteris species
Wood fern, shield fern

Fern
Dense to medium shade
Hardy to Zone 3

This large group of ferns includes many that are native to the forests of the United States and Canada. Most are very hardy, evergreen, and easy to grow.

All wood ferns need shade, moist soil, and a humus-rich soil. Many forms spread by underground runners and thus are easily propagated by division.

D. carthusiana (florist's fern) is widely distributed throughout eastern North America. Its fronds are harvested in summer and shipped in winter.

A good landscape accent plant also native to the Northeast is *D. marginalis* (leather wood fern). It grows in clumps to about 2 feet high and is hardy to -35° F.

D. arguta (coastal wood fern) is native to western North America. It grows to about 3 feet.

Duchesnea indica

Epimedium species

Duchesnea indica
Indian-strawberry, mock strawberry

Ground cover
Medium shade to sun
Hardy to Zone 4

This evergreen strawberry relative and look-alike is a versatile ground cover. The berries resemble strawberries. Like a strawberry plant, the Indian-strawberry spreads by runners, except more rapidly, to form a dense mat about 6 inches high, sometimes higher in heavy shade. Although in most areas it accepts sun, it is more at home in medium to open shade. It grows sparsely in dense shade and mats more densely in bright areas than in dark ones. Its pretty flowers, berries, and graceful runners make it a useful subject for hanging baskets.

Bright yellow flowers, ½ to 1 inch across, are held conspicuously above the foliage. They are followed by ½-inch scarlet berries, tasteless to birds as well as to people, so they remain to brighten the garden for weeks. The leaves, on slender stems, are composed of 3 soft green leaflets, more textured and less glossy than strawberry foliage.

Any well-drained soil suits Indian-strawberry. Once established, it tolerates drought with no lessening of attractiveness, but it thrives with moisture as well. Plants should be spaced 12 to 18 inches apart. Occasional foot traffic is acceptable. Hardier than strawberry, it is indifferent to neglect. Because it spreads rapidly, it can be a nuisance, although an easily controlled one.

Enkianthus species
Enkianthus

Deciduous shrub
Open to dappled shade
Hardiness varies according to species

These Japanese 6- to 8-foot shrubs have distinctive, whorled leaves, which give the plants a layered appearance. Strings of bell-shaped flowers appear in late spring. Brilliant fall color is one of the plant's greatest contributions to the shady garden. Like most members of the heath family, *Enkianthus* requires acid soil high in organic matter.

E. campanulatus, hardy to Zone 5, is the hardiest of the genus. It has dull green leaves that turn bright orange in fall. The red-veined flowers are yellow to bronze. 'Red Bells' has red flowers. The following two species are preferable where they are hardy, because they have larger flowers and better fall color.

E. cernuus rubens (hardy to Zone 7) grows 6 feet tall and has bright red flowers.

E. perulatus (hardy to Zone 7) has white flowers and resembles an elegant form of *Halesia.*

Epimedium species
Barrenwort, bishop's-hat

Ground cover
Dense shade to full sun
Hardy to Zone 3

Barrenwort is easy to grow, hardy, and too seldom used. Even in dry shade, it spreads with creeping roots to make a uniform, 9-inch ground cover. The plant is semievergreen; most of the leathery, heart-shaped leaves die back in winter, but a few last into January. In early spring the new leaves are pale green with some rose color. During midseason they are deep, glossy green; in fall they turn reddish. Tiny, ½-inch, orchidlike flowers (shaped like a bishop's hat) appear in May. Many colors are available; all last well when cut. The plant is very hardy, tolerating temperatures to -40° F.

Long lived and easy to grow, barrenwort prefers open shade but tolerates full sun if the soil (preferably acid) is rich and moist. It tolerates dense shade if drainage is good, although flower production will suffer. The creeping roots are close to the surface, so cultivating around them should be avoided. Plants spaced 10 inches apart will fill in without overcrowding. To propagate, the clumps should be divided in early spring. Cutting off old leaves allows the small flowers and new leaves to be more visible.

Barrenwort thrives in the open shade of other acid-soil plants such as the taller rhododendrons, camellias, and ferns. Barrenwort's roots compete well with those of other plants, so it is ideal under trees and shrubs.

Enkianthus campanulatus

Euonymus fortunei

E. grandiflorum is the most commonly cultivated form. It grows to about 1 foot. 'Rose Queen' has bright, rose-colored flowers with white-tipped spurs. The hybrid *E. ×versicolor* 'Sulphureum' has yellow flowers. *E. ×youngianum* 'Niveum' grows compactly and has white flowers.

Erythronium
Erythronium

Bulb
Medium shade to medium sun
Hardiness varies according to species

This picturesque group of bulbs comes mainly from North American woodlands, although the one European native, *E. denscanis,* is the best known. Its common name, dogtooth violet, has nothing to do with the appearance of the flower but is based on the resemblance of the corm to a dog's tooth. The delicate flower is purple or rose, rising from mottled leaves on a 6-inch stem. It is hardy to Zone 3.

A number of species, many of them with mottled foliage, are American natives. They are known by several descriptive names, most commonly fawn lily, trout lily, adder's-tongue, and Easter-bells. *E. grandiflorum* (hardy to Zone 6) has plain green foliage and 24-inch stems with yellow blossoms. *E. citrinum* also bears yellow flowers, but the stems are only 8 inches tall.

The other species grow to a height of about 12 inches with flower colors as follows: *E. albidum* (hardy to Zone 5), white to light blue; *E. americanum* (hardy to Zone 4), yellow tinged with pink; *E. californicum,* creamy white or yellow; *E. hendersonii,* purple; *E. oregonum,* creamy white; *E. revolutum,* white to purple; and *E. tuolumnense,* yellow with a greenish base. The latter five are all hardy to Zone 6. All bloom in spring, and many have a delicate fragrance. The foliage dies back in summer.

Erythronium is especially attractive in a woodland setting. It should be planted in fall in moist, well-drained soil and in medium to open shade in warm areas, or in medium sun where summers are cooler. It needs moisture all summer long even though dormant, and it does not like extreme heat. Fall mulching offers sufficient protection in cold regions.

Euonymus fortunei
Wintercreeper

Evergreen vine, prostrate shrub, ground cover
Medium shade to full sun
Zones 5 to 8

Hardy, tough wintercreeper grows in nearly every part of North America, in virtually any soil or exposure. The flowers are inconspicuous, but the evergreen foliage of this species and its varieties is attractive, even striking, and dependably fresh looking. It can be used as a vine, prostrate shrub, or ground cover. Stems root wherever they touch moist soil, spreading out to 4 feet, sometimes much farther, and forming a dense mass up to 2 feet high. When well established, it leaves no room for weeds. Deep roots bind soil on slopes or banks. It will cover rocky soil and stumps, fill in solidly under shrubs and trees, and serve as a lawn substitute in shade. Roots cling to rough surfaces, enabling wintercreeper to climb to 20 feet or more. It grows well everywhere except in desert areas, but even there it sometimes succeeds reasonably well. It prefers medium shade to full sun.

Care is easy, unless the plant is infested by scale. Scale can be controlled with dormant oil spray in early spring, followed by applications of diazinon or Orthene® when the orange-red crawlers first appear.

The species itself is less popular than the following varieties.

'Coloratus' (purpleleaf wintercreeper), the most popular, turns various shades of purple during autumn and winter. It forms a dense, even carpet 6 to 10 inches high and is a vigorous grower.

'Gracilis', smaller and less vigorous than 'Coloratus', has white or yellowish variegated leaves that turn rosy in winter.

'Kewensis' (Kew wintercreeper), sometimes sold as 'Minimus', is a dwarf form about 2 inches high. The ¼-inch-long leaves have near-white veins. It is appropriate as a ground cover or rock garden subject.

E. fortunei var. *radicans* is the fastest growing of the small-leafed varieties, making a quick ground cover or wall cover. It is confusing that the species, *E. fortunei,* is sometimes sold as *E. radicans*—not the same as diminutive cultivar *E. fortunei* var. *radicans.*

Fatsia japonica

Fragaria chiloensis

Fatsia japonica
Japanese aralia

Evergreen shrub
Dense to medium shade
Hardy to Zone 7

Japanese aralia is also listed as *Aralia japonica* or *A. sieboldii*. The gardener faced with a densely shaded entryway, an overhung north wall, an empty container in a recessed spot, or any other deep-shade problem situation that calls for bold greenery should consider this easy solution. A close relative of the common ivy, Japanese aralia can create a luxurious tropical effect in the darkest, most discouraging corner of the garden. It is one of the easiest shade plants to grow. A single plant can quickly fill an area 6 to 8 feet high and just as wide with handsome evergreen foliage and occasional blooms and fruit. In time it will fill an even larger area.

The blooms, which appear in fall and winter, are rather uninteresting individually but showy in their compound, milky white clusters up to 18 inches long. Round black berries, to ¼ inch in diameter, last through winter.

The leaves are deeply lobed, roundish, to 16 inches wide, and held on 12-inch stems. They are dark green and glossy.

Any spot in dense or medium shade that is sheltered from the wind is suitable. Virtually any soil is acceptable, although rich, moist, acid soil is best. The plant should be fertilized periodically. If the leaves are yellowish with dark green veins, feeding should be supplemented with chelated iron or iron sulfate. As the plant begins to lose its lower leaves, it should be pruned low to encourage sprouting from the base. For the best effect, one or more smaller plants should be placed in front of an older, larger one if space allows. Snails and slugs should be removed, and any aphids hosed off.

'Moseri' is low and compact. 'Variegata' has leaves with golden or creamy borders.

Fothergilla species
Fothergilla

Deciduous shrub
Open to dappled shade
Hardy to Zone 6

Beautiful flower spikes, reminiscent of bottle brushes, and bright fall foliage come with these native plants of the southeastern United States. Like azalea, fothergilla is suited to cool, acid soil high in organic matter,

and to the open or dappled shade of open woodlands or places next to taller shrubs. In heavy shade the fall color is less bright.

F. gardenii (dwarf fothergilla, witch-alder), only about 3 feet tall and wide, is ideal in foundation plantings by shady walls or in front of a row of taller shrubs. The creamy white flowers appear in spring before the leaves. The foliage turns bright yellow in fall.

F. major (large fothergilla) can reach 9 feet tall and an equal width. The white flowers grow in 2-inch spikes. The fall foliage is bright yellow to scarlet.

Fragaria chiloensis
Wild or sand strawberry

Ground cover
Open shade
Hardy to Zone 5

Rich, glossy foliage, not fruit, is this evergreen perennial's greatest asset in the garden. In open shade it creates a deep green ground cover for large or small areas, including slopes and the front of beds. Its runners trail gracefully over walls and banks. It will grow in medium shade but sparsely and with dull, not glossy, leaves.

White flowers 1 inch wide appear in spring (late winter in coastal areas). In the wild, red berries develop in spring and summer. Wild strawberry seldom fruits in the garden, and when it does the berries are usually dry and tasteless.

Leaves vary in size depending on soil and climate. Usually each leaflet of the 3-part leaf is 2 inches long. Leaves form a mat from 6 to 10 inches high.

In its native habitat, wild strawberry grows in sandy soil, sometimes covering dunes. In the garden it likes similar soil, sandy and fast draining. It can be planted from flats or sections of runners, spaced a foot or more apart. In early spring the plants should be clipped or mowed. If after 2 to 3 years the cover becomes sparse and uneven, the area should be raked vigorously in early spring to thin old growth and stimulate new. Then the area should be fertilized lightly with lawn fertilizer. Wild strawberry requires average watering in open shade, infrequent watering in dense shade. Infestations of spider mites can be controlled with sprays.

Fritillaria species

Fuchsia

Rancho Santa Ana Botanic Garden in California has developed Hybrid Ornamental Strawberry No. 25, a larger and more vigorous grower than the species, which produces delicious berries. It is virtually free of disease except for some mildew when it is overwatered in damp coastal areas.

F. californica (California wood strawberry; hardy to Zone 7) is sometimes available on the West Coast. It is best used in woodland plantings, not as a ground cover, in open to medium shade. Moderate to infrequent watering is best.

F. virginiana (Virginia strawberry; hardy to Zone 4), native to eastern North America, is occasionally available in specialty nurseries there. Its uses are similar to those of *F. californica,* but it requires more moisture.

Fritillaria species
Fritillary

Bulb
Open shade
Zones 3 to 8

Open shade and well-drained, moist, cool, acid soil rich in humus suit this woodland native. All forms have rather unusual drooping flowers and narrow leaves that die back with the hot weather of summer.

F. meleagris (snake's-head lily, checkered lily, guinea-hen-flower) is a hardy European bulb that grows to about 12 inches, sometimes higher, and bears curious but exquisite 2-inch, bell-shaped flowers in a solitary, pendulous habit. Their remarkable patterns and colors—subtly checkered in purples and maroons, yellow, and white—account for various common names. In a border, near the edge of a woodland, or in a shaded rock garden, *F. meleagris* creates a subtle but striking focal point during its April to May blooming. If it is well placed, it will naturalize. It particularly likes to grow in unmowed grass, perhaps because there its roots are cool. It may also be grown in containers.

Several North American species of this genus rank among the most beautiful of American wildflowers and are well worth locating and cultivating in the woodland garden. Like the calochortuses, they are disappearing from many areas where they were once numerous. However, commercial propagation, even if limited, makes these beauties available to the gardener who seeks out unusual and particularly pleasing flowers.

F. affinis (missionbells; hardy to Zone 5), native to California and northwestern North America, bears 1½-inch, bell-shaped flowers, chocolate brown to purple, mottled with greenish yellow. Flowers are borne atop a 1- to 3-foot purplish stem with whorls of rich green foliage.

F. pudica (yellowbell; hardy to Zone 3), less than 12 inches high, grows in dry, rocky soil in the Rocky Mountains and the Sierra Nevada. It is especially suited to rock garden and container culture.

F. recurva (scarlet fritillary; hardy to Zone 6), native to areas of open shade in California and southern Oregon, is

the showiest native fritillary. In habit and flower form, it resembles *F. affinis,* except that its flowers are scarlet, flecked yellow inside the bells and tinged with purple outside. Petals curve outward at the tips. Blooming begins in March. Like the other native fritillaries, this one is best planted in fall, and like them it grows best in California, the Northwest, or wherever the climate is similar.

Fuchsia
Fuchsia

Perennial sometimes used as annual
Dense to open shade
Hardy to Zone 9

The colorful magenta, white, and pink blossoms of fuchsia brighten any shaded spot. Upright varieties reach various heights, up to 10 feet, and lend themselves to use as specimens, components of shrub borders, or espaliers. Some are pruned to a single vertical stem to form graceful standards. Others, diminutive and trailing, are best grown in hanging planters or in raised beds. These are the types favored in places where fuchsia can be grown only as a summer annual or a houseplant or greenhouse plant.

Galium odoratum

Gaultheria procumbens

The flowers appear profusely from spring until winter in the mildest areas. They are pendulous on thin stems, usually 2 to 6 inches long, and often bicolored. Hummingbirds love the flowers in all their forms and colors.

Fuchsia should be planted in spring in well-drained soil high in organic matter. It is very sensitive to drought, so it should be watered regularly to keep the soil moist. A heavy feeder, it should be fertilized with a complete fertilizer every 2 weeks.

Fading blooms should be removed to encourage continual blossoming, and stem tips should be pinched back to prevent plants from becoming leggy. Each spring, fuchsia should be pruned back to the edge of its container or two thirds of the way back to the ground. Fuchsia grows fast and blooms only on new wood.

Many fuchsia species are cultivated, but the following two are particularly valuable in a shade garden.

F. magellanica (Magellan fuchsia), native to Chile and Argentina, is used as a specimen, or as a hedge in the more temperate parts of Britain and North America. A vigorous grower, it can reach 20 feet trained on walls, but it is seen more often as a shrub of 3 to 8 feet. Flowers are small (1½ inches) but very profuse. Sepals are bright red, and the corolla is blue. This is one of the hardiest fuchsias (to Zone 6); it is also one of the least finicky.

F. procumbens, from the North Island of New Zealand, is a prostrate ground cover whose many branched, aggressively spreading stems root freely. Its small blossoms are yellow, brownish red, and green, with blue pollen. The pink fruits are showy. It prefers moist, rich soil in medium shade and is hardy only in Zone 10.

Galax urceolata
Galax, wandflower, beetleweed, galaxy

Ground cover
Dense to dappled shade
Hardy to Zone 6

This evergreen ground cover is native to woodlands of the southeastern United States but is hardy farther north. Clumps 1 foot tall and equally wide of rounded, glossy, dark green leaves are crowned by spires of starry white flowers in early summer. The foliage turns partially bronze in fall. Galax spreads by rhizomes and is easy to propagate by division. It does best in moist, acid soil high in organic matter.

Galium odoratum
Sweet woodruff

Ground cover
Dense to open shade
Hardy to Zone 4

Also known as *Asperula odorata,* sweet woodruff is an old favorite in Europe, where it creates a 6-inch-thick carpet under deciduous trees. Its name suggests the fragrance of its small, starry white flowers that arise from the centers of the whorls of narrow, dark green leaves. When sweet woodruff has the moist, rich, organic soil and open shade it prefers, it can become invasive because of self-sowing, so it should be kept away from small plants that cannot take competition. Given a place of its own, without foot traffic, where it can spread undisturbed, it will create a beautiful effect from spring until fall.

Gaultheria procumbens
Wintergreen, teaberry, checkerberry

Ground cover
Dense to open shade
Hardy to Zone 3

Best known for the flavoring extracted from it, wintergreen is one of the densest evergreen ground covers for dense, medium, or open shade. A single plant spreads by underground stems to form a 3- to 6-inch-high mat covering about a square yard. Its ¼- to ½-inch flowers, resembling lily-of-the-valley but often tinged with pink, appear in May through early summer. The aromatic scarlet berries that follow last through winter unless eaten by birds, people, or field mice.

Oval leaves, 1 to 2 inches long, cluster toward the ends of upright stems. Their tops are glossy dark green and their undersides light green. In autumn some leaves remain green; others turn orange, crimson, or bronze.

Gelsemium sempervirens

Hakonechloa macra 'Aureola'

Rich, moist, acid soil and some shade are best for wintergreen. It is useful in woodland gardens, rock gardens, and the foreground of borders. If not planted in clumps, individual plants should be spaced 12 to 18 inches apart.

Wintergreen should be watered and weeded until well established. A light sprinkling of fine conifer needles from time to time will help keep the soil acid. Established plants can tolerate some drought but look better with regular watering.

G. ovatifolia (western teaberry, Oregon wintergreen) is an attractive but seldom available spreading ground cover to 8 inches high. It is similar to the species except that its leaves are thicker and more serrated, its blossoms are smaller, and it flowers later (June and July).

G. shallon (salal) is the largest wintergreen used in American gardens; it grows to about 5 feet high in a moist, shaded location, or 1 to 1½ feet in a dry, bright exposure. The leathery, rich green leaves are

evergreen and grow to 5 inches long and 1½ inches wide; they are used as greenery by florists. Flowers are like those of *G. procumbens* but larger, on reddish stems in 5- to 6-inch loose clusters. The ¼-inch berries are edible but bland and are very attractive to birds. Salal grows in open to medium shade. It tolerates poor soil and drought, although it looks better in rich, well-drained acid soil. It is a suitable ground cover beneath trees that tolerate summer drought, and it can become somewhat invasive where conditions suit it. However, it is not yet widely available beyond the West Coast of the United States.

Gelsemium sempervirens
Carolina jessamine

Climber
Dappled shade to full sun
Hardy to Zone 8

Suited to a wall, fence, or trellis in dappled shade, Carolina jessamine, the state flower of South Carolina, grows at a moderate rate to 20 to 30 feet. It climbs by twining and needs sturdy support and occasional tying to help it along. Masses of fragrant, tubular, buttery yellow flowers a little more than an inch long begin blooming in late

winter or early spring and last for 2 to 4 months. The buds require cool nights in order to open. The dense, attractive, glossy green leaves grow to 3 inches long and are somewhat evergreen. The vine should be thinned by pruning just after blooming. Every part of this plant is extremely poisonous to eat but safe to touch.

Geranium species
Cranesbill

Perennial, ground cover
Open shade to partial sun
Hardiness varies according to species

The genus *Geranium* includes a group of plants that are very different from the tender, sun-loving plants often called geraniums but whose genus name is *Pelargonium*. Cranesbills are hardy, most are tolerant of shade, and their flowers are relatively small. The plants often spread to become ground covers, and the foliage is attractive from spring to fall; so are good choices for the front of a shady border or along a pathway. Most flower in spring or early summer. There are at least a dozen good species for shade. The following are among the best.

G. endressii (hardy to Zone 4) is a European native whose bright pink flowers grow on stalks about 1½ feet tall. There are several cultivars with slightly different shades of pink flowers, such as 'A.T. Johnson' and 'Wargrave Pink'.

G. macrorrhizum (hardy to Zone 3) is a ground cover about 1 foot high. The species has magenta flowers, but more attractive are the white-blooming cultivars 'Album' and 'Ingwersen's Variety'.

G. pratense (meadow cranesbill, hardy to Zone 3) has blue flowers. 'Kashmire Purple', 'Kashmir White', and the cultivated double forms are less invasive and even more beautiful.

Hakonechloa macra
'Aureola'
Forestgrass

Ground cover
Open shade
Hardy to Zone 4

This grass is a relatively recent introduction to the United States from the mountains and forests of Japan. The long, arching, deciduous leaves are variegated creamy white. The plant spreads slowly by rhizomes and is never invasive. Equally effective in pots or planted in large drifts, the grass presents a tidy,

Halesia species

Hamamelis × intermedia

uniform appearance, reaching up to 12 inches high. This grass should be grown in acid soil that has both excellent drainage and plenty of organic matter. Bright, indirect light is best; full sun is not recommended.

Halesia species
Silverbell, snowdrop tree

Deciduous shrub
Open shade to full sun
Hardy to Zone 6

These native American shrubs or small trees are beautiful and loosely branched. *H. tetraptera* (Carolina silverbell) grows as tall as 25 feet and spreads equally wide. *H. monticola* (mountain silverbell, snowbell) is more vigorous, to about 40 feet high and 30 feet wide. In spring, before the foliage appears, there are thousands of ¾-inch, unscented, bell-shaped flowers, usually white, although *H. monticola* 'Rosea' has pale pink flowers. Silverbell needs rich, moist acid soil and should be sheltered from strong winds.

Hamamelis species
Witch hazel

Deciduous shrub
Open shade
Hardiness varies according to species

All witch hazels are delightful for their spicily fragrant, delicately showy winter flowers. During periods of extreme cold, the flower petals curl up into a tight ball and thus can withstand prolonged periods covered with ice in 0° F weather.

Witch hazel should be planted in deep, rich soil that has an abundant supply of moisture. Although it will not tolerate drought, it doesn't need to be pampered—it is virtually pest free. It can be used as a screen, background, or large focal point, or trained into a small tree. Because witch hazel performs well in open shade, it makes an excellent choice for a naturalized woodland understory. It should be planted near a window where its winter blooms can be seen from indoors.

The hybrid *H. × intermedia* is not as fragrant or as restrained in size as some others, but it is the showiest of all the witch hazels available in the United States. As early as February its leafless branches are covered with deep yellow blossoms

that last about a month. The red-flowered cultivars, such as 'Jelena' (the flowers are actually a coppery orange), although interesting, are not as outstanding from a distance as are the forms with yellow flowers.

Witch hazel is not a shrub for a small garden; it will eventually reach 15 to 20 feet in height with a comparable spread. It produces an outstanding show of fall color in reds, oranges, and yellows before the leaves drop.

H. vernalis (vernal witch hazel; Zones 6 to 9) has a tidy, small habit (6 to 10 feet high and usually much wider) that is round and dense. Powerfully fragrant, small yellow flowers appear in January and February. The leaves turn a clear yellow in fall. It is native to gravelly, often-flooded stream banks in the Ozark Mountains.

H. virginiana (common witch hazel; Zones 5 to 9) is the hardiest but also the largest and rangiest of the witch hazels, growing 20 to 30 feet high and

wide. Its yellow flowers in November and December often coincide with the clear yellow fall foliage, reducing their effectiveness, but they are quite fragrant. It is native to forest understories from Canada to Georgia and west to Nebraska.

Hedera helix
English ivy

Evergreen vine, ground cover
Dense shade to partial sun
Hardy to Zone 5

As a ground cover, English ivy does almost everything: stays green the entire year, spreads rapidly, lies flat, climbs and covers, prevents erosion, provides insulation, grows in sun or shade, adapts to most climates, requires minimal care, is easily propagated, and besides all that can be enormously attractive. It is evergreen where winters are mild, but the foliage browns in colder weather.

An ivy bed is most easily begun with well-established plants, which can be purchased in pots. Fast-growing cultivars should be planted one per square foot; small-leafed or slow-growing ivies should be planted two, three, or four to the square foot. Generally, self-branching and compact growers will cover more densely.

Hedera helix 'Baltica'

Helleborus niger

English ivy requires well-drained soil. It grows best in indirect light, but once it is established it will tolerate full sun. In dense shade, growth will be slow.

After the initial growth—English ivy spurts in spring and fall—it can be replenished or extended by taking cuttings. Ivy grows well despite adverse conditions. It roots easily, even in water.

Maintenance of an ivy bed is easy. It is a good practice to mow it every other year just before the new growth, with the mower at the highest setting. This prevents the growth from becoming so dense that it can harbor snails, slugs, and rats. The mowed plants will be covered with leaves with the first growth of spring.

If allowed to climb, English ivy grows moderately to quickly to 50 feet or higher. It climbs by roots that attach firmly to wood, concrete, or stone. The lobed, dark green leaves are 2 to 4 inches long. The vine forms dense, woody mats. It can be pruned vigorously at any time. Because it can damage wood and is an aggressive grower, in the garden as well as on structures, it is not a choice plant for house walls.

English ivy can be afflicted by leaf spot, which begins as ¼-inch brown or black spots. This condition is generally not serious, but it can become unsightly. If it does, the area should be sprayed with a fungicide containing copper. Spider mites can be troublesome. In hot, dry regions, care includes watering beds of ivy as much as you would a lawn.

Among the hardiest cultivars for cold areas are 'Bulgaria' and 'Hebron'. The many variegated cultivars are suitable only for warmer zones. The species *H. helix* has the most cultivars, due mainly to ivy's penchant for "sporting," in which it suddenly and for no apparent reason makes spontaneous changes in its genetic composition, producing leaves that differ from the original ones in color, shape, size, or growth pattern.

Helleborus niger
Christmas-rose

Evergreen perennial
Open shade
Hardy to Zone 3; evergreen to Zone 5

Christmas-rose produces splendid flowers, often out of the snow, sometime between November and March or April. Its substantial, glossy foliage enlivens otherwise drab garden areas during the bleakest months. Not a rose but a relative of the buttercup, it forms drifts of ground cover. Its clumps enlarge by spreading rhizomes, but it is slow growing and never invasive. It is also useful as a specimen, a foreground plant with border shrubs, and in scattered groupings in woodland gardens.

The flowers, 2 to 4 inches wide, resemble single roses and are usually pure white with bright yellow stamens. Some forms are pinkish or greenish, or become pinkish green or purple as they age. They usually last for several months. The uncommonly handsome leaves are divided into 7 or more glossy, dark leaflets, finely serrated toward the tips. The plant is bitter tasting and very poisonous to humans and animals.

Christmas-rose accepts most rich soils but prefers well-drained neutral or slightly alkaline soil with high organic content. Care is moderately easy as long as the plant is properly situated and kept moist. Fertilizer is not usually necessary, or even desirable, because nitrogen can damage the roots. Occasional leaf-spot fungus is easily treated. This plant dislikes being moved, but if division is necessary it should be done in spring, after blooming. The roots should be separated carefully so that each division has several eyes (leaf buds). Eyes should be buried about an inch.

H. foetidus (stinking hellebore), despite its forbidding name, is a graceful, 1½-foot plant with lush, shining, compound leaves that are usually semievergreen. From January to April it produces a profusion of pendulous, bell-shaped, 1-inch blooms, greenish on the lower parts of the plant and reddish higher up. It is drought tolerant and looks good in planters as well as in the garden situations described for *H. niger.*

H. argutifolius (Corsican hellebore), from Corsica and the Balearic Islands, grows to 2 to 3 feet in height. In late winter or early spring, it produces masses of large, apple green flowers that persist until summer. This is the best hellebore for the Southwest and similar climate areas. Like *H. foetidus* it is drought tolerant when established. This species is hardy to Zone 7.

Heuchera species

Hosta species

H. orientalis (lenten-rose), from Greece and Asia Minor, is the best hellebore for the Northeast. (Actually, several forms are sold under this name. Most have leaves that die during the coldest winter, although flowers appear in early to midspring.) It closely resembles *H. niger*, but its foliage is lighter green. Flowers may be deep red, purplish green, pink, or white. All are spotted in shades of green. Cultural requirements are essentially those of *H. niger*.

Heuchera species
Coralbells, alumroot

Perennial
Medium shade to full sun
Hardy to Zone 4

These North American plants have become the darlings of the English perennial border, because they are adaptable to cloudy and shady conditions, the flowers are charming and distinctive, and the foliage is attractively roundish or kidney shaped, marbled with white or bronze against medium green. They are natives of woodlands and mountains. Tiny, jewellike red or pink flowers grow above

the foliage on wiry stems 18 inches tall. Flowering may continue all summer. Given moist, rich soil with plenty of organic matter, most species can tolerate full sun, but all are more dependable in shade. They should be propagated by division, which should be done every 3 years to keep them growing well.

    H. sanguinea (coralbells) grows about 1 foot tall. Flowers are red. This is the parent of most garden strains, such as the Bressingham hybrids. *H. americana* (American alumroot) grows in small hills of mottled, glossy green leaves. *H. micrantha* 'Palace Purple' has showy bronze-red foliage and modest greenish white flowers.

Hosta species and hybrids
Hosta, plantain lily

Perennial, ground cover
Dense to open shade
Hardy to Zone 3

The lush, subtly colored foliage of hosta makes it a welcome addition to any shade garden. It is ideal around trees and shrubs and along walkways. It is a late bloomer—with tall stalks of

lilylike white to lilac blooms appearing from July to October—but the flowers are far less important than the foliage, and flowers are fewer in deeper shade. The slender to heart-shaped leaves grow in a basal rosette. Depending on the species, the clump may attain a height of 2 feet and sometimes measure up to 40 inches across.

    Hosta prefers rich, well-drained soil that is kept evenly moist. Crown rot can be a problem in soggy soil. New plantings can be established in spring with nursery plants or young divisions; the plants should be set 2 to 3 feet apart. Hosta grown from seed takes at least 3 years for sizable plants to develop. Hosta almost never requires division and may last 30 years or more in one spot. To propagate, only young plants up to 3 years of age should be divided; older plants develop a tough crown that is hard to separate and even more difficult to establish. Snails and slugs love to feast on hosta; it can be protected with bait available at a nursery.

Some nurseries specialize in hosta. There are several species and scores of cultivars. Leaves may be large or small, smooth or wrinkled, bright or dark green. They may have a powdery blue cast or be silvery white. Plants with white or yellow variegated leaves are very popular.

Hydrangea species
Hydrangea

Deciduous shrub
Dense shade to full sun
Hardiness varies according to species

The huge, mop-headed hydrangea commonly grown in pots by florists, *H. macrophylla* (bigleaf hydrangea, hardy to Zone 7), is just one of several shade-tolerant members of the genus. All of the following do best in rich, moist soil.

    H. macrophylla has an excellent late-summer floral display (July and August) and lustrous, tidy foliage in mild-winter areas. Generally, however, varieties suitable as container plants are not as satisfactory in the garden. Outdoors, this hydrangea is a round shrub with many erect, infrequently branched stems reaching 4 to 8 feet in height (sometimes 12 feet); it spreads freely, due to its tendency to sucker vigorously.

Hydrangea macrophylla

Ilex verticillata

The many available cultivars are generally divided between the hortensias, with sterile flowers forming large, globular heads, and the lace caps, which have a delicate ring of large, sterile flowers surrounding a cluster of tiny, fertile ones. Flowers, which can be single or double, are white, pink, or blue and are generally clustered in heads that are 5 to 10 inches in diameter.

Bigleaf hydrangea prefers, rather than just tolerates, seashore conditions, where it can be planted in full sun. Otherwise, it should be planted in medium shade in moist, rich, well-drained soil that is high in organic matter. In dense shade the plant is leggy and flowering is reduced.

Soil acidity affects the uptake of aluminum by the plant, which in turn determines whether the flowers are pink or blue. Blue flowers result from a pH of 5 to 5.5; pink flowers occur in soil with a pH of 6 or higher. Applying aluminum sulfate to the soil increases acidity for blue flowers; applying lime decreases acidity for pink flowers. Either must be accomplished well before blooming to achieve the color desired. Bigleaf hydrangea flowers on old wood, so pruning should

be done just after flowering. If the plant dies back from a hard winter, it will not produce flowers that season.

H. arborescens has the advantage of hardiness, to Zone 3, although flowers are not pink or blue but white. It grows 3 feet tall and is of easy culture, requiring only an annual pruning after flowering. It does best in open shade. In the northern part of its range, it winter-kills to the ground and regrows every spring. Flowers appear in June and last all season, gradually fading to green, then brown.

H. paniculata 'Grandiflora' is the usual cultivar, although 'Annabelle' is more compact and earlier to flower and thus is more attractive in most situations.

H. quercifolia (oakleaf hydrangea; hardy to Zone 6) grows in dense shade and reaches 3 to 6 feet high. The foliage is reason enough to grow it even in gardens too cool for the white flowers to bloom. The leaves are attractively corrugated and turn orange or plum in fall.

Ilex species
Holly

Evergreen and deciduous shrub
Medium shade to full sun
Hardiness varies according
to species

Holly is a highly ornamental tree or shrub that is notable for its leathery, shiny green leaves and clusters of mostly red (sometimes yellow or black) berries. Some hollies are self-fertile; others need both a male and a female plant to produce berries, which grow only on the female.

Holly thrives in good, well-drained garden soil in medium shade to full sun. Regular watering is needed throughout the year. It can be pruned to shape and control growth. Holly leaf-miner is its most serious insect pest; it can be controlled by spraying with Orthene® or diazinon when damage is first noticed. Mealybugs, whiteflies, and scale are occasional pests that are easily controlled.

I. cornuta (Chinese holly; hardy to Zone 7) is a large, upright shrub 10 to 15 feet tall; many smaller, denser cultivars of this shrub are available as well. The leaves are an extremely handsome, polished, dark green in all seasons; they are larger and coarser than those

of Japanese holly. Berries are profuse and normally red.

I. crenata (Japanese holly; hardy to Zone 7) is commonly mistaken for boxwood because of its tidy, rounded shape and dense, lustrous, fine-textured, dark green foliage. The berries of this species are black and inconspicuous. A slow-growing shrub that responds well to pruning, it will eventually reach 5 to 10 feet in height, usually with a greater spread; older specimens may reach a height of 20 feet or more. Japanese holly is an excellent selection for hedges, foundation planting, and massing, and for an evergreen, soft texture in the shrub border. It transplants easily into moist, well-drained, slightly acid soil, does well in shade or sun, and is quite tolerant of pollution.

I. glabra (inkberry; hardy to Zone 3) is the hardiest broadleaf evergreen available to northern gardeners. The handsome, dark green foliage grows densely on younger plants in all seasons. Older plants often reach 6 to 8 feet tall and 8 to 10 feet wide and develop a leggy openness, although this is quite variable. The berries are black and not particularly showy.

Impatiens with *Bergenia*

Iris kaempferi

I. × *meserveae* is a group of hollies hardy to Zone 5 developed by Mrs. Leighton Meserve of New York. 'Blue Prince' and 'Blue Princess' are the cultivars most commonly available. Both are necessary for the appearance of the bright red berries. The shrubs are slow growing but can reach 8 to 10 feet.

I. verticillata (common winterberry; Zones 4 to 8) is a deciduous holly that is unusual for its adaptability to wet, swampy soil, to which it is native. A popular plant in the eastern United States, it is an outstanding fruiting shrub that bears great quantities of bright red berries on bare branches far into the winter if planted in a fairly sunny location. Birds find the berries tasty, so the effective season often depends on their appetite. Winterberry can grow to 20 feet high in the wild but usually reaches only 6 to 9 feet in the garden, with a similar spread. A male holly must be planted within a few hundred feet of each female to ensure fruiting.

I. vomitoria (yaupon; hardy to Zone 8) is a small, evergreen tree, although several cultivars are available, such as 'Nana' and 'Stoke's Dwarf', which are effectively dwarf (18 inches or less) and compact. Popular in the southeastern United States, this holly is more tolerant of alkaline soil and drought than other hollies. Its fine-textured foliage can easily be sheared into formal shapes. Although the species is considered one of the heaviest fruiting of all the hollies, the dwarf forms are generally sterile.

Impatiens wallerana
Impatiens, busy-lizzie

Perennial used as annual
Dense to open shade
Impatiens is one of the most versatile flowering plants for shade. It is used for color under shrubs, along walkways, and tucked into corners by entranceways. It also grows readily in containers and window boxes and provides color in hanging baskets under eaves. It blooms continually from transplanting to the first fall frost, with showy single or double flowers in shades of pink, magenta, mauve, salmon, orange, white, and bicolors. The glossy, dark green leaves frequently have a bronze

hue. The erect, succulent stems, 6 to 18 inches tall, are very sensitive and wilt easily as the soil dries. Impatiens should be watered regularly, especially in hot weather, to keep the soil moist. It should be fertilized lightly each month with a complete fertilizer.

Impatiens grows easily from seed when started indoors 10 to 12 weeks before planting outdoors, at which time the plants should be set 10 to 15 inches apart. Impatiens transplants well from nursery packs. In addition, cuttings will root in water. Plants can be made bushy by cutting them back by a third when planting. Impatiens grows best in well-drained, sandy soil amended with plenty of organic matter.

I. hawkeri (New Guinea impatiens) is available with bicolored foliage and flowers. It does best in open shade but tolerates full sun.

Iris ensata
(*I. kaempferi*)
Japanese iris

Perennial
Open shade to full sun
Hardy to Zone 4
Massive, stately foliage and huge, beautiful flowers distinguish this iris. It is quite finicky about location, but once established in moist, acid soil rich with organic matter, it needs little attention for a long, colorful life. The plant tolerates and even thrives in boggy or frequently flooded areas, but lime and dry alkaline soil are usually fatal.

The flowers are white, blue, purple, lavender, or pink. They are often 6 inches or more across. The 3 overlapping outer falls are large, flat, and held horizontally; the inner standards are small and spreading. Japanese iris blooms in late June and July. The swordlike, dark green leaves often grow 3 to 4 feet tall and remain attractive all season. The leaves are graceful, upright, and slightly arching in clusters topped by tall, flowering stems, which usually grow 3 to 4 feet high. Heights of 6 feet are not uncommon in rich, boggy soil in mild climates. Japanese iris is restrained in growth and long

Kalmia latifolia

Kerria japonica

lived. Its rhizomes expand to form a clump.

Plants should be spaced 18 to 24 inches apart and watered abundantly. Acid soil conditions should be maintained by feeding occasionally with acid plant food. Japanese iris has no serious pests. Division is rarely needed for rejuvenation; most plants can be left undisturbed indefinitely. Division is an excellent means of increase, however, and is best performed in spring, although it can be done in late summer after flowering.

Many hybrids are available in white, reddish purple, rose, lavender, blue, violet, purple, and various combinations thereof. *I. pseudacorus* (water flat iris) is another large, beardless iris that prefers very moist, acid conditions. The flowers are yellow and appear in great quantities atop 36- to 40-inch stems. This iris will self-sow prolifically in boggy, wet locations and has become naturalized in many such areas in North America.

Jasminum polyanthum
Bridal jasmine

Evergreen climber
Medium shade to sun
Hardy to Zone 9

This Chinese climber grows quickly to 20 or 30 feet. It ascends by twining and may benefit from being tied to a support or being woven through structures. Dense clusters of deeprose buds open white and very fragrant in spring and summer, or periodically throughout the year in the warmest zones. The leaves, finely divided into 5 to 7 leaflets, are handsome the year around. The vine should be thinned and shaped yearly, after flowering. Bridal jasmine requires at least 4 weeks of winter temperatures below 50° F in order to flower; the vine will tolerate temperatures as low as 20° F in midwinter. Many other species of flowering jasmine are available regionally.

Kalmia latifolia
Mountain laurel

Broadleaf evergreen shrub
Open shade
Zones 5 to 8

For spectacular white to deep pink flowers and excellent evergreen foliage, this eastern native is an undisputed treasure in the garden. It can be used as a specimen and as a companion for azalea and rhododendron. Slow growing, in youth it is dense, rounded, and tidy, becoming gnarled, picturesque, and open in old age. In the wild it can reach 30 to 35 feet high, but under cultivation 7 to 15 feet is more common. In the harsher climate of the Midwest, it rarely grows above a rounded form 3 to 7 feet high.

Mountain laurel should be planted in cool, moist, welldrained acid soil that is high in organic matter. Open shade is appreciated, although full sun is tolerated. Because it is shallow rooted, mulching is recommended rather than cultivating around it. Mountain laurel is not a good choice for dry, Mediterranean climates or areas without frost (Zones 9 and 10).

Kerria japonica
Japanese kerria

Deciduous shrub
Dense to open shade
Zones 5 to 8

This deciduous shrub has several appealing aspects. In winter its thin, pistachio green stems brighten the garden. If planted against a shaded wall or among more rampantly growing plants, it can assume a graceful, semivining habit, growing to 6 to 8 feet, sometimes much higher. Its flowers appear in early spring and continue sporadically into summer in even the most shaded garden, although the plant may become sparse and leggy in dense shade. In autumn its leaves turn bright yellow. Its usual size, if unrestrained, is 4 to 6 feet tall and nearly as wide, but Japanese kerria can be maintained at 2 to 3 feet in open shade. It is dense and suitable for the foreground of a shrub border. Kept low, it can help hide the dying foliage of bulbs. Its most effective use is often not as an accent but as a softener of bare trunks or walls.

Flowers of the species are single, golden yellow, and up to 2 inches wide. They are borne singly and, in spring, profusely. The leaves are up to 4 inches long, tapering, and rich green on top and lighter underneath. They are pendulous on arching branches, contributing to an especially graceful effect.

Japanese kerria is indifferent to soil and exposure, accepting dense shade, drought, and rather poor soil. Unless thinned, kerria can sucker heavily and

Leucojum aestivum

Leucothoe fontanesiana

become brambly. It is more attractive when kept open. It should be pruned immediately after spring flowering, since it blooms on last year's wood. It should be fertilized only occasionally, and lightly; richness encourages rampant growth.

K. japonica 'Aureo-variegata', seldom seen but worth looking for, is like the species except that it has yellow-edged leaves. *K. japonica* 'Variegata' has white-edged leaves. *K. japonica* 'Pleniflora', the most common kerria, has double golden yellow flowers 1½ inches wide, like pom-poms; they last longer than the single flowers of the species.

Lamium galeobdolon (*Lamiastrum galeobdolon*)
Golden deadnettle, yellow-archangel

Evergreen ground cover
Open shade to full sun
Hardy to Zone 5

Golden deadnettle (*L. galeobdolon*) differs from spotted deadnettle (*L. maculatum*), described below, in having longer, 3-inch leaves and bright yellow flowers. Sometimes called *Galeobdolon luteum*, golden deadnettle is invasive, so it should be

kept in wild gardens where it can run rampant, covering rocks and small shrubs. It thrives in wooded places. More attractive but less vigorous and hence easy to control are cultivars such as 'Silver Angel', with silver-speckled leaves, and 'Variegatum', with silver-marbled leaves.

Lamium maculatum
Spotted deadnettle

Evergreen ground cover
Open shade to full sun
Hardy to Zone 5

Pink or white flowers distinguish spotted deadnettle from golden deadnettle, described above. Spotted deadnettle is another easy-care ground cover; its cultivars, such as the silver-leafed 'Beacon's Silver', are easier to control than the species, which has marbled leaves and mauve flowers. 'White Nancy' has silver leaves and white flowers. The brilliance of the silver-leafed cultivars brightens up dark places and makes a strong contrast to dark green plants.

Spotted deadnettle is easy to propagate from soft tip cuttings to create a carpet under shrubs and trees. Plants grow into a loose mat about 8 inches high.

Leucojum species
Snowflake, leucojum

Bulb
Open shade to full sun
Hardy to Zone 6

Snowflakes are among the easiest bulbs to grow and are especially attractive in a woodland setting. They should be planted in open shade to full sun in fall. No special care is necessary; the bulbs flower best if left undisturbed for several years at a time. The fall snowflake does not fare well in warm climates.

The earliest blooming of the 3 species is *L. vernum* (spring snowflake), with single, bell-shaped flowers tipped in green on 6- to 9-inch stems. Slightly larger and bearing 4 to 8 similar blossoms per stem is *L. aestivum* (summer snowflake). In early fall *L. autumnale* (autumn snowflake) puts in an appearance. There are usually 2 or 3 white blossoms on each of the 4- to 6-inch stems. All snowflake bulbs send out several grassy leaves.

Leucothoe fontanesiana
Drooping leucothoe

Broadleaf evergreen
Dense to medium shade
Zones 5 to 7

Most commonly planted in moist, acid soil in eastern gardens, drooping leucothoe makes an ideal companion to rhododendron, azalea, and mountain laurel because of its dark, lustrous, evergreen foliage and graceful form. Important assets are the bright green or bronze new foliage in spring; the fragrant, delicate white flowers in spring; and the purplish winter color. Leucothoe can be used to front leggy shrubs; as a graceful, high ground cover for shady slopes; or for massing, grouping, or integrating into the shrub border. It is a perfect shrub to naturalize in a shady, woodland wildflower garden.

Drooping leucothoe transplants easily from a container in early spring, but it is fastidious about its requirements. If given a moist, well-drained acid soil that is high in organic matter, as well as dense to medium shade, ample moisture, and protection from drought and drying winds, it will prove to be a basically trouble-free plant, although leaf spot can be a problem. Pruning

Ligularia dentata

Ligustrum japonicum

should be done directly after flowering, although it is seldom necessary due to the natural, graceful, fountainlike form of the plant, which grows 3 to 5 feet high and often wider. Older plants can be rejuvenated by pruning them clear to the ground.

'Rainbow' ('Girard's Rainbow') has yellow, green, and copper-variegated foliage. 'Nana' is a dwarf form that is 2 feet high and 6 feet wide.

Ligularia dentata
Golden groundsel

Perennial
Open shade to full sun
Hardy to Zone 4

Large, bold leaves and tall spires of flowers make golden groundsel a useful specimen or border plant. The small flowers are orange-yellow to bright yellow, about 2 inches across, and appear in large quantities held tightly against the tall flower stalks. The cultivars 'Desdemona' and 'Othello' are somewhat smaller with purple leaves. The plant blooms in August. The deep green leaves are effective all season but are prone to droop and wilt in hot sun and during periods of high heat and high humidity.

The plant forms dense basal clumps of leaves up to 18 inches high. From these arise 30- to 40-inch stiffly vertical flower stalks. Clumps expand at a moderate rate through the growth of short rhizomes. The plant is fairly restrained in growth and is long lived.

Golden groundsel needs moist, rich soil that is high in organic matter. Although dry soil is quickly fatal, the plant also resents sogginess. Open shade is best, although full sun is tolerated, especially in cool climates and moist soil. The plants should be spaced 24 inches apart.

Care is moderately easy. Water abundantly and feed regularly. If necessary, bait for slugs and snails. Division, which is rarely necessary for maintenance, is most successful if performed in spring. The flowers should be deadheaded to prolong blooming.

Ligustrum species
Privet

Evergreen and deciduous shrubs
Medium shade to full sun
Hardiness varies according to species

Pest free, highly adaptable, and low in maintenance, the shrubby privets are most often used as formal and informal hedges, backgrounds, and screens. Most have spiky clusters of white flowers in early summer, their heavy scent variously described as offensive to pleasant. All privets transplant easily in the bare-root form, are adaptable to nearly any soil except a wet one, and take medium shade to full sun. They perform well under adverse conditions of pollution and drought. All privets grow rapidly and respond well to pruning and shaping.

Deciduous Types

L. amurense (Amur privet; hardy to Zone 4), a hardy privet that is excellent for hedges, has attractive foliage that is medium to fine in texture.

L. × *ibolium* (Ibolium privet; hardy to Zone 5) is a shrub similar to the California privet but hardier.

L. obtusifolium (border privet; hardy to Zone 4), in addition to being one of the hardiest privets, is also one of the most

attractive because of its broad, horizontal growth habit and dark green foliage. It grows 10 to 12 feet tall and 12 to 15 feet wide, although it can easily be kept much smaller. The variety *regelianum* is a low, 4- to 5-foot-high shrub with unusual, horizontally spreading branches that are most attractive if allowed to grow naturally.

L. ovalifolium (California privet; hardy to Zone 6) has glossy, semievergreen leaves that often tempt gardeners to grow this plant north of its range, where it dies to the ground every winter. Where hardy, it is a deservedly popular hedge plant.

L. × *vicaryi* (golden privet; hardy to Zone 6) is a popular plant whose leaves in full sun are a glaring yellow; in shade they are yellow-green to light green. Clipped hedges remain yellow-green, since the shaded inner leaves are constantly exposed by clipping. 'Hillside Strain' is a hardier variety that is useful in Zone 5, although it is a gaudy plant, difficult to integrate into the landscape.

Lilium species

Liriope muscari

L. vulgare (common privet; hardy to Zone 5) is a plant to avoid because of its susceptibility to anthracnose. To lose mature hedge plants is an annoyance, to say the least.

Evergreen Types

L. japonicum (Japanese privet; hardy to Zone 7) makes an excellent hedge or screen in southern and western gardens. Because of its lustrous, evergreen leaves, its dense, compact habit (it grows rapidly 6 to 12 feet high), and its responsiveness to pruning, this privet is also commonly trained into topiary or small standards. An excellent container plant, it looks best when given plenty of water and protection from the hot sun. Many forms are available. This plant is frequently sold incorrectly to nurseries as *L. texanum.*

L. lucidum (glossy privet; hardy to Zone 7), often confused with the Japanese privet, is more treelike, growing 35 to 40 feet high. It can be differentiated from *L. japonicum* among young nursery plants by feeling the undersides of the leaves. If the veins are raised, it is *L. japonicum;* if they are sunken, it is *L. lucidum.*

L. 'Suwannee River' is an evergreen hybrid that eventually grows 4 to 6 feet high, with a compact, tight habit. Its wavy, dark green leaves make the shrub useful as a low hedge or in a foundation planting.

Lilium species
Lily

Perennial
Medium shade to medium sun
Hardy to Zone 4

Some wild lilies not only thrive in open shade but also look best there. Their petals seem to shine in subdued light. They bring a welcome splash of late-summer color to the dappled shade at the edges of deciduous trees, or in an east-facing perennial border that receives only morning sun. Most of the hybrids, however, appreciate full sun.

There are almost 100 species and countless cultivars, which vary in plant height (generally 3 to 6 feet), flower size and color, and flower habit—facing downward, outward, or upward. The long, narrow leaves grow almost horizontally from the stems. Some nurseries specialize in lilies; a glance through a catalog will give you an idea of the possibilities.

All lilies do best in rich, well-drained soil. They grow from bulbs, which should be planted in fall. An exception is *L. candidum,* the Madonna lily, which must be planted no later than August. The turkscaps are also good in shade. This group is named for the reflexed shape of the flowers, which are usually orange, yellow, or red. *L. martagon* var. *album* is an attractive white form. Some of the North American turkscap lilies, such as *L. michiganense* and *L. superbum,* do best in moist valleys and by streams. From Asia come *L. speciosum* and *L. auratum,* both of which thrive in acid soil and dappled shade.

Liriope species
Lilyturf

Ground cover
Medium shade to medium sun
Hardy to Zone 6

Lilyturf is characterized by clumps of coarse, grasslike, mostly dark green leaves up to 24 inches long and ¼ to ¾ inch wide. Like *Ophiopogon,* with which it is sometimes confused, lilyturf is a member of the lily family. One difference between the two is that lilyturf is hardier. *L. muscari* 'Big Blue' gets its name from its 4- to 8-inch-long, spikelike clusters of flowers that

are, in fact, more violet than blue. They appear in good number among the leaves from about July into September and are followed by a few blue-black berries. This is the tallest lilyturf, growing rather slowly to a height of 2 feet. It is sometimes listed as *Ophiopogon jaburan.*

L. spicata (creeping lilyturf) is smaller in all respects, forms a dense cover that spreads by underground stems, has pale lavender flowers, and grows at a moderate rate up to a foot high. Creeping lilyturf is excellent under trees, in rock gardens, as a border along paths, or as fill-in ground cover in small areas.

Although lilyturf has no special soil or light requirements, it is probably grown most often in medium to open shade, if only for reasons of landscape design. It needs only light summer watering. Both forms are easily propagated by division. In extremely cold weather the leaves of both forms turn yellow and should be clipped off before new growth starts in spring. *L. spicata* is the hardier of the two, tolerating temperatures to -20° F.

Lobelia erinus

Lonicera species

L. muscari is damaged by temperatures below 0° F. Variegated types are somewhat less hardy but very attractive. Cultivars include 'Gold-banded' and 'Silvery Midget'.

Lobelia cardinalis
Cardinal flower

Perennial
Open shade to full sun
Hardy to Zone 2

Cardinal flower is a tall, stately plant with brilliant scarlet flowers in mid- to late summer. It is a fine choice for moist, shady spots, especially in natural gardens.

The individual flowers are small and grow in a spike along the upper 6 to 8 inches of the stem. They bloom from late July to September and are attractive to hummingbirds. The medium to dark green leaves, which grow to 4 inches, are oblong or lance shaped and are arranged opposite each other or in whorls along the stalks. The tall, vertical stems grow 3 to 4 feet high and are topped with the blazing red flowers.

Cardinal flower is short lived, although it may self-sow under optimum conditions. It is seldom if ever invasive.

Native to the wet soils along streams, in boggy meadows, and in woodland bottomlands, cardinal flower does best in well-drained, sandy loam that is high in organic matter and kept evenly moist. Although in moist soil it is tolerant of full sun, it does best in open shade. It does not perform well in regions with mild winters.

Care is moderately difficult. Keep the plants well watered. Remove faded flower stalks. Mulch in summer to retain moisture and in winter to protect the crowns.

Although several insects and fungal diseases may attack cardinal flower, they are seldom serious enough to warrant protection. The plant should be divided annually to perpetuate it. The clump should be lifted, then the outside clusters of new basal growth should be removed and reset. The plants should be spaced 12 to 18 inches apart. This is best done in early fall.

Lobelia erinus
Lobelia

Annual
Dense to open shade

Annual lobelia has small, ½-inch-wide flowers in jewel-like shades of blue, mauve, purple, and pink. There are also white cultivars. The trailing type of this fragile ground cover, *L. erinus* 'Pendula', is best used in window boxes and hanging baskets in shade, where it drapes gracefully over the edges of the pots and fills in the spaces between larger plants. It can also be used to edge a shady border of perennials or impatiens. Stems are about 8 inches long but are so relaxed that the ground cover is only about 3 inches high.

Annual lobelia requires shade and moist, rich soil. Given these conditions it will tolerate heat, although it is more dependable in cool weather. It often stops blooming during the hottest summer weather and resumes in fall. It does not tolerate frost.

Annual lobelia is easy to grow from seed, although growth is slow. To save time, it is best bought as a bedding plant.

Lonicera species
Honeysuckle, woodbine

Deciduous or evergreen climbers and shrubs
Medium shade to sun
Hardiness varies according to species

These fast-growing vines, to 20 feet or more, are most appreciated for the fragrant, tubular flowers that appeal to butterflies and bees. The vines have twining stems that can climb a trellis or cover an arbor in shade or sun. They prefer rich garden soil but are tolerant of less than ideal conditions. Aphids are sometimes a problem. There are species of honeysuckle for every area, including the following.

L. × *brownii* 'Dropmore Scarlet' (hardy to Zone 2) has unscented, bright red flowers from June until frost. Some sun is required for full flower production.

L. henryi (hardy to Zone 4) is less vigorous than Hall's honeysuckle and is therefore often preferred in places where Hall's is too rampant.

Lysimachia nummularia

Mahonia aquifolium

L. hildebrandiana (Burmese honeysuckle; hardy to Zone 9) is evergreen. It is slightly twining but does best tied or woven onto a firm support. The highly fragrant, 7-inch, tubular flowers open white, aging to gold or bronze, throughout the summer. The glossy, dark leaves are beautiful the year around.

L. japonica 'Halliana' (Hall's honeysuckle; hardy to Zone 4) is widely available. It is a semi-evergreen climber with fragrant white flowers followed by black fruits that bring birds. It has become weedy in the South but is still appreciated as an ornamental in more northerly gardens, where its growth is more restrained.

L. periclymenum (woodbine; hardy to Zone 8) is a climber with sweetly perfumed white flowers touched with purple from June to October. It is a strong twiner that will climb wires or a trellis.

L. tatarica (Tatarian honeysuckle: hardy to Zone 2) is a deciduous shrub 9 feet tall, tolerant of conditions from dense shade to full sun. Several cultivars offer flowers from dark red to pink to white. The fruits are yellow or red.

Lysimachia nummularia
Creeping-jenny, moneywort, loosestrife

Evergreen ground cover
Dense shade to sun
Hardy to Zone 4

An evergreen plant of moist woodlands, creeping-jenny will also tolerate sun and fairly dry soil. The leaves are roundish and 1 inch wide. The cup-shaped yellow flowers bloom along the stems, which trail and root as they go, forming a mat just 2 inches high. It can be invasive, so it is best grown in a woodland where it can wander at will, or in a bed where it can be confined by lawn or pavement. The cultivar 'Aurea' has golden leaves that are striking in dense shade.

Mahonia species
Mahonia, Oregon grape

Evergreen shrubs and ground covers
Medium to open shade
Hardiness varies according to species

The Lewis and Clark expedition brought *M. aquifolium* (*Berberis aquifolium*, Oregon grape; hardy to Zone 5) to the East

Coast of the United States, where it has been popular ever since. This and related species are among the most adaptable and useful plants for the shade garden. They survive nearly anywhere, most of them in any soil and in any degree of shade, and they provide evergreen foliage, seasonal flowers, and edible fruit. Oregon grape is not really a grape but a member of the barberry family.

As an informal foundation planting, a specimen, or even a large-scale ground cover, Oregon grape is one of the most dependable shrubs. Its whorls of foliage grow on woody stems that can reach 6 to 8 feet but are usually shorter. The height of the plant can be kept at 2 feet or less. Planted at 2-foot intervals, Oregon grape will form a tough, thick ground cover that chokes out even the most pernicious weeds. It creates an effective barrier yet is graceful and delicate as a container plant. 'Compacta' stays about 2 feet high and spreads freely. It is bronze in winter.

The pinkish or bronze new foliage of Oregon grape matures into leathery, spiny, compound leaves up to 10 inches long, with 5 to 9 leaflets per leaf. In the Northwest they are cut and sold as Christmas greens.

The waxy yellow flowers form in clusters at the tips of branches from March to May. Clusters of ¼-inch, deep blue berries with a bloom succeed the flowers. These "grapes" were once marketed on the West Coast; they taste something like currants.

Oregon grape thrives virtually anywhere except in the full sun of the hottest climates. Acid soil is best. It accepts summer water, as long as drainage is good, but tolerates long periods of drought. It should be pruned to maintain the desired height. If attacked by the barberry looper, a defoliating caterpillar, spraying is necessary.

M. bealei (leatherleaf mahonia; hardy to Zone 8), native to China, grows in a strongly vertical habit from 6 to 12 feet high. Its fragrant yellow flowers in late winter and dense clusters of "grapes" are beautiful, but the most striking aspect of the plant is its symmetrical, horizontally held, compound leaves—up to 15 inches long, dark blue-green, and spiny. It

Matteuccia pensylvanica

Mertensia virginica

strongly prefers rich soil and moisture; medium to open shade is necessary.

M. lomariifolia (Burmese mahonia; hardy to Zone 7) has leaves to 24 inches long and 6 inches wide. The flowers are similar to those of *M. aquifolium* and *M. bealei.* It grows to 12 feet high and, unlike *M. bealei,* branches with age. It too likes rich, moist soil and medium to open shade. If you want a bold, tropical effect in a shaded entryway and your climatic zone doesn't allow tree ferns or other tropicals, perhaps this or *M. bealei* is the solution. Burmese mahonia lends itself to container culture.

M. nervosa (longleaf mahonia; hardy to Zone 7) has 10- to 20-inch leaves, erect stems 2 feet or taller, and a more polished appearance than *M. aquifolium.* This native of northwestern North American woodlands spreads to make an excellent ground cover with tidy, 12- to 18-inch, glossy green leaves. It does best in rich, moist soil and open to medium shade. *M. pinnata* (California hollygrape) closely resembles *M. aquifolium* except that its leaves are spinier

and more crinkly. It does best in open shade. Native to southern and central California, it is particularly tolerant of poor soil, drought, and heat—a tough plant that makes an excellent barrier.

M. repens (creeping mahonia; hardy to Zone 3), a 10-inch-tall, bluish green ground cover from the American Northwest, stays uniformly low and spreads quickly to form a dense mat over medium or small areas, including slopes, in any degree of shade. Except in size, it resembles *M. aquifolium.*

Matteuccia pensylvanica
Ostrich fern

Fern
Dense shade to medium sun
Hardy to Zone 2

The ostrich fern is one of the largest ferns native to central and northern North America. Under optimum growing conditions the fronds grow at least 4 to 6 feet tall and sometimes taller. The fronds are a lustrous dark green and grow from a central crown. Underground runners grow outward rapidly from the crown and spread easily into nearby areas. This fern

should be planted only in large areas where it can grow freely. The sterile fronds are deciduous and turn brown with the first fall frost. The fertile fronds are bronze and stand erect throughout the winter.

Native to marshes, swamps, and shallow creeks, the ostrich fern grows best in sandy, slightly acid (pH 5.5 to 6.5) soil that is high in organic matter. The soil should be kept moist. Easy to grow, this fern thrives in areas with open shade but in moist soil can tolerate some sun. Because of its height, it is most effective as a background plant. To allow room for spreading, the plants should be set 3 feet apart.

Mentha requienii
Corsican mint

Ground cover
Open shade to full sun
Hardy to Zone 7

Corsican mint is the lowest growing of the many species and dozens of cultivars of mint. It spreads rapidly by underground stems, forming a soft green carpet 1 to 3 inches high. Tiny, oval leaves, about $\frac{1}{8}$ inch across, grow opposite each other on slender stems and give off a

strong, minty fragrance when bruised. Tiny lavender flowers appear in midsummer.

Corsican mint grows equally well in open shade or sun. In a fairly rich, moist but well-drained soil, it is a vigorous grower. It self-sows and is also easily propagated by division; new plants should be spaced 6 inches apart.

Mertensia virginica
Virginia bluebells

Perennial
Dense to open shade
Hardy to Zone 3

Virginia bluebells has drooping, bell-shaped flowers that bloom in April and May. The erect, leafy plants are most attractive in an informal or a wild garden.

The flowers, each about an inch long, are produced in clusters that hang gracefully at the ends of branching stems. The outer portion of each petal is sky blue; the inner part is pinkish or purplish. The foliage dies back usually by July. Virginia bluebells is restrained in growth and not invasive, but it can self-sow here and there.

The plant prefers dense shade and cool, moist soil high in organic matter. It does best in the cool-summer climates of the northern latitudes.

Mimulus 'Calypso Gold'

Myosotis sylvatica

Mulching helps keep the soil cool and moist in summer and also provides a continual supply of decaying organic matter. The soil should be kept evenly moist but never soggy. The foliage should not be removed when it starts to degenerate but allowed to die down naturally, as with bulbs. Plants should be spaced 8 to 12 inches apart.

Mimulus species and hybrids
Monkeyflower

Annuals and perennials
Dense to open shade
Hardiness varies according
to species

These three species of *Mimulus* are moisture-loving annuals and perennials that thrive in some degree of shade. They are not to be confused with *M. aurantiacus* and *M. puniceus* (formerly *Diplacus*), dry-growing, sun-loving species also called monkeyflower.

All the moisture-loving monkeyflowers have bright, tubular flowers and repeat bloom if cut back after the first flowering. Otherwise, species and their cultural requirements are so varied that they are discussed individually below. These are the most widely available forms.

M. cardinalis (scarlet monkeyflower; hardy to Zone 7), a perennial native to the western United States, produces slender, 2-inch scarlet flowers with 2 lips from midsummer into autumn. Heavily branched and loose growing to 2½ feet tall, it requires open shade and constant moisture. In its native habitat it often grows in seeps and shallow streams. Beds, borders, and bogs are suitable settings. Kept wet, it withstands extreme heat.

M. × hybridus, native to Chile, is an annual that grows 6 to 12 inches tall in bogs. This group of popular, large-flowered, hybrid annuals has blooms in shades of yellow, bronze, and red, with some speckled or striped. Hybrids, 6 to 8 inches high, start easily from seed cast on the surface of damp soil. Useful in planters, in beds and borders, along streams, or beside garden pools, this group of plants adapts easily to boggy conditions. Medium shade is best, but both open and dense shade are tolerated. All plants in this group prefer a cool location, rich soil, and regular fertilizing.

M. lewisii, a British Columbian perennial often grown as an annual, is quite similar to *M. cardinalis* in culture and appearance, except that it has pink flowers beautifully spotted with maroon and lined with yellow. The variety 'Albus' has white flowers. *M. lewisii* likes open shade and moisture with good drainage. It is hardy to Zone 7.

Myosotis species
Forget-me-not

Biennial often treated as annual
Medium shade to full sun
Hardy to Zone 3

In late summer or early fall, after planting a bed of bulbs, if you cast about a generous supply of seeds of *M. sylvatica,* you will be rewarded in spring with a beautiful blue haze. It is the perfect backdrop for daffodils and tulips, one that will keep the bed colorful well into early summer.

Forget-me-not reseeds abundantly to perform year after year. The tiny blue, pink, or white flowers bloom generously on delicate, multi-branched stems that are 6 to 12 inches tall.

Forget-me-not should be watered and fertilized liberally. It prefers fertile, moist, well-drained soil that is rich in organic matter. It performs well in wet soil. Although it prefers open shade, it will tolerate full sun. It does best in regions with long, cool springs. Elsewhere, it will set seed and die out. Then, after late-summer rains, a second crop will come up to give you fall color.

Nandina domestica
Nandina, heavenly-bamboo

Evergreen or
semideciduous shrub
Medium shade to full sun
Hardy to Zone 7

Not even remotely related to true bamboo, nandina is a popular shrub in southern gardens for its variety of ornamental assets and easy care.

Its strongly vertical form contrasts nicely with delicate, wispy foliage that is evergreen in mild climates. Erect, creamy white flower spikes borne on the ends of the vertical branches in June are followed by clusters of bright red berries.

Nicotiana alata 'Nicki Rose'

Nierembergia hippomanica

With a few hours of sun a day, nandina frequently has brilliant crimson to purple foliage in fall and winter. Often reaching 8 feet in height and 2½ to 3 feet in width, nandina is effective as a hedge or screen, in a mass or grouping, or as a solitary specimen in an entryway or container. It is particularly effective when backlit. Nandina loses its leaves at 10° F and dies back to the ground at 0° F, although it quickly recovers the following season. In the northern limits of its range, it is best used as an herbaceous perennial.

Since cross-fertilization improves fruiting, nandina should be planted in groups. It performs well in nearly any soil and in medium shade to full sun, although some protection is required in particularly hot climates. Established plants tolerate drought well. Old, leggy canes should be removed annually to encourage density. Nandina competes well with tree roots and is little troubled by pests, although it exhibits chlorosis in alkaline soil.

Several cultivars are offered for form, dwarf size, foliage color, and improved hardiness.

Nicotiana species
Nicotiana,
flowering tobacco

Annual
Medium shade to full sun

The bedding plant *N. alata* is by far the best-known member of the genus. It reaches the height of grace when massed in a large bed. Each plant is anchored by a low rosette of large leaves from which spring tall, slender stems. Long, thin tubes at right angles to the stem open into star-shaped flowers in white and shades of mauve, red, maroon, pink, yellow, green, and yellow-green. The nodding, delicate effect is enhanced by planting in great masses, especially in areas with a gentle wind.

Often touted as powerfully fragrant, the day-blooming hybrids available today are sorely disappointing. Occasionally a fresh, sweet scent can be detected in the vicinity of a bed, especially on cool evenings, but the famous perfume can usually be found only in the tall, old-fashioned, evening-blooming white nicotiana.

Nevertheless, nicotiana makes a tall (12 to 36 inches), delicate statement in the mixed border. It is surprisingly effective when planted in clumps in large pots. It should not be grown near where tomatoes may be placed; it attracts many pests and diseases that may attack tomatoes, such as tobacco mosaic virus. Although the hardy nicotiana will be little troubled, the tomatoes may not survive.

Nicotiana is gaining favor as an alternative to petunias in areas where the humidity-related disease botrytis can snip off the petunia blossoms for several weeks in late summer.

Far taller than *N. alata,* sometimes reaching 5 feet in a few weeks, is the dramatic *N. sylvestris,* which has 4-inch-long, tubular white flowers. It is as easy to grow from seed as *N. alata,* but it is much more stately under a high, leafy canopy or at the back of a shady border.

Both types of nicotiana do best in fertile, well-drained, moist soil that is high in organic matter. Medium to open shade is preferred, but full sun is tolerated in humid climates; flowers will fade in full sun in dry climates. Nicotiana should be fertilized regularly and the soil kept moist. Although this plant self-sows freely, it is not difficult to control.

Nierembergia
hippomanica
Cupflower

Tender perennial grown as annual
Open shade to full sun

Although little known and usually hard to find, cupflower is a diminutive delight in the garden. Tidy, spreading mounds of the fine-textured foliage are smothered with blue-violet or purple flowers all summer long. There is also a white cultivar, 'Mont Blanc'. Flowers hold their color without fading even in the brightest sun.

Cupflower is outstanding in large beds or as a 6- to 12-inch ground cover, but it is even more elegant and appropriate grown in small patches in the rock garden. It behaves well as an edging to a border or walkway, and can be planted in pots, hanging baskets, and window boxes. It is also a logical substitute for trailing lobelia where the latter dies out in the heat.

For its long-season, blue-violet color, easy care, and restrained size, cupflower deserves greater popularity. It needs fertile, sandy, moist, well-drained soil that is high in organic matter, and open shade to full sun. Shade is preferred in areas with hot summers. The

Ophiopogon japonicus

Osmanthus fragrans

plants should be kept moist but not soggy. Cupflower is easy to grow from seed started indoors 2 months before the date of the last spring frost.

Ophiopogon japonicus
Mondograss

Ground cover
Medium to open shade
Hardy to Zone 7

Mondograss is the most grasslike of the lilyturfs. It is identified by dense clumps of long, 1/8-inch-wide leaves that arch over into mounds 8 to 10 inches high. The leaves are dark green and coarse in texture. Small, pale purple flowers, mostly hidden among the leaves, appear in July and August, followed by pea-sized blue fruit. Mondograss spreads by means of fleshy subsurface stems. The growth rate is quite slow until the plant is well established.

A miniature version of *O. japonicus,* growing about half as high, is *O. japonicus* 'Nanus'.

O. jaburan is similar in size and growth habit to *Liriope muscari* and is often mistaken for it. The chief observable differences are that *O. jaburan* has green instead of brownish stems, and more drooping, less tightly clustered white flowers.

O. jaburan 'Variegatus' is a low-growing variety with striated white leaves.

Mondograss is adaptable to most well-drained soils. In coastal areas it will grow in full sun; elsewhere it looks and grows best in medium to open shade. It needs regular summer watering, and frequent watering if exposed to full sun in a mass planting. New plants can be started by dividing clumps. Divisions of *O. japonicus* should be set 6 inches apart, *O. jaburan* 12 inches apart.

Mondograss looks attractive as a sizable planting under a large shade tree. In a shaded patio setting, a few dozen plants, placed about 8 inches apart with baby's tears (*Soleirolia soleirolii*) in between, produce a lovely, cool effect. Mondograss also makes a handsome border along paths and is useful in defining and separating lawns from flower beds. *O. jaburan* is most effective where its attractive flowers (good for cutting) and violet-blue fruits can be seen close up, as in entryways, near fences and buildings, and under trees.

Osmanthus fragrans
Sweet olive

Broadleaf evergreen shrub
Medium to open shade
Hardy to Zone 8

Although its powerfully fragrant, nearly year-round flowers are an attraction, sweet olive is also a compact, tidy plant with glossy evergreen foliage that makes an outstanding hedge, screen, background, espalier, or container plant. It is very easy to care for and quite adaptable. Planted in any soil, from sand to clay, in medium to open shade, it will grow at a moderate rate to a 10-foot-wide and equally high shrub with a rounded outline. It can easily be kept lower, however, and responds well to shearing. It can be pruned anytime of year; pinching the growing tips encourages denseness.

O. fragrans aurantiacus has powerfully fragrant orange blossoms most abundant in October.

O. heterophyllus (holly olive; hardy to Zone 7) is perhaps the handsomest of the *Osmanthus* species. Its opposite leaves distinguish it from English holly, with which it is often confused. (English holly has alternate leaves.) Holly olive has lustrous, spiny, dark green leaves and fragrant, hidden yellow flowers in

fall. It is unusually shade tolerant. A number of cultivars with variegated foliage are available.

O. delavayi (Delavay osmanthus; hardy to Zone 8) is distinguished by its small, fine-textured leaves and graceful, arching habit, along with the largest white flowers of the genus. They are profuse and fragrant from late March to May. Particularly handsome on banks and walls where branches can cascade, Delavay osmanthus also responds well to pruning as a hedge or as a foundation plant.

Osmunda cinnamonea
Cinnamon fern

Fern
Dense shade to medium sun
Hardy to Zone 4

Native to boggy areas of the eastern United States and Canada, the cinnamon fern is one of the earliest ferns to emerge in spring. Young fronds are covered with woolly white hair before they unfurl. When full grown, the waxy fronds are yellow-green and grow 24 to 36 inches tall and 6 to 8 inches wide.

Osmunda cinnamonea

Pachysandra terminalis

There are two distinctly different types of fronds—fertile and sterile. The fertile frond resembles a cinnamon stick. It emerges first, and after releasing its spores it turns golden brown, withers, and lies on the ground through the summer. The sterile fronds appear in late spring, stay green all summer, and turn brown with the first fall frost. This fern requires a slightly acid (pH 5.5 to 6.5) soil that is kept evenly moist. It spreads slowly. Because of its height, it is best used as a background plant.

Pachysandra terminalis
Pachysandra, Japanese spurge

Ground cover
Dense to open shade
Hardy to Zone 4

Pachysandra is reportedly the most popular shade ground cover in the United States. This is not surprising, because it has a lot going for it: It is evergreen, hardy, lush, fast covering, perfect for large or small areas in medium or dense shade, indifferent to tree roots, attractively flowering, and long lived. It spreads by branching underground runners. In dense shade it grows almost 12 inches high;

in open to medium shade, 6 to 8 inches high.

Pachysandra produces small, fluffy spikes of greenish white flowers in spring. Established plants occasionally produce whitish berries in fall. It makes a dense, even cover of 4-inch-long leaves that grow in whorls at the tops of the stems.

Pachysandra prefers moist, acid, well-drained soil but will tolerate somewhat compacted, root-matted soil. Because its runners are rather invasive, it should be planted only where it is contained or where its spreading will do no harm to the design of the garden or to less vigorous plants. It can compete all too successfully with broadleaf evergreens for food and moisture, but it will not tolerate foot traffic.

Spring feeding with a complete fertilizer is helpful. Tree leaves settle down into it and should be left alone, as they form a beneficial mulch. If the planting becomes open, it should be cut back lightly to encourage denser growth.

'Green Carpet' is hardier, more compact, and denser than the species. It is darker green and flowers more heavily. 'Silver Edge' has lighter green leaves with a silvery white margin of ¼ inch or less.

P. procumbens (Allegheny spurge), native to the Appalachians, is clumping and erect, growing to a foot high. In colder regions it is deciduous. Its fragrant white or pinkish spring flowers are especially attractive.

Parthenocissus species
Virginia creeper, Boston ivy

Climber
Medium shade to sun
Hardiness varies according to species

Responsible for the description of many of the "Ivy League" colleges in places too cool for *Hedera helix,* these related vines can cover a wall quickly and densely, holding on with tendril adhesive disks that attach to any surface, no matter how smooth.

P. quinquefolia (Virginia creeper, woodbine; hardy to Zone 4) is named for its 5-sectioned leaves, which grow to 6 inches wide and are bright green in spring and summer and brilliant red in fall. After a slow

start the vine grows rapidly to 60 feet. Flowers and fruit are inconspicuous, though birds are attracted to the fruit. When the woody stems are bare in winter, their tracery on a wall is attractive. Virginia creeper is a rampant vine that can be difficult to control, but it is useful where little else will succeed. It tolerates even poor soil. *P. quinquefolia* var. *engelmannii* has smaller foliage.

P. tricuspidata (Boston ivy; hardy to Zone 5) is the same in nearly every respect except that it is less vigorous, and its shiny green leaves are shaped more like those of maples. There are several cultivars.

Pericallis × hybrida
Cineraria

Annual
Medium to dense shade

Cineraria is an easy-to-grow, shade-loving plant. Its daisylike flowers are 2 to 4 inches across and bloom in a wide range of colors, including blue, pink, red, purple, lavender, and white. The oval, bright green leaves and slightly woolly stems set off the bright flowers.

Native to the Canary Islands, cineraria is grown as an annual or a houseplant in all but the warmest areas of the country.

Pittosporum tobira

Polygonatum odoratum 'Variegatum'

The plant, which reaches 18 inches and thrives in deep to open shade, can be grown directly in the ground among shrubs, in beds, and as a border plant. It also grows well in containers and window boxes for brightening patios and porches; for best growth, the plant should be kept slightly pot bound.

Cineraria grows easily from seeds if they are sprouted and grown in a cool (45° to 55° F) area. Seed should be started indoors from late spring to early fall for bloom the following spring and summer. If you don't have cool growing conditions with plenty of light, it is best to purchase the plant from a nursery or florist. The plants should be spaced 10 to 12 inches apart. Cineraria prefers well-drained soil that is high in organic matter. The plant wilts easily as the soil dries, so it should be kept evenly moist with regular waterings.

Pieris japonica
Japanese pieris, Japanese andromeda

Broadleaf evergreen shrub
Medium to open shade
Zones 6 to 9

This refined cousin of the rhododendron and azalea mixes beautifully with its relatives and various acid growers such as ferns and other woodland plants. A tidy, evergreen shrub with a compact habit, Japanese pieris requires no pruning. It grows slowly to 6 to 12 feet high and 6 to 8 feet wide, with a slightly drooping habit. It is singularly beautiful throughout the year, with its delicate sprays of buds, white or pink flowers, seed capsules, brilliantly colored bronze red new foliage in spring, and attractive, deep green mature foliage. As a specimen, part of a shrub border, a mass planting, or a container subject, it is a classic for medium to open shade.

Several cultivars are available, including a variegated compact form with white-edged leaves. Buds appear in autumn and develop in late winter or early spring into gracefully pendulous, 6-inch clusters of bell-shaped white or pinkish blossoms resembling lily-of-the-valley—hence one of its common names, lily-of-the-valley shrub. The flowers are long lasting.

In most climates open shade is preferable, but in very hot climates medium shade is best. Japanese pieris should be sheltered from the wind and winter sun in cold areas. The soil should be rich, high in organic content, acid, and fast draining. If pruning is ever necessary—and it seldom is, except to shape the plant—it should be done immediately after flowering. Crown rot, fungus leaf spot, a dieback fungus, lace bug, scale, and mites can be severe problems unless controlled by appropriate sprays. Lace bugs and mites are usually a problem if shrubs are sited in too much sun.

P. floribunda (mountain pieris, mountain andromeda; Zones 5 to 8), native to the eastern United States, is quite similar to *P. japonica* in appearance and requirements but blooms in April (flowers are pure white) and is more compact and smaller (2 to 6 feet high and wide), although a very old specimen in a garden in England is 6 feet high and 15 feet wide.

P. floribunda is less vulnerable to pests than is *P. japonica*.

'Forest Flame', a 6- to 7-foot hybrid of *P. japonica* and *P. formosa* var. *forrestii*, has vivid scarlet new growth and is hardier than *P. formosa* var. *forrestii*.

P. formosa var. *forrestii* (Chinese pieris) is more tender than other species. It closely resembles them but is denser and larger, and its new growth is more brilliantly colored. It is hardy to Zone 8.

Pittosporum tobira
Tobira, Japanese pittosporum

Broadleaf evergreen shrub
Dense shade to full sun
Zones 8 to 10

Leathery, evergreen foliage; fragrant, early, creamy yellow spring flowers with a scent like orange blossoms; and a broad, dense habit all have made this a popular plant in southern and western gardens for screens, massed plantings, borders, and foundation plantings. It is particularly effective in containers or trained as a small, crooked-stemmed tree. Smaller cultivars, some of which have variegated instead of dark green foliage, are available for ground covers.

Polypodium species

Polystichum munitum

This plant is not suitable for a formal hedge; it does not respond well to hard pruning or shearing, although frequent light pinching can help to maintain a compact habit. Allowed to grow naturally, it reaches 6 to 15 feet in height and is usually slightly wider. Fairly drought resistant, it nevertheless appreciates adequate water and an annual light fertilization. Aphids and scale can be a problem. Medium shade to full sun is best, although it tolerates dense shade well.

Polygonatum biflorum
Great Solomon's-seal

Perennial
Dense to open shade
Hardy to Zone 4

This subtle woodland native has long, attractive, arching stems and hanging clusters of tiny flowers. It is one of the rare plants that will thrive in dry shade.

The flowers are yellowish green to greenish white, about ½ inch long, and bell shaped; they droop in small clusters all along the undersides of the stems in May and early June. Foliage is the chief attraction of this plant. The rich green to bluish green leaves grow up to

7 inches long. They are held perpendicular to the stem and alternate along its length.

Great Solomon's-seal is best grown in cool, moist soil well amended with organic matter. However, it will tolerate dry soil and intensive root competition quite well. It prefers dense to open shade. Plants should be spaced 18 to 36 inches apart. They should be watered adequately and mulched over the summer. This plant has no serious pests. Although division is not required for rejuvenation, for increase it is easily performed in early spring.

Also worth searching for are the European species *P. multiflorum,* which grows about 3 feet all, and *P. odoratum* 'Variegatum', which has green-and-white–striped foliage.

Polypodium virginianum
Common polypody

Fern
Open shade to light sun
Hardy to Zone 4

Common polypody creeps over rocks and boulders and is sometimes called rock-cap fern. It is native to northern and central North America. The leathery yellow-green fronds grow 10 inches long and 2 inches wide. They are evergreen, even in severe winters, and curl up and turn dark green as the temperature drops. These fronds remain on the plant long after new fronds emerge in spring. The fronds leave a scar on the rhizome when they break off. The rhizomes form a dense mat that is partially exposed above the soil surface.

This fern grows best in loamy woodland soil. It tolerates short periods of drought, but regular watering improves the appearance. It prefers open shade but can withstand intermittent sun if the soil is kept constantly moist. Common polypody is most ideally planted in crevices between rocks, where the rhizomes can creep in their characteristic manner.

Polystichum species
Sword fern

Fern
Dense shade
Hardy to Zone 4

This large group of ferns, including many natives of North American forests, are hardy and usually evergreen, with sword-shaped fronds, and are similar to wood fern (*Dryopteris*). However, the rough, sawtoothed edges of shield fern fronds are a distinguishing characteristic. Shady woodlands and rock gardens are the most appropriate places for these plants.

Christmas fern (*P. acrostichoides*) is native from Nova Scotia to Florida. The common name is due to the commercial availability of its fronds for use in Christmas decorations. It is also used as a houseplant.

Western sword fern (*P. munitum*) is native to a range extending from Alaska south to California and east to Montana. Its fronds are leathery, 2 to 3½ feet long, and up to 10 inches wide at the base.

Moisture, shade, and humus-rich soil are the most important needs of these ferns. Dividing the underground runners in spring is the best means of propagating them.

Primula vialii

Primula species

Pratia angulata
Pratia

Ground cover
Medium shade to full sun
Hardy to Zone 7

English gardeners, with their keen eyes for the beautiful and useful, began growing pratia (formerly *Lobelia angulata*) in the nineteenth century, but it is still a sleeper in the United States. This lushest of low ground covers is attractive the year around, with its evergreen foliage, liberal sprinkling of lobelia-like flowers through summer and autumn, and pea-sized violet to purple berries.

In sun or very open shade, with proper feeding and watering, pratia forms a tight carpet to 5 inches tall that usually keeps out weeds and grasses. In medium shade its habit is looser and taller, to a foot high. Particularly valuable to West Coast gardeners who want a bright green ground cover for areas beneath oaks, pratia can grow—but only in the shade—in dry soil with an occasional light sprinkling once it is established. Autumn planting assures that it

will become established during the rainy season. Its appropriateness for the rock garden should not be overlooked. Wherever it is planted, it will spread rapidly by rooting stems if the soil is moist.

The flowers, ½ to ¾ inch wide, are white and strikingly similar to those of *Lobelia erinus*. The leaves, ¾ inch long with slightly serrated edges, are rich, lustrous green, and, like the stems, rather succulent.

In hotter areas pratia must have at least open shade. The soil must drain rapidly. High sand content is desirable but not mandatory. Plugs spaced at 6- to 12-inch intervals fill in rapidly.

In bright, warm spots moisture is necessary and richness is desirable. Occasional feeding with mild fertilizer such as fish emulsion benefits pratia grown in such spots. Grown in medium shade pratia prefers a more austere regimen—not only less watering but less feeding. It will not withstand foot traffic.

Primula species
Primrose, primula

Perennial
Medium to open shade
Hardy to Zone 5

The genus *Primula* offers the shade gardener flowers in an assortment of colors, including white, magenta, pink, yellow, and orange. Some are bicolored and others are fragrant. There are several hundred species, varying in height from a few inches to 3 feet tall. Flowers appear in February in mild-winter areas and in April and May in northern climates. The crinkly, tongue-shaped leaves form basal rosettes and are evergreen where temperatures do not drop below 15° F. For an array of spring color, primula can be interplanted with bulbs.

New plantings can be established from nursery bedding plants, divisions, or seed started indoors in late winter or early spring. Primula grows best in medium to open shade in rich, well-drained soil that is kept evenly moist. The plants should be fertilized occasionally with a complete fertilizer. Crowded plantings should be divided every 2 to 3 years after flowering. Although new plants appear

in the garden from self-sown seed and from surface roots, primula is not considered invasive.

The easiest-to-grow primulas are *P. vulgaris* (English primrose), *P. × polyantha* (Polyanthus primula), *P. japonica* (Japanese primula), and *P. sieboldii*.

Prunus laurocerasus
Cherry-laurel

Evergreen shrub
Open shade to sun
Hardy to Zone 7

Cherry-laurel, a native of the eastern Mediterranean, is best known not for its fruits, which are small and dark purple, but for its shiny, leathery, dark green leaves. The spring blossoms are white. Cherry-laurel looks attractive in the dappled shade of an eastern exposure or at the edge of a woodland. Like all cherries, it resents heavy clay soil and wet feet. Where the species is hardy, it usually grows 15 feet tall and is so vigorous that it may crowd out nearby plants. It should be pruned heavily every spring. In places where it is not quite hardy, it winterburns badly.

Pulmonaria saccharata 'Mrs. Moon' with *hostas*

Rehmannia elata

The species can grow as tall as 30 feet, but there are several smaller, spreading cultivars, including 'Zabeliana', which reaches 4 to 5 feet, and 'Otto Luyken', just 3 feet tall. 'Schipkaensis' and the narrow-leafed 'Magnifolia' ('Latifolia') are hardier, to Zone 6.

Pulmonaria saccharata
Bethlehem-sage

Ground cover
Dense to open shade
Hardy to Zone 4

Bethlehem-sage's deep green leaves speckled with white make an attractive ground cover in the shade. Small flowers in early spring are a decided extra advantage, and the plant is easy to grow.

The flowers are blue (often pink in bud), reddish violet, or white. Individually they are trumpetlike and about ½ inch long. They appear in early April and May as relaxed clusters on stalks 10 to 12 inches tall. They should be removed when spent. The attractive, glossy leaves are oval to heart shaped and grow to about 6 inches long. The basal rosette of leaves reaches 6 to 8 inches in height. From each crown arise several flowering stalks. The foliage remains attractive all season. 'Mrs Moon' has larger flowers that are pink in bud and bright blue when they are open.

The crowns gradually expand by producing more leaves at the outer edge of the clump. The plant is long lived, restrained in growth, and is not invasive.

Bethlehem-sage has no serious pests and requires little attention. It prefers moist soil that is high in organic matter although not necessarily fertile. It does best in dappled to dense shade and benefits from being watered during dry spells. The plants should be spaced 10 inches apart and watered heavily after transplanting. Although division is seldom required, it is an excellent means of increase. It is best done in late summer or very early spring, although success is common even during full bloom.

P. angustifolia (blue lungwort) has plain, dark green leaves that are quite hairy, almost bristly. The flowers are showy, pink in bud, opening to blue, and appear in April and May. Several varieties are available, including pink, salmon, white, and red. It may be listed as *P. saccharata.*

Rehmannia elata
Rehmannia

Perennial
Medium to open shade
Hardy to Zone 9

It is curious that this spectacular perennial is so little known in the more moderate climatic zones. Its blossoms are no less beautiful than those of its cousin the foxglove, to which it bears a clear family resemblance. The dusky rose-pink flowers, to 3 inches long, are tubular with widely flaring lips. Yellowish or golden throats are heavily speckled with deep red. Like typical foxglove flowers, these are rather pendulous on the spikes. In borders and planters these slim, 2- to 4-foot spikes of sparse but showy flowers create casual beauty. They are useful in arrangements. Deeply cut, irregular leaves, to 8 inches long, are concentrated beneath the flowers.

From spring to late autumn, an established plant blooms continually. As it becomes established, what began as a modest plant spreads by underground stems to become a sizable clump. Where there is little frost it is evergreen.

Rehmannia prefers open shade. In dense shade it holds its own but blooms sparsely on spindly stems, and the clumps enlarge slowly. Moist soil rich in organic matter is best. Occasional feeding with high-phosphorus fertilizer during the long blooming season is beneficial. In cold areas it should be covered with mulch as it goes dormant.

'Alba', a creamy white variety, is occasionally sold.

Rhododendron with *Azalea*

Rhododendron

Rhododendron species
Rhododendron, azalea

Evergreen and deciduous shrubs
Medium to dappled shade
Hardiness varies according
to species

Probably no other group of plants, other than roses, elicits as much devotional praise and obsessional frustration as the genus *Rhododendron*. Where they can be grown, few plants can match their bewildering variety of striking, profuse, often brilliant flowers, outstanding form, and attractive foliage.

Rhododendron is an extensive genus, with more than nine hundred species and ten thousand varieties. *Azalea* is a series within the *Rhododendron* genus. There are evergreen and deciduous, small- and large-leafed, and dwarf and tall forms of these plants. The range of colors is endless, including solid and bicolored blossoms; some have a heady perfume. Depending on the variety and location, rhododendrons and azaleas bloom from late winter to mid-summer.

Botanists have not yet settled exactly what anatomical characteristics separate *Azalea* from *Rhododendron*. Although many azaleas are deciduous and most rhododendrons are evergreen, both azaleas and rhododendrons have deciduous and evergreen species. A common misconception is that azaleas are always smaller in form and leaf than rhododendrons, when in fact several rhododendrons are tiny, rock-garden dwarfs with leaves smaller than any azalea. Sizes of both plants can vary from 8 to 80 inches.

There is, however, one significant difference between rhododendrons and azaleas—namely, where the buds are located. Rhododendron buds are found just above the leaf rosette; on azaleas, the buds are concealed under the bark along the entire branch. This difference influences the kind of pruning each type needs (see page 34).

The reputation of rhododendrons and azaleas as finicky, frustrating plants is misleading. If planted in a favorable location and given proper growing conditions, these plants are easy, carefree, and long lived. The trick is in creating favorable growing conditions.

Because these plants grow best in a cool climate with high atmospheric moisture and moist, acid soil, they are difficult to grow in the central United States and in the dry desert areas of the West and Southwest. They are most widely adapted to the mid-Atlantic, northeastern, and Pacific northwestern states. Depending on species, rhododendrons and azaleas are hardy in Zones 2 to 8.

Rhododendrons and azaleas grow best in the filtered shade of high tree branches in both summer and winter. The eastern side of a sheltering structure is also a good planting location. Protection from winter sun and wind and excessive summer heat is especially important for the evergreen varieties. Because of their shallow root systems, rhododendrons cannot reach below the frost line to transmit water to their leaves when the soil is frozen. Yet their evergreen leaves constantly transpire water, even in the coldest winter. Sun and wind at this vulnerable time can be deadly. Destructive rapid freezing and thawing can be lessened by protection from the sun during winter. A 3-inch layer of organic mulch applied in fall will moderate winter soil temperature and add needed organic matter to

the soil. Where flower spot or petal blight is a problem, the mulch must be replaced each year.

Rhododendrons and azaleas require acid soil (pH 4.5 to 6.5) that is well drained and retains moisture well. If you are amending the soil to provide these conditions, you should use a mixture of ¼ soil, ½ peat moss, and ¼ coarse sand. Volcanic sand, if available, is highly recommended, because it is porous and retains moisture well. Avoid using sand from near the sea; it may be high in deadly salts. Adding some slow-release fertilizer is also beneficial. If you have very heavy soil, raised beds may be the best answer, although simply mounding the soil and planting high can improve drainage enough to mean the difference between death and survival for your rhododendrons.

If you have neutral or alkaline soil, you may want to choose a plant other than a rhododendron. Although you can acidify soil, it is a tricky operation to keep it perpetually acid. Rhododendrons let you know when the soil has reverted to its alkaline state by declining

Rhododendron

Rodgersia aesculifolia

in vigor and developing chlorosis (leaves turn yellow while the veins remain green)—actually an iron deficiency caused either by alkalinity, which makes the iron in the soil unusable, or by an actual lack of iron. The best way to acidify soil is with ferrous sulfate. A soil test report can tell you exactly how much to apply.

Adequate atmospheric and soil moisture are essential for these plants. They will not tolerate drought for any length of time. During dry periods they should be watered regularly, but the soil should not be allowed to become soggy. Water that is alkaline or high in salts should be avoided. Rainwater is ideal; you might try capturing it in a barrel to help the plants through dry periods.

Overfeeding is a common error. Rhododendrons and azaleas are highly sensitive to excessive levels of nitrogen around their fibrous roots. They do benefit, however, from infrequent light feedings with a fertilizer formulated for acid-loving plants. In good garden soil, little fertilizer should be necessary. If

you are using an organic mulch such as wood chips, sawdust, or shredded oak leaves, additional nitrogen will be needed. Manure should not be used; it is usually high in salts, to which rhododrons are extremely sensitive.

Rhododendrons and azaleas have shallow roots, so cultivating around them should be avoided. Instead, weeds can be controlled with a mulch or gentle pulling. Adequate hardening off of any new growth before the onset of winter is advised; this is best done by ceasing to apply fertilizer 2 months before the first frost date. Plants should be prepared for winter by giving them a deep, thorough watering just before the first hard freeze.

The difference between a rhododendron and an azalea causes them to need different types of pruning. Since a rhododendron bud is found just above the leaf rosette, they must be cut there, just above the bud. An azalea, on the other hand, can be cut anywhere along the branch and still be near a bud, which will then begin to grow.

Rhododendrons and azaleas require more grooming than pruning. Seedpods that are left on rhododendrons consume much of the energy that could go into flowers or leaves. The spent flower heads should be removed—this is called deadheading. Many rhododendrons tend to bloom in alternate years if they are not deadheaded. The best means of removing a flower is by holding the branch with the faded flower in one hand, and with the other hand carefully snapping off the flower head with a slight sideways pressure, taking care not to harm the growth buds below. These buds are next year's flowers and leaves; if injured, they will not open. If your plant is too tall to handpick thoroughly, try using a hose to wash away the dead petals.

To make azaleas bushier, the tips of the branches should be pinched off within a couple of weeks after the plant blooms, being careful not to take next year's buds with the flowers.

Your fingertips will do nicely for most of the pruning of these plants. Only older plants that have become leggy, sparse, or damaged will require a few cuts with hand pruners or loppers.

Rodgersia species
Rodgersia

Perennial
Medium shade to sun
Hardy to Zone 6

These are big, eastern Asian plants for moist, leaf-strewn soil and sheltered places, preferably by a pond or stream or in a damp corner where their dramatic appearance can be appreciated. Rodgersia forms clusters of tall, hairy stalks, each of which culminates in a leaf 8 to 10 inches long. Plants are 3 to 6 feet tall and 2 to 3 feet wide. Spikes of small flowers, which resemble astilbe, ascend above the leaves. Most forms bloom in July.

R. aesculifolia is the largest. Its glossy leaves are purple-bronze, resembling those of the horse chestnut. The flowers are creamy or pink. *R. pinnata* has paired, wrinkled leaves and pink flowers. *R. pinnata* 'Superba' has bigger leaves and bright pink flowers. 'Irish Bronze' has bronze leaves and light pink flowers.

Sagina subulata

Saxifraga stolonifera

Ruscus aculeatus
Butcher's-broom

Evergreen shrub
Dense shade to full sun
Hardy to Zone 8

This low, spreading shrub, 2 to 4 feet tall and 3 feet wide, is an unlikely-looking member of the lily family. It has leathery, pointed leaves and tiny flowers followed by bright red fruits in fall, if there are male and female plants close to one another. The branches, which are stiff and have shoots tipped with spines, are sometimes used in dried floral arrangements. Butcher's-broom grows well in dense shade and also in dry, sunny places. It spreads by underground rhizomes and is easily propagated by division.

Sagina subulata
Irish-moss, Scotch-moss

Ground cover
Open shade
Hardy to Zone 5

Dark green Irish-moss and its golden green form, *S. subulata* 'Aurea' (Scotch-moss), have a pair of look-alikes that wrongly bear the same common names and are used similarly in the garden: *Minuartia verna* and *M. verna* 'Aurea', both formerly *Arenaria.* The more common genus is *Sagina.* Neither genus is a true moss. *Sagina* is a relative of *Dianthus.* A close look at the tiny white flowers sprinkled over it in summer and the tiny, awl-like leaves reveals a family resemblance.

Scotch- and Irish-moss are useful in lightly shaded gardens as fine-textured evergreen ground covers or lawn substitutes for small areas, as fillers between stepping-stones, and as accents among rocks. They form a soft, mossy carpet 1 to 4 inches high.

Open shade and rich, moist, well-drained soil are best. Occasional foot traffic is not very damaging. In mild-summer areas Irish- and Scotch-moss accept medium to full sun. The plugs should be planted 6 to 8 inches apart. They spread quickly, and humps can be leveled somewhat by pressing gently with your foot. Occasional fertilizing with a mild liquid fertilizer keeps them looking their best. They require constant moisture but not wetness.

Sarcococca ruscifolia
Fragrant sarcococca

Evergreen shrub
Dense to open shade
Hardy to Zone 7

Fragrant sarcococca is as undemanding and reliable as any shrub in the garden. Even in dense shade, and in the drabness of late winter and early spring, it provides evergreen foliage, fragrant flowers, and bright, showy berries. Properly situated, it can endure neglect quite happily. Its slow growth rate and drought tolerance make it easy to maintain. Sarcococca grows 3 to 6 feet high and spreads as wide. It is especially valuable in dark entryways, beneath low trees, espaliered, or placed around the shade garden as a high ground cover.

Small white flowers appear in late winter or early spring, nearly hidden by foliage but very noticeably fragrant. Even as it blooms, the plant retains the fleshy ¼-inch scarlet berries produced the year before. The waxy, wavy-edged, deep green leaves, to 2 inches long and ½ inch wide, are consistently attractive throughout the year.

Any degree of shade is acceptable. Rich, acid soil is best, but almost any well-drained soil will do. The only pest to watch for is scale.

S. hookerana var. *humilis* (*S. humilis*) can reach 4 feet high but seldom exceeds 1½ feet. A more vigorous spreader than *S. ruscifolia,* it can spread several feet slowly by underground stems. To foster quicker growth, plants should be spaced 9 to 12 inches apart. Berries are blue-black. Otherwise it is quite similar in appearance, and in requirements, to *S. ruscifolia.*

Saxifraga stolonifera
Strawberry-geranium, creeping-sailor

Perennial
Medium shade to sun
Hardy to Zone 7

This species, formerly *S. sarmentosa,* is best known as a plant for indoor hanging baskets. In places where it is not hardy, it can be kept going with a few rooted plants brought indoors for the winter. Like a strawberry, it spreads by runners and grows new plants at the tips. The veined leaves are marbled green on top, reddish beneath. Starry white flowers 1 inch wide bloom in summer. The cultivar 'Tricolor', which

Scilla hispanica

Soleirolia (Helxine soleirolii)

has leaves variegated yellow and pink, is less vigorous than the species. Strawberry-geranium deserves a place near the front of the border or by a pathway. It grows 1½ feet tall and will tolerate some dryness and sun. It prefers rich soil.

Scilla species
Bluebells

Bulb
Open shade to full sun

Not all bluebells are blue; some are purple, violet, pink, rose, or white. But all the following members of the *Scilla* genus produce bell-shaped blossoms borne in clusters on leafless stalks. Some produce as many as a hundred blooms per stalk; others no more than a few. The basal leaves of the plants are strap shaped. Although beautiful when sprinkled throughout a woodland garden, they are also attractive in pots.

S. bifolia (two-leafed squill) is the earliest-blooming bluebell. Blooms resemble open bells or stars in turquoise, white, violet, or purplish pink. Up to 8 flowers about 1 inch across are carried on stems that grow to 8 inches.

The Spanish bluebell, now called *Hyacinthoides hispanica* but sometimes still listed as *Scilla hispanica* or *S. campanulata,* is the most popular species of the genus. Its 15- to 20-inch stems carry about 12 nodding bells each ½ inch across. There are white and pink varieties as well as blue.

The English bluebell, now called *Hyacinthoides non-scripta* but sometimes still listed as *Scilla non-scripta* or *S. nutans,* is also known as wood hyacinth. Its bells are smaller than those of the Spanish bluebell, and the stalks grow to only 12 inches. It forms a carpet of blue in spring, or you may choose white or pink variations.

In spite of its name, the Peruvian bluebell, or squill, is native to the Mediterranean region. *S. peruviana* flowers are bluish purple and borne in a dramatic, dome-shaped cluster instead of the gentle, elongated clusters of the other bluebells. Stalks are 10 to 12 inches high. A single plant in a large pot makes a striking patio accent.

S. mischtschenkoana blooms in late winter or early spring. It produces only 1 to 4 flowers clustered along 5-inch stalks, but each bulb sends up several stalks.

Cold-weather gardeners take special delight in *S. siberica* (Siberian squill), with its dainty, flaring, intense-blue bells on 3- to 6-inch stems. This is one of the best for naturalizing, especially under deciduous trees.

To use bluebells for a cut flower, they should be snipped when open flowers cover half the spike. They will last as long as a week.

Bluebells should be planted in fall in sun or open shade. All species need plenty of moisture during the growing season. They prefer being left alone for several years.

Soleirolia soleirolii
Baby's tears

Ground cover
Dense to open shade
Zone 10

Baby's tears, sometimes listed as *Helxine soleirolii,* is a creeping, mosslike plant that forms a dense, soft carpet 1 to 3 inches high. The foliage is composed of tiny, rounded, light green leaves growing in a tight mat.

This is a plant for shade, rich soil, and moisture in a warm climate. It is quickly killed by too much direct sun, drought, or subfreezing temperatures. It can be propagated by division, with the plant sections set 6 to 12 inches apart. A variant with golden yellow foliage is also available.

Baby's tears provides a cool, delicate effect when planted at the base of trees or shade plants such as ferns, camellias, and azaleas. The plant is well named, for it seems as fragile as a baby's tear. A few steps will not kill it, but the footprint will remain for at least several days.

Solenostemon scutellaroides
Coleus

Perennial used as annual
Medium to open shade

S. scutellaroides, formerly *Coleus hybridus,* offers a wide diversity of foliage color, shape, and size. The leaves may be velvety or rough and crinkled, deeply notched or round and full. They may be one solid color or several colors in varying shades of pink, red, bronze, yellow, maroon, green, and chartreuse. Coleus is ideal as an edging plant as well as in flower beds, pots, and window boxes.

Thalictrum

Tiarella cordifolia

Coleus grows best in rich, well-drained soil that is kept evenly moist. The square stems grow 6 to 36 inches tall. Small blue or lilac flower spikes, which appear throughout summer, are not showy and should be removed to conserve the plant's energy. Keep coleus bushy by periodically cutting back the stems several inches. Some new cultivars stay dense without being pinched back.

Native to Java and the Philippines, coleus is grown as an annual in most areas of the country, since it is damaged by even the lightest frost. It is propagated easily from stem cuttings. Fall cuttings can be grown indoors in winter as houseplants, then set outdoors in spring after the last frost. Coleus can also be grown from seed, but no two plants will be alike.

Taxus species
Yew

Coniferous shrub
Dense shade to sun
Zones 4 to 8

Although the species are 40- to 50-foot trees, the many cultivars available are among the most useful coniferous evergreen shrubs for the landscape. Hardy and trouble free, they have

handsome, dark green foliage and come in a variety of dense, refined forms. Their only drawback may be overuse.

As with junipers, yews are often planted without consideration for their ultimate size. A nursery can help you select the appropriate variety, but you should be sure to ask how big it will grow. Yews accept formal pruning well and are often clipped into hedges or other shapes. They should also be considered for massing, as an evergreen touch to the shrub border, and as a foundation plant. When allowed to develop their natural forms, the effect is usually graceful and appealing.

Given soil with excellent drainage in dense shade to filtered sun, they generally prove to be easy to grow and pest free. In heavy, wet soil they will be stunted and sickly if they survive at all. They need adequate moisture and protection from wind. In hot, dry climates, they do best given a northern exposure; they should be hosed frequently during the driest periods. The inner portions of their attractive red fruits are poisonous.

T. baccata (English yew; hardy to Zone 7), the least hardy yew, has several cultivars that are excellent for southern gardens.

T. cuspidata (Japanese yew; hardy to Zone 5), a species with many excellent cultivars, ranges from a low, 1-foot-high and 3-foot-wide form with yellow new growth ('Aurescens') to a 40- to 50-foot pyramidal form ('Capitata').

T. × media (Anglojap yew; hardy to Zone 4), a hybrid between the above two species, has an extremely wide variety of cultivars, from low, spreading types to tall, narrow ones.

Thalictrum rochebrunianum
Meadowrue, lavender mist

Perennial
Open shade
Hardy to Zone 5

Growing 3 to 6 feet high or more, meadowrue makes a splendid background in a shady perennial border. The tall, airy plants have fine-textured foliage topped with delicate sprays of lavender flowers. Individually the flowers are minute, but they appear in great quantities in loose, compound clusters, blooming in the months of July

and August. They have no petals; the showy parts are the purplish sepals and yellow stamens.

The plant prefers deep, rich, moist soil that is high in organic matter. Open shade is best, but full sun is tolerated if the soil is kept moist. The plants should be spaced 24 inches apart. Meadowrue appreciates abundant water. It has few serious pests, but powdery mildew and rust are occasionally reported. It is best to divide the plant about every fourth or fifth year to relieve crowding of the root mass.

Tiarella cordifolia
Foamflower

Evergreen ground cover
Dense to medium shade
Hardy to Zone 5

Foamflower is a North American wildflower suited to shady, moist soil rich in organic matter. It forms a loose mat under shrubs or along a shady path. The heart-shaped green leaves, up to 4 inches wide, turn bronze in winter. In May 9-inch spikes of foamy white flowers appear. The species spreads by runners, but *T. wherryi* forms clumps. Its flowers are light pink and the foliage is spotted with brown.

Torenia fournieri

Tradescantia virginiana

Torenia fournieri
Wishbone flower

Annual
Medium to open shade

Quiet and unassuming, wishbone flower is a little-known gem that should be a favorite of the discerning shade gardener. The individual flowers are especially interesting viewed up close. Their structure is similar to that of the snapdragon, to which they are related, but the coloring is more reminiscent of the pansy. The upper and lower petals are light blue, dark blue, or rose, and the center is yellow. There is also a white form. Two yellow stamens arch over the center of the flower in the shape of a wishbone, from which the plant receives its common name.

In the garden the plant forms a loose clump 8 to 10 inches tall and 6 inches wide. Not a flashy plant by any means, it prefers a cool, damp retreat in a shady corner. Flowers fade quickly in bright sun and a dry climate. Planted in dappled shade either in large beds as a ground cover, or dabbed here and there, the deep, cool colors with a slight yellow sparkle are particularly pleasing. Wishbone flower prefers medium to open shade and fertile, moist, fluffy soil that is high in organic matter. It should be kept well watered. Before the first frost in fall, it can be dug, potted, and brought indoors for winter color.

Tradescantia virginiana
Spiderwort

Perennial
Medium shade to full sun
Hardy to Zone 4

Adaptable to many difficult situations, including infertile soil, dense shade, and boggy conditions, spiderwort provides colorful blooms over a long season. However, it has a tendency to sprawl and ramble through the garden when it is not restrained. Named cultivars are usually superior to the species.

The flowers are usually bright purple, although varieties are white, blue, pink, or red. The inch-wide blossoms are composed of 3 petals and last individually for only a day; however, they are produced in clusters at the ends of the stems and bloom over a long season, from June to September.

The deep green leaves are straplike, growing to 1 inch wide and as long as 15 inches. The lower portion of the leaf is wrapped around the stem, giving the plant the appearance of a coarse grass. The form is variable but mostly upright; the plant grows from 18 to 36 inches tall. From midseason on it tends to sprawl into an open, tangled structure. If the stems flop badly, they can be cut clear to the ground; the revived plant will flower again in fall.

This long-lived plant spreads enthusiastically by underground stems; aboveground stems will also root where their joints contact the soil. Frequent division will restrain its rampant growth.

Spiderwort tolerates nearly any soil but grows most vigorously in moist, rich soil, which should be avoided by gardeners who desire to restrain it.

It grows in medium shade to full sun and looks best with adequate water. It has few serious pests, although several types of caterpillars have been reported. Botrytis blight may attack the blossoms. Division in spring is best performed every other year; it should be done at least every third or fourth year to restrain spreading or for increase. Plants should be spaced 15 to 30 inches apart.

Trillium species
Trillium, wood lily

Perennial
Medium to open shade
Hardiness varies according to species

It is hard to imagine a woodland perennial more delightful than trillium. In earliest spring, its smooth stems and furled foliage break through the leaf mold, and soon its handsome leaves, 3 to the stem, and its 3-petaled flower, centered among the leaves, provide one of the year's most special garden displays. Usually planted in informal clumps or groupings, it is at home among ferns and other woodland plants, around rocks in a shady nook, or nestled in a shaded border. Height varies from 1 to nearly 3 feet. Trillium should be grown from seed (difficult sometimes) or purchased from a propagator, not dug from its dwindling numbers in the wild. It should be planted in autumn.

Flowers are solitary, and white, pink, or purplish. Like the petals, the sepals come in threes. The fruit is a large berry. The trio of leaves is clear green in some varieties and bronzy green or mottled in others. Foliage lasts through spring and summer.

Trillium grandiflorum

Tsuga canadensis 'Pendula'

Good drainage and deep, rich, moist soil with a high organic content are necessary. Medium shade in a cool spot is optimal, although most species grow well in somewhat denser shade.

Care is easy, as long as trillium is properly situated and the soil is kept moist. It should be mulched annually. Snails and slugs like these juicy plants, so bait is often necessary.

Many species are available but not always easy to find. The following are among the easiest to locate and grow.

T. chloropetalum (giant trillium; hardy to Zone 7), native to Washington and California, is a showy plant. Its 12- to 30-inch stem bears big, dark green leaves mottled with bronze, and a flower whose 4-inch petals are erect and greenish, cream, rose, or mahogany.

T. erectum (purple trillium; hardy to Zone 4), from eastern North America, actually bears deep red rather than purple flowers; some strains have white or yellowish flowers. Height is 10 to 12 inches. Each leaf is about 7 inches long. *T. erectum* is the most popular species for gardens.

T. grandiflorum (trinity-flower, wakerobin; hardy to Zone 4), another popular species, is one of the showiest. To 1½ feet high, it begins with shiny bronze growth and yellow buds, which develop into bright green foliage and a white flower, sometimes turning pinkish. Hard-to-find 'Flore pleno' is many petaled.

T. ovatum (western trillium; hardy to Zone 8), native from British Columbia to California, grows to 1 to 1½ feet and has a large flower that opens white and turns rosy as it ages.

T. sessile (toadshade; hardy to Zone 6) is the eastern cousin of the western *T. chloropetalum*. Foliage is heavily mottled and veined. The maroon flower, growing directly out of the axis of the leaves, is erect and 2 inches long.

T. undulatum (painted trillium; hardy to Zone 3) is named for its white flowers, which are veined, mottled, or streaked with purple or rose. Petals are wavy. This foot-high species is from eastern North America. It is rare and may be difficult to find.

Trollius europaeus
Common globeflower

Perennial
Medium shade to full sun
Hardy to Zone 3

Common globeflower is a leafy, bushy plant that produces rounded, globular blossoms in many shades of yellow and orange. Blooming in late spring and early summer, it is an excellent choice for the moist, heavy soil that most other perennials abhor.

Flowers come in many shades of yellow and orange, according to variety. They are 1 to 3 inches across and are composed of 5 to 15 showy sepals in a rounded, ball-like mass that looks as if it has not fully opened. The flowers appear on the ends of 1- to 3-foot stems. The dark green leaves are deeply divided into 3 to 5 lobes and are attractive all season. The stems grow in upright clusters, creating bushy, rounded masses. Globeflower is long lived and restrained in growth. The clumps gradually expand by sending up new shoots on the outside perimeter of the crown.

Very moist, fertile soil that is high in organic matter is best; boggy conditions should be avoided. Although preferring medium to open shade, common globeflower will tolerate full sun if the soil is kept moist. The plants should be spaced 12 inches apart. Removing faded flowers prolongs bloom. This plant should be well watered and never allowed to dry out. It has no serious pests. Division is usually required every 5 years or so to reduce crowding, but if necessary the plant can survive much longer without disturbance. An excellent means of increase, division should be done in late August or September.

Tsuga canadensis 'Pendula'
Sargent's weeping hemlock

Coniferous evergreen shrub
Open shade
Zones 4 to 8

This is the most commonly grown garden hemlock. It displays a graceful, pendulous habit and refined, evergreen foliage. Although it can reach 5 to 6 feet in height and two or three times that in spread in extreme old age, a more reasonable size to expect is 3 to 4 feet high by 8 to 9 feet wide. This plant makes an outstanding focal specimen in a border, by an entryway, or in a raised bed or container.

Vancouveria chrysantha

Vinca minor

It prefers well-drained, moist, acid soil. Unlike most conifers it tolerates shade well and in fact prefers open shade; however, if drainage is good, the soil is moist, and there are no drying winds, it will tolerate full sun. Hemlock will not tolerate wind, drought, or waterlogged soils, and in areas where summer temperatures exceed 95° F it is likely to develop leaf scorch. This is not a plant for heavily polluted areas. If the location is right, however, hemlock is usually a hardy, trouble-free, and long-lived plant.

Vaccinium species
Blueberry, huckleberry

Deciduous shrubs and ground covers
Open shade to sun
Hardiness varies with species

These lovers of wet, acid soil grow well in open shade. In denser shade flowering and fruiting are reduced. The coloring of the leaves in fall is also brighter with some sun. Early spring pruning keeps these shrubs bushy.

V. angustifolium var. *laevifolium* (blueberry; hardy to Zone 2) is a deciduous, fruit-bearing shrub of which many varieties are available. It requires open shade and moist, well-drained, acid soil.

V. vitis-idaea (cowberry; hardy to Zone 2) is a creeping evergreen, to 1 foot high, suitable for small-area ground cover. *V. vitis-idaea* var. *minus* (mountain cranberry, lingonberry; hardy to Zone 1), native to the northern United States and Canada, is a dwarf that forms dense mats 8 inches or lower and spreads by underground runners. The red berries of both forms make good preserves. Both are useful in wet, shaded areas.

Vancouveria species
American barrenwort

Ground cover
Medium to open shade
Hardy to Zone 6

This Pacific Northwest native is closely related to epimedium. American barrenwort (*V. hexandra*) grows to 1 to 1½ feet tall. The ½-inch white flowers appear in May and June. Its delicate, light green leaves die to the ground each winter.

American barrenwort grows naturally in the shade of the coast redwoods, where the soil is acid and high in organic matter, temperatures are cool, and there is plenty of moisture.

This is an excellent ground cover where it is well adapted. It combines well with ferns and epimediums around the base of trees and in shaded beds. The cut foliage is attractive in bouquets.

V. chrysantha is evergreen but somewhat less hardy than *V. hexandra*.

Vinca minor
Periwinkle, running myrtle

Ground cover
Medium to open shade
Hardy to Zone 4

There is no more useful and versatile ground cover for the shade garden than periwinkle. This 6-inch-tall evergreen thrives in medium to open shade; it produces healthy foliage, if few flowers, in denser shade. Tall enough to hide withering bulb foliage, it is an excellent companion plant for large bulbs such as daffodils and tulips. Its fast-growing runners can fill medium to large beds in a season. For covering shady slopes and trailing gracefully over walls and the edges of raised beds and planters, it is without equal.

Lavender-blue (periwinkle) flowers, an inch wide, appear toward the stem ends throughout spring and often longer. Their 5 fused petals seem to float starlike over the dark foliage. Oblong, glossy, deep green leaves are spaced at 1-inch intervals along the trailing stems. They remain evenly green throughout the year.

Periwinkle prefers shade and rich, moist, well-drained soil. Desert climates are too hot for it to flourish, even in the shade. Moderately aggressive, it is best used away from small, delicate plants. Divisions or rooted cuttings should be set out 12 to 18 inches apart, preferably in spring.

During the warm months, some moisture and about 3 feedings with a lawn fertilizer keep the foliage richly green and thick. Runners that grow out of bounds can be trimmed. Edges can be kept informal by pruning stems individually. Occasional foot traffic does no harm.

V. minor 'Alba' has white flowers; *V. minor* 'Atropurpurea' has purple flowers. *V. minor* 'Aureomarginata' has blue flowers and leaves with bright, irregular yellowish margins. The flowers of 'Bowles's Variety' are deeper blue and larger than those of the species, and it is

Vinca minor

Viola odorata

a more prolific bloomer. However, its growth is slower because it spreads from expansion of the crown rather than rooting of trailing stems. 'Gertrude Jekyll' is small leafed, dainty, and very dwarf. All the cultivars are somewhat less hardy than the species.

V. major is a larger and more upright and vigorous version of *V. minor,* growing 12 to 24 inches tall. It accepts more sun, more dryness, and less cold. Because it is so invasive, it should be used judiciously.

Viola species
Violet

Perennial
Medium to open shade
Hardiness varies with species

Literary references to sweet violet (*V. odorata*), the most famous of the violas, may be found from Homer to modern literature. Although not cultivated as widely as the pansy (*V. × wittrockiana*), it is probably most flower lovers' favorite viola—or violet, as most species except pansy are usually called. Scent alone would be reason enough for the popularity of this violet

and its varieties, but it has additional virtues. A broadly clumping perennial that spreads by runners, it is often used in open shade as a woodland ground cover or container plant. In all but the coldest winter climates, it is evergreen. Heaviest flowering is in spring, but flowers may appear in other seasons.

The 5-petaled flowers vary from deep purple to rose and white, depending on the variety. Most are single; some are variegated and some are double. Most varieties have flowers ¾ inch across or larger. The leaves are heart shaped and borne on stems 2 to 8 inches long, depending on the variety.

Sweet violet likes reasonable drainage and cool, moist soil; moisture is especially important in open shade or hot, dry spots. A winter covering of fallen leaves is beneficial. It prefers shade—ideally, open shade in cool climates, medium shade in hot climates, even dense shade (with brightness) in desert areas. Pockets of sweet violet can grow quite well beneath shallow-rooted trees. Acid, neutral, and slightly alkaline soils are all acceptable as long as they are rich and friable. Air circulation aids in blooming. Spider mites occasionally require spraying.

V. odorata 'Red Giant' has long-stemmed leaves, flower stems up to 10 inches, and red-violet flowers. 'Rosina' is 5 to 6 inches high. Its rosy pink flowers are profuse and especially fragrant; the leaves are downy. 'Royal Robe' grows up to 8 inches high and has large, glossy leaves and deep blue-violet or purple flowers.

The following are various species of identical culture.

V. alba (Parma violet; hardy to Zone 6) is popular for its intensely fragrant double flowers. It rapidly forms carpets of inch-wide leaves. Varieties are 'Lady Hume Campbell' (lavender flowers marked with white) and 'Swanley White' (pure white flowers).

V. cornuta (horned violet, tufted violet, viola; hardy to Zone 6), from the Pyrenees, is a bedding plant quite close to the pansy in appearance but smaller flowered. Numerous hybrid forms are available. It can be grown from seed or set out as seedlings, 8 inches apart. Unlike most violas, it is treated as an annual. Open shade is preferred.

V. hederacea (Australian violet; hardy to Zone 7), a diminutive shade ground cover, is often available in nursery flats. It spreads rapidly by rooting

runners. Leaves are tiny. Blue-and-white flowers are less than ½ inch wide, borne on 1- to 4-inch stems. It requires rich soil, moisture, and open shade. It is dormant in winter.

V. pedata (bird's-foot violet; hardy to Zone 5), bearing 1½-inch violet to lilac-purple flowers with darker upper petals, is a striking spring bloomer. It thrives in well-drained but poor soil in open shade. A rock garden setting is appropriate. In horticultural literature it is commonly referred to as the most beautiful of North American violets. Its name refers to the shape of its leaves.

V. sororia (confederate violet; hardy to Zone 5), which was formerly known as *V. papilionacea,* is a wildflower of the Northeast that bears large, substantial, blue-veined white blossoms on long stems. Its heart-shaped leaves are 4 to 5 inches wide. It reseeds freely and makes a suitable ground cover for shrubs and larger woodland plants in medium shade. 'White Czar' has delicately penciled purplish markings against a yellow blush at the center of large white flowers.

Climate Zone Map

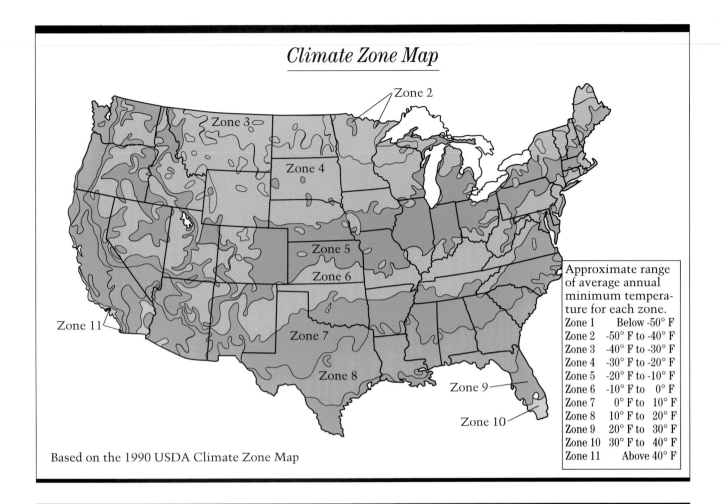

Zone 2

Zone 3

Zone 4

Zone 5

Zone 6

Zone 11

Zone 7

Zone 8

Zone 9

Zone 10

Approximate range of average annual minimum temperature for each zone.

Zone 1   Below -50° F
Zone 2   -50° F to -40° F
Zone 3   -40° F to -30° F
Zone 4   -30° F to -20° F
Zone 5   -20° F to -10° F
Zone 6   -10° F to   0° F
Zone 7   0° F to 10° F
Zone 8   10° F to 20° F
Zone 9   20° F to 30° F
Zone 10   30° F to 40° F
Zone 11   Above 40° F

Based on the 1990 USDA Climate Zone Map

U.S. Measure and Metric Measure Conversion Chart

	Symbol	When you know:	Multiply by:	To find:			
		Formulas for Exact Measures			**Rounded Measures for Quick Reference**		
Mass	oz	ounces	28.35	grams	1 oz		= 30 g
(weight)	lb	pounds	0.45	kilograms	4 oz		= 115 g
	g	grams	0.035	ounces	8 oz		= 225 g
	kg	kilograms	2.2	pounds	16 oz	= 1 lb	= 450 g
					32 oz	= 2 lb	= 900 g
					36 oz	= 2¼ lb	= 1000 g (1 kg)
Volume	pt	pints	0.47	liters	1 c	= 8 oz	= 250 ml
	qt	quarts	0.95	liters	2 c (1 pt)	= 16 oz	= 500 ml
	gal	gallons	3.785	liters	4 c (1 qt)	= 32 oz	= 1 liter
	ml	milliliters	0.034	fluid ounces	4 qt (1 gal)	= 128 oz	= 3¾ liter
Length	in.	inches	2.54	centimeters	⅜ in.		= 1.0 cm
	ft	feet	30.48	centimeters	1 in.		= 2.5 cm
	yd	yards	0.9144	meters	2 in.		= 5.0 cm
	mi	miles	1.609	kilometers	2½ in.		= 6.5 cm
	km	kilometers	0.621	miles	12 in. (1 ft)		= 30.0 cm
	m	meters	1.094	yards	1 yd		= 90.0 cm
	cm	centimeters	0.39	inches	100 ft		= 30.0 m
					1 mi		= 1.6 km
Temperature	° F	Fahrenheit	⅝ (after subtracting 32)	Celsius	32° F		= 0° C
	° C	Celsius	⅝ (then add 32)	Fahrenheit	212° F		= 100° C
Area	in.²	square inches	6.452	square centimeters	1 in.²		= 6.5 cm²
	ft²	square feet	929.0	square centimeters	1 ft²		= 930 cm²
	yd²	square yards	8361.0	square centimeters	1 yd²		= 8360 cm²
	a.	acres	0.4047	hectares	1 a.		= 4050 m²

Nursing Leadership and Management
REVIEW MODULE EDITION 9.0

Contributors

Alissa Althoff, Ed.D, MSN, RN

Laurie F. Fontenot, MSN, RN

Lori Grace, MSN, RN

Norma Jean Henry, MSN/Ed., RN

Honey C. Holman, MSN, RN

Janean Johnson, DNP, RN, CNE

Beth Cusatis Phillips, PhD,
RN, CNE, CHSE

Pamela Roland, MSN, MBA, RN

Consultants

Julie Traynor, MS, RN, CNE

Director of content review: Kristen Lawler

Director of development: Derek Prater

Project management: Meri Ann Mason

Coordination of content review: Alissa Althoff, Honey C. Holman

Copy editing: Kelly Von Lunen, Tricia Lunt, Bethany Robertson, Kya Rodgers, Rebecca Her, Sam Shiel, Alethea Surland, Graphic World

Layout: Bethany Robertson, Maureen Bradshaw, Haylee Hedge, scottie. o

Illustrations: Randi Hardy, Graphic World

Online media: Brant Stacy, Ron Hanson, Britney Frerking, Trevor Lund

Interior book design: Spring Lenox

IMPORTANT NOTICE TO THE READER

User's Guide

Welcome to the Assessment Technologies Institute® Nursing Leadership and Management Review Module Edition 9.0. The mission of ATI's Content Mastery Series® Review Modules is to provide user-friendly compendiums of nursing knowledge that will:
- Help you locate important information quickly.
- Assist in your learning efforts.
- Provide exercises for applying your nursing knowledge.
- Facilitate your entry into the nursing profession as a newly licensed nurse.

This newest edition of the Review Modules has been redesigned to optimize your learning experience. We've fit more content into less space and have done so in a way that will make it even easier for you to find and understand the information you need.

ORGANIZATION

Chapters in this Review Module use a nursing concepts organizing framework, beginning with an overview describing the central concept and its relevance to nursing. Subordinate themes are covered in outline form to demonstrate relationships and present the information in a clear, succinct manner. Some chapters have sections that group related concepts and contain their own overviews. These sections are included in the table of contents.

ACTIVE LEARNING SCENARIOS AND APPLICATION EXERCISES

Each chapter includes opportunities for you to test your knowledge and to practice applying that knowledge. Active Learning Scenario exercises pose a nursing scenario and then direct you to use an ATI Active Learning Template (included at the back of this book) to record the important knowledge a nurse should apply to the scenario. An example is then provided to which you can compare your completed Active Learning Template. The Application Exercises include NCLEX-style questions (multiple-choice and multiple-select items), providing you with opportunities to practice answering the kinds of questions you might expect to see on ATI assessments or the NCLEX. After the Application Exercises, an answer key is provided, along with rationales.

NCLEX® CONNECTIONS

To prepare for the NCLEX, it is important to understand how the content in this Review Module is connected to the NCLEX test plan. You can find information on the detailed test plan at the National Council of State Boards of Nursing's website, www.ncsbn.org. When reviewing content in this Review Module, regularly ask yourself, "How does this content fit into the test plan, and what types of questions related to this content should I expect?"

To help you in this process, we've included NCLEX Connections at the beginning of each unit and with each question in the Application Exercises Answer Keys. The NCLEX Connections at the beginning of each unit point out areas of the detailed test plan that relate to the content within that unit. The NCLEX Connections attached to the Application Exercises Answer Keys demonstrate how each exercise fits within the detailed content outline.

These NCLEX Connections will help you understand how the detailed content outline is organized, starting with major client needs categories and subcategories and followed by related content areas and tasks. The major client needs categories are:
- Safe and Effective Care Environment
  - Management of Care
  - Safety and Infection Control
- Health Promotion and Maintenance
- Psychosocial Integrity
- Physiological Integrity
  - Basic Care and Comfort
  - Pharmacological and Parenteral Therapies
  - Reduction of Risk Potential
  - Physiological Adaptation

An NCLEX Connection might, for example, alert you that content within a chapter is related to:
- Management of Care
  - Advance Directives
    - Provide clients with information about advance directives.

QSEN COMPETENCIES

As you use the Review Modules, you will note the integration of the Quality and Safety Education for Nurses (QSEN) competencies throughout the chapters. These competencies are integral components of the curriculum of many nursing programs in the United States and prepare you to provide safe, high-quality care as a newly licensed nurse. Icons appear to draw your attention to the six QSEN competencies.

Safety: the minimization of risk factors that could cause injury or harm while promoting quality care and maintaining a secure environment for clients, self, and others.

Patient-Centered Care: the provision of caring and compassionate, culturally sensitive care that addresses clients' physiological, psychological, sociological, spiritual, and cultural needs, preferences, and values.

Evidence-Based Practice: the use of current knowledge from research and other credible sources, on which to base clinical judgment and client care.

Informatics: the use of information technology as a communication and information-gathering tool that supports clinical decision-making and scientifically based nursing practice.

Quality Improvement: care-related and organizational processes that involve the development and implementation of a plan to improve health care services and better meet clients' needs.

Teamwork and Collaboration: the delivery of client care in partnership with multidisciplinary members of the health care team to achieve continuity of care and positive client outcomes.

ICONS

Icons are used throughout the Review Module to draw your attention to particular areas. Keep an eye out for these icons.

(N) This icon is used for NCLEX Connections.

(G) This icon indicates gerontological considerations, or knowledge specific to the care of older adult clients.

Qs This icon is used for content related to safety and is a QSEN competency. When you see this icon, take note of safety concerns or steps that nurses can take to ensure client safety and a safe environment.

QPCC This icon is a QSEN competency that indicates the importance of a holistic approach to providing care.

QEBP This icon, a QSEN competency, points out the integration of research into clinical practice.

QI This icon is a QSEN competency and highlights the use of information technology to support nursing practice.

QQI This icon is used to focus on the QSEN competency of integrating planning processes to meet clients' needs.

QTC This icon highlights the QSEN competency of care delivery using an interprofessional approach.

QSDoH This icon highlights content related to social determinants of health.

M◇ This icon appears at the top-right of pages and indicates availability of an online media supplement (a graphic, animation, or video). If you have an electronic copy of the Review Module, this icon will appear alongside clickable links to media supplements. If you have a hard copy version of the Review Module, visit www.atitesting.com for details on how to access these features.

FEEDBACK

ATI welcomes feedback regarding this Review Module. Please provide comments to comments@atitesting.com.

As needed updates to the Review Modules are identified, changes to the text are made for subsequent printings of the book and for subsequent releases of the electronic version. For the printed books, print runs are based on when existing stock is depleted. For the electronic versions, a number of factors influence the update schedule. As such, ATI encourages faculty and students to refer to the Review Module addendums for information on what updates have been made. These addendums, which are available in the Help/FAQs on the student site and the Resources/eBooks & Active Learning on the faculty site, are updated regularly and always include the most current information on updates to the Review Modules.

Table of Contents

When reviewing the following chapter, keep in mind the relevant topics and tasks of the NCLEX outline, in particular:

Management of Care

ASSIGNMENT, DELEGATION AND SUPERVISION
Evaluate delegated tasks to ensure correct completion of activity.

Evaluate effectiveness of staff members' time management skills.

CASE MANAGEMENT: Practice and advocate for cost effective care.

CONCEPTS OF MANAGEMENT
Manage conflict among clients and health care staff.

Identify roles/responsibilities of health care team members.

ESTABLISHING PRIORITIES
Apply knowledge of pathophysiology when establishing priorities for interventions with multiple clients.

Prioritize the delivery of client care.

PERFORMANCE IMPROVEMENT (QUALITY IMPROVEMENT):
Participate in performance improvement projects and quality improvement processes.

CHAPTER 1 Leading and Managing Client Care

To lead and manage client care effectively, a nurse must develop knowledge and skills in multiple areas. Specific areas include leadership, management, critical thinking, clinical reasoning, clinical judgment, prioritization, time management, assigning, delegating, supervising, staff education, quality improvement, performance appraisal, peer review, disciplinary action, conflict resolution, and cost-effective care.

Leadership and management

- Management is the process of planning, organizing, directing, and coordinating the work within an organization.
- Leadership is the ability to inspire others to achieve a desired outcome.
- Effective managers usually possess good leadership skills. However, effective leaders are not always in a management position.
- Managers have formal positions of power and authority. Leaders might have only the informal power afforded them by their peers.
- One cannot be a leader without followers.

LEADERSHIP THEORIES (STYLES)

Early leadership theories focused on the traits the leader possessed, but as time went on, the focus shifted to the actions the leader performed or the style of leadership the leader portrayed. These first styles were categorized as autocratic/authoritarian, democratic, or laissez-faire. The nurse might need to use a variety of these leadership styles depending on the situation.

Autocratic/authoritarian

- Makes decisions for the group
- Motivates by coercion
- Communication occurs down the chain of command, or from the highest management level downward through other managers to employees.
- Work output by staff is usually high: good for crisis situations and bureaucratic settings.
- Effective for employees with little or no formal education.

Democratic

- Includes the group when decisions are made Q︎TC
- Motivates by supporting staff achievements
- Communication occurs up and down the chain of command.
- Work output by staff is usually of good quality when cooperation and collaboration are necessary.

Laissez-faire

- Makes very few decisions, and does little planning
- Motivation is largely the responsibility of individual staff members.
- Communication occurs up and down the chain of command and between group members.
- Work output is low unless an informal leader evolves from the group.
- Effective with professional employees.

From these various leadership styles, types of leaders have been identified. Some of the most referred to include transactional, transformational, laissez-faire, bureaucratic, and situational.

TYPES OF LEADERS

- **Transactional leaders** focus on immediate problems, maintaining the status quo and using rewards to motivate followers.
- **Transformational leaders** empower and inspire followers to achieve a common, long-term vision.
- **Laissez-faire leaders** are permissive and encourage decision making to take place throughout the group.
- **Bureaucratic (Authentic) leaders** inspire others to follow them by modeling a strong internal moral code
- **Situational leaders** are flexible and can adapt their leadership style based on the situation at hand, often combining both autocratic and democratic leadership styles.

Emotional intelligence

- Emotional intelligence is the ability of an individual to perceive and manage the emotions of self and others.
- The nurse must be able to perceive and understand their own emotions and the emotions of the client and family in order to provide client-centered care. Q︎PCC
- Emotional intelligence is also an important characteristic of the successful nurse leader.
- Emotional intelligence is developed through understanding the concept and applying it to practice in everyday situations.

The emotionally intelligent leader:
- Has insight into the emotions of members of the team.
- Understands the perspective of others.
- Encourages constructive criticism and is open to new ideas.
- Manages emotions and channels them in a positive direction, which in turn helps the team accomplish its goals.
- Is committed to the delivery of high-quality client care.
- Refrains from judgment in controversial or emotionally-charged situations until facts are gathered.

MANAGEMENT

The five major management functions are the following.
- PLANNING: The decisions regarding what needs to be done, how it will be done, and who is going to do it
- ORGANIZING: The organizational structure that determines the lines of authority, channels of communication, and where decisions are made
- STAFFING: The acquisition and management of adequate staff and staffing mix
- DIRECTING: The leadership role assumed by a manager that influences and motivates staff to perform assigned roles
- CONTROLLING: The evaluation of staff performance and evaluation of unit goals to ensure identified outcomes are being met

CHARACTERISTICS OF MANAGERS

- Hold formal positions of authority and power
- Possess clinical expertise
- Network with members of the team
- Coach subordinates
- Make decisions about the function of the organization, including resources, budget, hiring, and firing

CLINICAL DECISION-MAKING

Clinical decision-making is the product of a process involving critical thinking, clinical reasoning, and clinical judgment.

CRITICAL THINKING

Critical thinking is the foundation for clinical decision-making. Skills used to critically think include analyzing client issues and problems. Critical thinking skills align with the nursing process and include questioning, synthesis, intuition, application, creativity, interpretation, analysis, evaluation, inference, inductive and deductive reasoning, and explanation. These cognitive skills assist the nurse to determine the most appropriate action to take.
- Critical thinking reflects upon the meaning of statements, examines available data, and uses reason to make informed decisions.
- Critical thinking is necessary to reflect and evaluate from a broader scope of view.
- Sometimes one must think "outside the box" to find solutions that are best for clients, staff, and the organization.

Clinical reasoning

- Clinical reasoning is the mental process used when analyzing the elements of a clinical situation and making decisions. The nurse continues to use clinical reasoning for subsequent decisions as the client's situation changes.
- Clinical reasoning is the accumulation of skills and knowledge over time and leads to clinical decision making.
- Clinical reasoning supports the clinical decision-making process by:
  - Guiding the nurse through the process of assessing and compiling data.
  - Selecting and discarding data based on relevance.
  - Using nursing knowledge to make decisions about client care. Problem solving is a part of decision-making.

Clinical judgment

- Clinical judgment is the decision made regarding a course of action based on a critical analysis of data.
- Clinical judgment considers the client's needs when deciding to take an action, or modify an intervention based on the client's response.
- The nurse uses clinical judgment to complete these tasks.
  - Analyze data and related evidence.
  - Ascertain the meaning of the data and evidence.
  - Apply knowledge to a clinical situation.
  - Determine client outcomes desired and/or achieved as indicated by evidence-based practices. Q EBP

CLINICAL JUDGMENT MODELS (1.1)

Includes Assessment, Analysis, Planning, Implementation, and Evaluation.
- This process at the PN level includes Data Collection, Planning, Implementation, and Evaluation and is always done and Evaluation with the PN working under the supervision of the RN.

The steps of the nursing process are completed in order initially but then can be alternated or often revisited while providing care to achieve the best results. Tanner's Clinical Judgment Model describes the skills of Noticing, Interpreting, Responding, and Reflecting in teaching moral reasoning and client engagement.

The National Council of State Boards of Nursing (NCSBN) developed the Clinical Judgment Measurement Model (CJMM) as a framework to measure at what level NCLEX candidates possess clinical judgment skills. Q EBP

The ATI Clinical Judgment Action Module (CJAM) was based on the NCSBN CJMM, Tanner's Clinical Judgment Model (Tanner, 2006), and the Nursing Process (Smeltzer, 1980). It was developed to show correlation between what is measured by the NCLEX and what is being taught in nursing education. Nurse educators can use this model to develop and implement learning materials to teach clinical judgment skills to nursing students.

1.1 ATI guide for clinical judgment

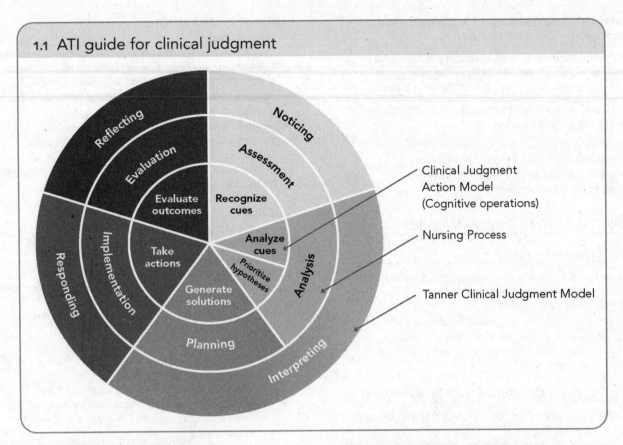

Clinical Judgment
Action Model
(Cognitive operations)

Nursing Process

Tanner Clinical Judgment Model

PRIORITIZATION AND TIME MANAGEMENT

- Nurses must continuously set and reset priorities in order to meet the needs of multiple clients and to maintain client safety. Qs
- Priority setting requires that decisions be made regarding the order in which:
  - Clients are seen.
  - Assessments are completed.
  - Interventions are provided.
  - Steps in a client procedure are completed.
  - Components of client care are completed.
- Establishing priorities in nursing practice requires that the nurse make these decisions based on evidence obtained:
  - During shift reports and other communications with members of the health care team,
  - Through careful review of documents, and
  - By continuously and accurately collecting client data.

PRIORITIZATION PRINCIPLES IN CLIENT CARE

Prioritize systemic before local ("life before limb").

Prioritizing interventions for a client in shock over interventions for a client who has a localized limb injury

Prioritize acute (less opportunity for physical adaptation) before chronic (greater opportunity for physical adaptation).

Prioritizing the care of a client who has a new injury/illness (mental confusion, chest pain) or an acute exacerbation of a previous illness over the care of a client who has a long-term chronic illness

Prioritize actual problems before potential future problems.

Prioritizing administration of medication to a client experiencing acute pain over ambulation of a client at risk for thrombophlebitis

Listen carefully to clients and don't assume.

Asking a client who has a new diagnosis of diabetes mellitus what they feel is most important to learn about disease management.

Recognize and respond to trends vs. transient findings.

Recognizing a gradual deterioration in a client's level of consciousness and/or Glasgow Coma Scale score

Recognize indications of medical emergencies and complications vs. expected findings.

> Recognizing indications of increasing intracranial pressure in a client who has a new diagnosis of a stroke vs. the findings expected following a stroke

Apply clinical knowledge to procedural standards to determine the priority action.

> Recognizing that the timing of administration of antidiabetic and antimicrobial medications is more important than administration of some other medications

PRIORITY-SETTING FRAMEWORKS

Maslow's hierarchy (1.2) Qpcc

The nurse should consider this hierarchy of human needs when prioritizing interventions. For example, the nurse should prioritize a client's:

- Need for airway, oxygenation (or breathing), circulation, and potential for disability over need for shelter.
- Need for a safe and secure environment over a need for socialization.

Airway Breathing Circulation (ABC) Framework

- The ABC framework identifies, in order, the three basic needs for sustaining life.
  - An open airway is necessary for breathing, so it is the highest priority.
  - Breathing is necessary for oxygenation of the blood to occur.
  - Circulation is necessary for oxygenated blood to reach the body's tissues.
- The severity of manifestations should also be considered when determining priorities. A severe circulation problem can take priority over a minor breathing problem.
- Some frameworks also include a "D" for disability and "E" for exposure.

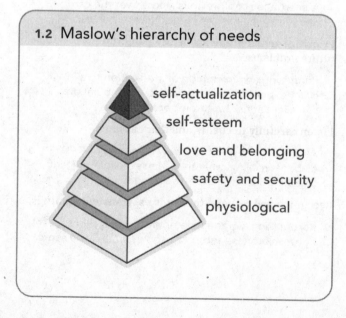

1.2 Maslow's hierarchy of needs

- self-actualization
- self-esteem
- love and belonging
- safety and security
- physiological

PRIORITY INTERVENTIONS

- **First: Airway**
  - Identify an airway concern (obstruction, stridor).
  - Establish a patent airway if indicated.
  - Recognize that 3 to 5 min without oxygen causes irreversible brain damage secondary to cerebral anoxia.
- **Second: Breathing**
  - Assess the effectiveness of breathing (apnea, depressed respiratory rate).
  - Intervene as needed (reposition, administer naloxone).
- **Third: Circulation**
  - Identify circulation concern (hypotension, dysrhythmia, inadequate cardiac output, compartment syndrome).
  - Institute actions to reverse or minimize circulatory alteration.
- **Fourth: Disability**
  - Assess for current or evolving disability (neurological deficits, stroke in evolution).
  - Implement actions to slow down development of disability.
- **Fifth: Exposure**
  - Remove the client's clothing to allow for a complete assessment or resuscitation.
  - Implement measures to reduce the risk for hypothermia (provide warm blankets and IV solutions or use cooling measures for clients exposed to extreme heat).

Safety/Risk Reduction Qs

- Look first for a safety risk. For example, is there a finding that suggests a risk for airway obstruction, hypoxia, bleeding, infection, or injury?
- Next ask, "What's the risk to the client?" and "How significant is the risk compared to other posed risks?"
- Give priority to responding to whatever finding poses the greatest (or most imminent) risk to the client's physical well-being.

Assessment/Data Collection First

Use the nursing process to gather pertinent information prior to making a decision regarding a plan of action. For example, determine if additional information is needed prior to calling the provider to ask for pain medication for a client.

Survival Potential

- Use this framework for situations in which health resources are extremely limited (mass casualty, disaster triage).
- Give priority to clients who have a reasonable chance of survival with prompt intervention. Clients who have a limited likelihood of survival even with intense intervention are assigned the lowest priority.

Least Restrictive/Least Invasive

- Select interventions that maintain client safety while posing the least amount of restriction to the client. For example, if a client who has a high fall risk index is getting out of bed without assistance, move the client closer to the nurses' work area rather than choosing to apply restraints.
- Select interventions that are the least invasive. For example, bladder training for the incontinent client is a better option than an indwelling urinary catheter.

Acute vs. Chronic, Urgent vs. Nonurgent, Stable vs. Unstable

- A client who has an acute problem takes priority over a client who has a chronic problem.
- A client who has an urgent need takes priority over a client who has a nonurgent need.
- A client who has unstable findings takes priority over a client who has stable findings.

Evidence-Based Practice

- Use current data to make informed clinical decisions to provide the best practice. Best practice is determined by current research collected from several sources that have desirable outcomes.
- Use knowledge of evidence-based practice to guide prioritization of care and interventions (responding to clients experiencing wound dehiscence or crisis). For example, initiating CPR in the proper steps for a client experiencing cardiac arrest.

Methods to promote evidence-based practice
- Use a variety of sources of research.
- Keep current on new research by reading professional journals and collaborating with other nurses and professionals in other disciplines.
- Change traditional nursing practice with new research-based practices.

TIME MANAGEMENT

Organize care according to client care needs and priorities. ○PCC
- What must be done immediately (administration of analgesic or antiemetic, assessment of unstable client)?
- What must be done by a specific time to ensure client safety, quality care, and compliance with facility policies and procedures (routine medication administration, vital signs, blood glucose monitoring)?
- What must be done by the end of the shift (ambulation of the client, discharge and/or discharge teaching, dressing change)?
- What can the nurse delegate?
  - What tasks can only the RN perform?
  - What client care responsibilities can the nurse delegate to other health care team members (practical nurses [PNs] and assistive personnel [APs])?

Use time-saving strategies and avoid time wasters. (1.3)
- **Good time management:**
  - Facilitates greater productivity.
  - Decreases work-related stress.
  - Helps ensure the provision of quality client care.
  - Enhances satisfaction with care provided.

1.3 Time management examples

Time savers
- Documenting nursing interventions as soon as possible after completion to facilitate accurate and thorough documentation
- Grouping activities that are to be performed on the same client or are in close physical proximity to prevent unnecessary walking
- Estimating how long each activity will take and planning accordingly
- Mentally envisioning the procedure to be performed and gathering all equipment prior to entering the client's room
- Taking time to plan care and taking priorities into consideration
- Delegating activities to other staff when client care workload is beyond what can be handled by one nurse
- Enlisting the aid of other staff when a team approach is more efficient than an individual approach
- Completing more difficult or strenuous tasks when energy level is high
- Avoiding interruptions and graciously but assertively saying "no" to unreasonable or poorly-timed requests for help
- Setting a realistic standard for completion of care and level of performance within the constraints of assignment and resources
- Completing one task before beginning another task
- Breaking large tasks into smaller tasks to make them more manageable
- Using an organizational sheet to plan care
- Using breaks to socialize with staff

Time wasters
- Documenting at the end of the shift all client care provided and assessments done
- Making repeated trips to the supply room for equipment
- Providing care as opportunity arises regardless of other responsibilities
- Missing equipment when preparing to perform a procedure
- Failing to plan or managing by crisis
- Being reluctant to delegate or under-delegating
- Not asking for help when needed or trying to provide all client care independently
- Procrastinating: delaying time-consuming, less desirable tasks until late in the shift
- Agreeing to help other team members with lower priority tasks when time is already compromised
- Setting unrealistic standards for completion of care and level of performance within constraints of assignment and resources
- Starting several tasks at once and not completing tasks before starting others
- Not addressing low level of skill competency, increasing time on task
- Providing care without a written plan
- Socializing with staff during client care time

- **Poor time management:**
  - Impairs productivity.
  - Leads to feelings of being overwhelmed and stressed.
  - Increases omission of important tasks.
  - Creates dissatisfaction with care provided.

Time management is a cyclic process.
- Time initially spent developing a plan will save time later and help to avoid management by crisis.
- Set goals and plan care based on established priorities and thoughtful utilization of resources.
- Complete one client care task before beginning the next, starting with the highest priority task.
- Reprioritize remaining tasks based on continual reassessment of client care needs.
- At the end of the day, perform a time analysis and determine if time was used wisely.

TIME MANAGEMENT AND TEAMWORK

- Be cognizant of assistance needed by other health care team members.
- Offer to help when unexpected crises occur.
- Assist other team members with provision of care when experiencing a period of down time. Qᴛᴄ

TIME MANAGEMENT AND SELF-CARE

- Take time for yourself.
- Schedule time for breaks and meals.
- Take physical and mental breaks from work and the unit.

Assigning, delegating, and supervising

Assigning is the process of transferring the authority, accountability, and responsibility of client care to another member of the health care team. Qᴛᴄ

Delegating is the process of transferring the authority and responsibility to another team member to complete a task, while retaining the accountability.

Supervising is the process of directing, monitoring, and evaluating the performance of tasks by another member of the health care team.

Nurses must delegate appropriately and supervise adequately to ensure that clients receive safe, quality care. **(1.4)** Qs
- Delegation decisions are based on individual client needs, facility policies and job descriptions, state nurse practice acts, and professional standards. The nurse should consider legal/ethical concerns when assigning and delegating.
- The nurse leader should recognize limitations and use available information and resources to make the best possible decisions at the time. The nurse must remember that it is their responsibility to ensure that clients receive safe, effective nursing care even in tasks delegated to others.
- Nurses must follow the ANA codes of standards in delegating and assigning tasks.

ASSIGNING

Assigning is performed in a downward or lateral manner with regard to members of the health care team.

CLIENT FACTORS

- Condition of the client and level of care needed
- Specific care needs (cardiac monitoring, mechanical ventilation)
- Need for special considerations (isolation precautions, fall precautions, seizure precautions)
- Procedures requiring a significant time commitment (extensive dressing changes or wound care)

HEALTH CARE TEAM FACTORS

- Knowledge and skill level of team members
- Amount of supervision necessary
- Staffing mix (RNs, PNs, APs)
- Nurse-to-client ratio
- Experience with similar clients
- Familiarity of staff member with unit

ADDITIONAL FACTORS

Unsafe assignments are those that:
- Assign the nurse to care for an excessive number of clients or a mix including too many clients with high acuity.
- Assign the nurse to care for clients in specialty areas where the nurse lacks the knowledge, skills, and ability to provide safe and competent care.

When a nurse receives an unsafe assignment, they should take the following actions:
- Bring the unsafe assignment to the attention of the scheduling/charge nurse and negotiate a new assignment.
- If no resolution is arrived at, take the concern up the chain of command.
- If a satisfactory resolution is still not arrived at, the nurse should file a written protest to the assignment (an assignment despite objection [ADO] or document of practice situation [DOPS]) with the appropriate administrator.
- Failure to accept the assignment without following the proper channels can be considered client abandonment.

1.4 The health care team

LICENSED PERSONNEL: Nurses who have completed a course of study, successfully passed either the NCLEX-PN® or NCLEX-RN® exam, and have a nursing license issued by a board of nursing

ASSISTIVE PERSONNEL: Specifically trained to function in an assistive role to licensed nurses in client care activities
- These individuals can be nursing personnel (certified nursing assistants [CNAs] or certified medical assistants [CMAs]), or they can be non-nursing personnel to whom nursing activities can be delegated (dialysis technicians, monitor technicians, and phlebotomists).

Some health care entities can differentiate between nurse and non-nurse assistive personnel by using the acronym NAP for nursing assistive personnel.

MAKING CLIENT ROOM ASSIGNMENTS

The nurse should consider client age and diagnosis, as well as client safety, comfort, privacy, and infection control needs when planning client room assignments. Qpcc

Private rooms

Private rooms are required for clients who have an infectious disease that requires airborne precautions, or clients who require a protective environment.

Private rooms are preferred for clients who are on droplet and contact precautions. These clients can cohort if no private rooms are available and if all of the following are true.
- The clients have the same active infection with the same micro-organisms.
- The clients remain at least 3 feet away from each other.
- The clients have no other existing infection.

A private room is also preferred for the following clients.
- Clients who are agitated
- Clients who have dementia and a history of wandering
- Clients who require a quiet environment (those at risk for increased intracranial pressure [stroke, traumatic brain injury])
- Clients who are at risk for sensory overload (those who are having pain, are acutely ill, have invasive tubes [nasogastric, IVs, endotracheal], or have reduced cognitive function [head injury])
- Clients who require privacy (those who are near death)

Other considerations
- A client who is confused or disoriented should be assigned a room away from noise and away from exits.
- Children who are transitioning from a critical care unit to a lower level of care should be assigned a room near the nurses station and with a roommate of similar age.

1.5 The five rights of delegation

RIGHT task
RIGHT circumstance
RIGHT person
RIGHT direction and communication
RIGHT supervision and evaluation

DELEGATING AND SUPERVISING

A licensed nurse is responsible for providing clear directions when a task is initially delegated and for periodic reassessment and evaluation of the outcome of the task.
- RNs delegate to other RNs, PNs, and APs.
  - RNs must be knowledgeable about the applicable state nurse practice act and regulations regarding the use of PNs and APs.
  - RNs delegate tasks so that they can complete higher level tasks that only RNs can perform. This allows more efficient use of all members of the health care team. Qtc
- PNs can delegate to other PNs and APs.

DELEGATION FACTORS

- Nurses can only delegate tasks appropriate for the skill and education level of the health care team member who is receiving the assignment.
- RNs cannot delegate the nursing process, client education, or tasks that require clinical judgment to PNs or APs.
- PN and RN scope of practice differs from state to state, and it is important to know and comply with the state's practice rules.

TASK FACTORS

Prior to delegating client care, consider the following.

Predictability of outcome
- Will the completion of the task have a predictable outcome?
- Is it a routine treatment?
- Is it a new treatment?

Potential for harm
- Is there a chance that something negative can happen to the client (risk for bleeding, risk for aspiration)?
- Is the client unstable?

Complexity of care
- Are complex tasks required as a part of the client's care?
- Is the delegatee legally able to perform the task and do they have the skills necessary?

1.6 Examples of tasks nurses can delegate to practical nurses and assistive personnel*

TO PN	TO AP	
• Monitoring findings (as input to the RN's ongoing assessment)	• Activities of daily living (ADLs)	• Positioning
• Reinforcing client teaching from a standard care plan	• Bathing	• Routine tasks
• Performing tracheostomy care	• Grooming	• Bed making
• Suctioning	• Dressing	• Specimen collection
• Checking NG tube patency	• Toileting	• Intake and output
• Administering enteral feedings	• Ambulating	• Vital signs (for stable clients)
• Inserting a urinary catheter	• Feeding (without swallowing precautions)	
• Administering medication (excluding IV medication in some states)		

Provided the facility's policy and state's practice guidelines permit.

Need for problem solving and innovation
- Is nursing judgment required while performing the task?
- Does it require nursing assessment skills?

Level of interaction with the client
- Is there a need to provide psychosocial support or education during the performance of the task?

DELEGATEE FACTORS

Considerations for selection of an appropriate delegatee include the following.
- Education, training, and experience
- Knowledge and skill to perform the task
- Level of critical thinking required to complete the task
- Ability to communicate with others as it pertains to the task
- Demonstrated competence
- The delegatee's culture
- Agency policies and procedures and licensing legislation (state nurse practice acts)

DELEGATION AND SUPERVISION GUIDELINES

- Use nursing judgment and knowledge related to the scope of practice and the delegatee's skill level when delegating.
- Use the five rights of delegation. **(1.5)** Q℠
  - What tasks the nurse delegates (right task)
  - Under what circumstances (right circumstance)
  - To whom (right person)
  - What information should be communicated (right direction/communication)
  - How to supervise/evaluate (right supervision/evaluation)

Right task

- Identify what tasks are appropriate to delegate for each specific client.
- A right task is repetitive, requires little supervision, and is relatively noninvasive for the client.
- Delegate tasks to appropriate levels of team members (PN, AP) based on standards of practice, legal and facility guidelines, and available resources.

> **RIGHT TASK:** Delegate an AP to assist a client who has pneumonia to use a bedpan.

> **WRONG TASK:** Delegate an AP to administer a nebulizer treatment to a client who has pneumonia.

Right circumstance

- Assess the health status and complexity of care required by the client.
- Match the complexity of care demands to the skill level of the health care team member.
- Consider the workload of the team member.

> **RIGHT CIRCUMSTANCE:** Delegate an AP to measure the vital signs of a client who is postoperative and stable.

> **WRONG CIRCUMSTANCE:** Delegate an AP to measure the vital signs of a client who is postoperative and received naloxone to reverse respiratory depression.

Right person

- Assess and verify the competency of the health care team member.
  - The task must be within the team member's scope of practice.
  - The team member must have the necessary competence/training.
- Continually review the performance of the team member and determine care competency.
- Assess team member performance based on standards and, when necessary, take steps to remediate a failure to meet standards.

> **RIGHT PERSON:** Delegate a PN to administer enteral feedings to a client who has a head injury.

> **WRONG PERSON:** Delegate an AP to administer enteral feedings to a client who has a head injury.

Right direction/communication

Communicate either in writing or orally.
- Data that needs to be collected
- Method and timeline for reporting, including when to report concerns/findings
- Specific task(s) to be performed; client-specific instructions
- Expected results, timelines, and expectations for follow-up communication

> **RIGHT DIRECTION AND COMMUNICATION:** Delegate an AP to assist the client in room 312 with a shower before 0900 and to notify the nurse when complete.

> **WRONG DIRECTION AND COMMUNICATION:** Delegate an AP to assist the client in room 312 with morning hygiene.

The delegating nurse must:
- Provide supervision, either directly or indirectly (assigning supervision to another licensed nurse).
- Provide clear directions and expectations of the task to be performed (time frames, what to report).
- Monitor performance.
- Provide feedback.
- Intervene if necessary (unsafe clinical practice).
- Evaluate the client and determine if client outcomes were met.
- Evaluate client care tasks and identify needs for quality improvement activities and/or additional resources.

> **RIGHT SUPERVISION:** Delegate the ambulation of a client to an AP. Observe the AP to ensure safe ambulation of the client, and provide positive feedback to the AP after completion of the task.

> **WRONG SUPERVISION:** Delegate the ambulation of a client to an AP and delegate the supervision of the AP to a more experienced AP.

SUPERVISION

Supervision occurs after delegation. A supervisor oversees a staff member's performance of delegated activities and determines if:
- Completion of tasks is on schedule.
- Performance was at a satisfactory level.
- Unexpected findings were documented and reported or addressed.
- Assistance was required to complete assigned tasks in a timely manner.
- Assignment should be re-evaluated and possibly changed. Qs

Staff development

Staff development refers to the nurse's involvement in the orientation, socialization, education, and training of fellow health care workers to ensure the competence of all staff and to help them meet standards set forth by the facility and accrediting bodies.
- The quality of client care provided is directly related to the education and level of competency of health care providers. Q℮ᴮᴾ
- The nurse leader has a responsibility in maintaining competent staff.
- Nurse leaders work with a unique, diverse workforce. The nurse should respect and recognize the health care team's diversity. Q℞

ORIENTATION

Orientation helps newly licensed nurses translate the knowledge, skills, and attitudes learned in nursing school into practice.

ORIENTATION TO THE INSTITUTION

- The newly licensed nurse is introduced to the philosophy, mission, and goals of the institution and department.
- Policies and procedures that are based on institutional standards are reviewed.
- Use of and access to the institution's computer system is a significant focus.
- Safety and security protocols are emphasized in relation to the nurse's role. Qs

ORIENTATION TO THE UNIT

- Classroom orientation is usually followed by orientation to the unit by an experienced nurse.
- Preceptors assist in orienting newly licensed nurses to a unit and supervising their performance and acquisition of skills.
- Preceptors are usually assigned to newly licensed nurses for a limited amount of time.
- Mentors can also serve as a newly licensed nurse's preceptor, but their relationship usually lasts longer and focuses more on assumption of the professional role and relationships, as well as socialization to practice.
- Coaches establish a collaborative relationship to help a nurse establish specific individual goals. The relationship is often task-related and typically time limited.

NEWLY LICENSED NURSES

- The first two years of a nurse's career is a vulnerable time for leaving their first job and the profession of nursing. More than 20% of newly licensed nurses leave their job within the first year.
- A successful orientation and mentoring program can increase retention of new nursing staff. Qʟ
- Transition to practice programs are used to transition the newly licensed nurse to a nursing role in practice.
- Nurse preceptors/mentors are frequently used to assist newly licensed nurses with the orientation process on the clinical unit.

> **1.7 Staff education**
>
> | CHARACTERISTICS | IDENTIFIED/ PROVIDED BY |
> |---|---|
> | Involves methods appropriate to learning domain and learning styles of staff. | Peers, unit managers, staff development educators |
> | Initiated in specific situations
• New policies or procedures implemented
• New equipment becomes available
• Educational need identified | Unit managers, staff development educators |
> | Can focus on one-on-one approach | Unit manager, charge nurse, preceptor |
> | Can use "just in time" training to meet immediate needs for client care | Staff members, supervisors |
> | Higher education degree or certification | Staff |

SOCIALIZATION

Socialization is the process by which a person learns a new role and the values and culture of the group within which that role is implemented.
- Successful socialization helps new staff members fit in with already established staff on a client care unit.
- Staff development educators and unit managers can begin this process during interviewing and orientation.

EDUCATION AND TRAINING

Staff education, or staff development, is the process by which a staff member gains knowledge and skills. The goal of staff education is to ensure that staff members have and maintain the most current knowledge and skills necessary to meet the needs of clients. (1.7)

Steps in providing educational programs Q EBP

1. Identify and respond: Determine the need for knowledge or skill proficiency.

2. Analyze: Look for deficiencies, and develop learning objectives to meet the need.

3. Research: Resources available to address learning objectives based on evidence-based practice.

4. Plan: Program to address objectives using available resources.

5. Implement: Program(s) at a time conducive to staff availability; consider online learning modules.

6. Evaluate: Use materials and observations to measure behavior changes secondary to learning objectives.

Improved nursing ability

An increase in knowledge and competence is the goal of staff education.

Competence is the ability of an employee to meet the requirements of a particular role at an established level of performance. Nurses usually progress through several stages of proficiency as they gain experience in a particular area.

The five stages of nursing ability were identified by Patricia Benner (1984), and are based on level of competence. Level of competence is directly related to length of time in practice and exposure to clinical situations. When nurses move to a new clinical setting that requires acquisition of new skills and knowledge, their level of competence will return to a lower stage. (1.8)

Quality improvement

- Quality improvement (performance improvement, quality control) is the process used to identify and resolve performance deficiencies. Quality improvement includes measuring performance against a set of predetermined standards. In health care, these standards are set by the facility and consider accrediting and professional standards. Q QI
- Standards of care should reflect optimal goals and be based on evidence.
- The quality improvement process focuses on assessment of outcomes and determines ways to improve the delivery of quality care. All levels of employees are involved in the quality improvement process.
- The Joint Commission's accreditation standards require institutions to show evidence of quality improvement in order to attain accreditation status.

1.8 Five stages of nursing ability

Novice nurse

Novice nurses can be students or newly licensed nurses who have minimal clinical experience. They approach situations from theoretical perspective relying on context-free facts and established guidelines. Rules govern practice.

Advanced beginner

Most new nurses function at the level of the advanced beginner. They practice independently in the performance of many tasks and can make some clinical judgments. They begin to rely on prior experience to make practice decisions.

Competent nurse

These are usually nurses who have been in practice for 2 to 3 years. They demonstrate increasing levels of skill and proficiency and clinical judgment. They exhibit the ability to organize and plan care using abstract and analytical thinking. They can anticipate the long-term outcomes of personal actions.

Proficient nurse

These are nurses who have a significant amount of experience upon which to base their practice. Enhanced observational abilities allow nurses to be able to conceptualize situations more holistically. Well-developed critical thinking and decision-making skills allow nurses to recognize and respond to unexpected changes.

Expert nurse

Expert nurses have garnered a wealth of experience so they can view situations holistically and process information efficiently. They make decisions using an advanced level of intuition and analytical ability. They do not need to rely on rules to comprehend a situation and take action.

Source: http://www.scribd.com/doc/27103958/Benner-Theory-Novice-to-Expert

---

QUALITY IMPROVEMENT PROCESS

The quality improvement process begins with identification of standards and outcome indicators based on evidence.

Outcome (clinical) indicators reflect desired client outcomes related to the standard under review. Q**EBP**

Structure indicators reflect the setting in which care is provided and the available human and material resources.

Process indicators reflect how client care is provided and are established by policies and procedures (clinical practice guidelines).

Benchmarks are goals that are set to determine at what level the outcome indicators should be met.

While process indicators provide important information about how a procedure is being carried out, an outcome indicator measures whether that procedure is effective in meeting the desired benchmark. For example, the use of incentive spirometers in postoperative clients can be determined to be 92% (process indicator), but the rate of postoperative pneumonia can be determined to be 8% (outcome indicator). If the benchmark is set at 5%, the benchmark for that outcome indicator is not being met and the structure and process variables need to be analyzed to identify potential areas for improvement.

STEPS IN THE QUALITY IMPROVEMENT PROCESS

A standard is developed and approved by a facility committee.

- Standards are made available to employees by way of policies and procedures.
- Quality issues are identified by the staff, management, or risk management department.
- An interprofessional team is developed to review the issue.
- The current state of structure and process related to the issue is analyzed.
- Data collection methods are determined.
  - Quantitative methods are primarily used in the data collection process, although client interview is also an option.
- Data is collected, analyzed, and compared with the established benchmark.
- If the benchmark is not met, possible influencing factors are determined. A root cause analysis can be done to critically assess all factors that influence the issue. A root cause analysis: Q**EBP**
  - Focuses on variables that surround the consequence of an action or occurrence
  - Is commonly done for sentinel events (client death, client care resulting in serious physical injury) but can also be done as part of the quality improvement process.
  - Investigates the consequence and possible causes
  - Analyzes the possible causes and relationships that can exist
  - Determines additional influences at each level of relationship
  - Determines the root cause or causes

- Potential solutions or corrective actions are analyzed and one is selected for implementation.
- Educational or corrective action is implemented.
- The issue is reevaluated at a pre-established time to determine the efficacy of the solution or corrective action.

Core measures

National standardized measures are developed by the Joint Commission to improve client outcomes. It is used to measure client outcomes and provides information to support accreditation of hospitals.

Core measures developed include stroke, venous thromboembolism, heart failure, acute myocardial infarction, and substance use.

Audits

Audits can produce valuable quantitative data.

Types of audits
- Structure audits evaluate the influence of elements that exist separate from or outside of the client-staff interaction.
- Process audits review how care was provided and assume a relationship exists between nurses and the quality of care provided.
- Outcome audits determine what results, if any, occurred as a result of the nursing care provided.
  - Some outcomes are influenced by aspects of care (the quality of medical care, the level of commitment of managerial staff, and the characteristics of the facility's policies and procedures).
  - Nursing-sensitive outcomes are those that are directly affected by the quality of nursing care. Examples include client fall rates and the incidence of nosocomial infections.

Timing of audits
- Retrospective audits occur after the client receives care.
- Concurrent audits occur while the client is receiving care.
- Prospective audits predict how future client care will be affected by the current level of services.

NURSE'S ROLE IN QUALITY IMPROVEMENT

- Serve as unit representative on committees developing policies and procedures.
- Use reliable resources for information (Centers for Disease Control and Prevention, professional journals, evidenced-based research). Q**EBP**
- Enhance knowledge and understanding of the facility's policies and procedures.
- Provide client care consistent with these policies and procedures.
- Document client care thoroughly and according to facility guidelines.
- Participate in the collection of information/data related to staff's adherence to selected policy or procedure.
- Assist with analysis of the information/data.
- Compare results with the established benchmark.

- Make a judgment about performance in regard to the findings.
- Assist with provision of education or training necessary to improve the performance of staff.
- Act as a role model by practicing in accordance with the established standard.
- Assist with re-evaluation of staff performance by collection of information/data at a specified time

Nursing strategies to promote evidence-based approach to client care

- Remain aware of current trends in research.
- Incorporate evidence into clinical practice.
- Question traditional nursing practice to promote change.
- Collaborate with other disciplines to enrich practice.
- Use the PICO model (population, intervention, comparison, and outcome) to find current evidence to guide best practice.

Quality improvement tools for tracking outcomes

Structured care methodologies are used to track variances, measure outcomes, improve quality, and facilitate best practices.

Standards of care: Baseline of quality care a client should receive

Algorithms: Series of progressive treatment based on client response (advanced cardiac life support)

Critical or clinical pathway: Projected path of treatment based on a set time frame for clients who have comparable diagnoses

Protocols: Standard guidelines for a specific intervention (stroke protocol)

Guidelines: Evidence-based information to provide quality care and improve outcomes

Performance appraisal, peer review, and disciplinary action

A performance appraisal is the process by which a supervisor evaluates an employee's performance in relation to the job description for that employee's position as well as other expectations the facility can have. Qᵔ

- Performance appraisals are done at regular intervals and can be more frequent for new employees.
- Performance expectations should be based on the standards set forth in a job description and written in objective terms.
- Performance appraisals allow nurses the opportunity to discuss personal goals with the unit manager as well as to receive feedback regarding level of performance. Performance appraisals can also be used as a motivational tool.
- Deficiencies identified during a performance appraisal or reported by coworkers might need to be addressed in a disciplinary manner.

PERFORMANCE APPRAISAL AND PEER REVIEW

- A formal system for conducting performance appraisals should be in place and used consistently. Performance appraisal tools should reflect the staff member's job description and can be based on various types of scales or surveys.
- Various sources of data should be collected to ensure an unbiased and thorough evaluation of an employee's performance.
  - Data should be collected over time and not just represent isolated incidents.
  - Actual observed behavior should be documented/used as evidence of satisfactory or unsatisfactory performance. These can be called anecdotal notes and are kept in the unit manager or equivalent position's files.
  - Peers can be a valuable source of data. Peer review is the evaluation of a colleague's practice by another peer. Peer review should:
    - Begin with an orientation of staff to the peer review process, their professional responsibility in regard to promoting growth of colleagues, and the disposition of data collected.
    - Focus on the peer's performance in relation to the job description or an appraisal tool that is based on institutional standards.
    - Be shared with the peer and usually the manager.
    - Be only part of the data used when completing a staff member's performance appraisal.
  - The employee should be given the opportunity to provide input into the evaluation.
- The unit manager should host the performance appraisal review in a private setting at a time conducive to the staff member's attendance. The unit manager should review the data with the staff member and provide the opportunity for feedback. Personal goals of the staff member are discussed and documented, including avenues for attainment. Staff members who do not agree with the unit manager's evaluation of their performance should have the opportunity to make written comments on the evaluation form and appeal the rating.

DISCIPLINARY ACTION

- Deficiencies identified during a performance appraisal or the course of employment should be presented in writing, and corrective action should be based on institutional policy regarding disciplinary actions and/or termination of employment. Evidence regarding the deficiency must support such a claim. **(1.9)**
- Some offenses (mistreatment of a client or use of alcohol or other substances while working) warrant immediate dismissal. Lesser infractions should follow a stepwise manner, giving the staff member the opportunity to correct unacceptable behavior.
- Staff members who witness an inappropriate action by a coworker should report the infraction up the chain of command. At the time of the infraction, this might be the charge nurse. The unit manager should also be notified, and written documentation by the manager is placed in the staff member's permanent file.

1.9 Steps in Progressive Discipline

First infraction
Informal reprimand
Manager and employee meet
Discuss the issue
Suggestions for improvement/correction

Second infraction
Written warning
Manager meets with employee to distribute written warning
Review of specific rules/policy violations
Discussion of potential consequences if infractions continue

Third infraction
Employee placed on suspension with or without pay. Time away from work gives the employee opportunity to:
Examine the issues
Consider alternatives

Fourth infraction
Employee termination
Follows after multiple warnings have been given and employee continues to violate rules and policies

Conflict resolution

Conflict is the result of opposing thoughts, ideas, feelings, perceptions, behaviors, values, opinions, or actions between individuals.

- Conflict is an inevitable part of professional, social, and personal life and can have constructive or destructive results. Nurses must understand conflict and how to manage it.
- Nurses can use problem-solving and negotiation strategies to prevent a problem from evolving into a conflict. Q℡
- Lack of conflict can create organizational stasis, while too much conflict can be demoralizing, produce anxiety, and contribute to burnout.
- Conflict can disrupt working relationships and create a stressful atmosphere.
- If conflict exists to the level that productivity and quality of care are compromised, the unit manager must attempt to identify the origin of the conflict and attempt to resolve it.

Common causes of conflict

- Ineffective communication
- Unclear expectations of team members in their various roles
- Poorly defined or actualized organizational structure
- Conflicts of interest and variance in standards
- Incompatibility of individuals
- Management or staffing changes
- Diversity related to age, gender, race, or ethnicity

CATEGORIES OF CONFLICT

INTRAPERSONAL CONFLICT

Occurs within the person and can involve internal struggle related to contradictory values or wants.

> Example: A nurse wants to move up on the career ladder but is finding that time with their family is subsequently compromised.

INTERPERSONAL CONFLICT

Occurs between two or more people with differing values, goals, or beliefs.
- Interpersonal conflict in the health care setting involves disagreement among nurses, clients, family members, and within a health care team. Bullying and incivility in the workplace are forms of interpersonal conflict.
- Incivility is a significant issue in nursing and can especially impact new nurses.
- Interpersonal conflict contributes to burnout and work-related stress.

> Example: A new nurse is given a client assignment that is heavier than those of other nurses, and when the new nurse asks for help, it is denied.

INTERGROUP CONFLICT

Occurs between two or more groups of individuals, departments, or organizations and can be caused by a new policy or procedure, a change in leadership, or a change in organizational structure.

> Example: There is confusion as to whether it is the responsibility of the nursing unit or dietary department to pass meal trays to clients.

STAGES OF CONFLICT

Five stages of conflict exist. If the nurse manager is familiar with the stages there is an increased chance that the conflict can be resolved effectively.

STAGE 1: LATENT CONFLICT

The actual conflict has not yet developed; however, factors are present that have a high likelihood of causing conflict to occur.

> Example: A new scheduling policy is implemented within the organization. The nurse manager should recognize that change is a common cause of conflict.

STAGE 2: PERCEIVED CONFLICT

A party perceives that a problem is present, though an actual conflict might not actually exist.

> Example: A nurse perceives that a nurse manager is unfair with scheduling. The nurse might not be aware that, in reality, it is only because the nurse manager misunderstood the nurse's scheduling request.

STAGE 3: FELT CONFLICT

Those involved begin to feel an emotional response to the conflict.

> Example: A nurse feels anger towards the nurse manager after finding out that they are scheduled to work two holidays in a row.

STAGE 4: MANIFEST CONFLICT

The parties involved are aware of the conflict and action is taken. Actions at this stage can be positive and strive towards conflict resolution, or they can be negative and include debating, competing, or withdrawal of one or more parties from the situation.

> Example: The nurse manager and nurses on a unit agree that the current scheduling system is causing a conflict and agree to work together to come up with a solution.

STAGE 5: CONFLICT AFTERMATH

Conflict aftermath is the completion of the conflict process and can be positive or negative.

> Example: Positive conflict aftermath: the nurse manager and nurses on a unit are satisfied with the newly revised scheduling system and feel valued for being included in the conflict resolution process.

> Example: Negative conflict aftermath: the nurse manager and nurses are unable to come up with a scheduling solution that meets the needs of both parties. They agree to continue with the current system; however, tensions still remain, increasing the risk of a recurrence of the conflict.

CONFLICT RESOLUTION STRATEGIES

PROBLEM-SOLVING

- Open communication among staff and between staff and clients can help defray the need for conflict resolution. Qтс
- When potential sources of conflict exist, the use of open communication and problem-solving strategies are effective tools to de-escalate the situation.

Actions nurses can take to promote open communication and de-escalate conflicts

- Use "I" statements, and remember to focus on the problem, not on personal differences.
- Listen carefully to what others are saying, and try to understand their perspective.
- Move a conflict that is escalating to a private location or postpone the discussion until a later time to give everyone a chance to regain control of their emotions.
- Share ground rules with participants. For example, everyone is to be treated with respect, only one person can speak at a time, and everyone should have a chance to speak. Qтс

Steps of the Problem-Solving Process

Identify the problem. State it in objective terms, minimizing emotional overlay.

Discuss possible solutions. Brainstorming solutions as a group can stimulate new solutions to old problems. Encourage individuals to think creatively, beyond simple solutions.

Analyze identified solutions. The potential pros and cons of each possible solution should be discussed in an attempt to narrow down the number of viable solutions.

Select a solution. Based on this analysis, select a solution for implementation.

Implement the selected solution. A procedure and timeline for implementation should accompany the implementation of the selected solution.

Evaluate the solution's ability to resolve the original problem. The outcomes surrounding the new solution should be evaluated according to the predetermined timeline. The solution should be given adequate time to become established as a new routine before it is evaluated. If the solution is deemed unsuccessful, the problem-solving process will need to be reinstituted and the problem discussed again.

NEGOTIATION

- Negotiation is the process by which interested parties:
  - Resolve ongoing conflicts.
  - Agree on steps to take.
  - Bargain to protect individual or collective interests.
  - Pursue outcomes that benefit mutual interests.
- Most nurses use negotiation on a daily basis.
- Negotiation can involve the use of several conflict resolution strategies.
- The focus is on a win-win solution or a win/lose-win/lose solution in which both parties win and lose a portion of their original objectives. Each party agrees to give up something and the emphasis is on accommodating differences rather than similarities between parties. Qтс

Example

> One nurse offers to care for Client A today if the other will care for Client B tomorrow.

Strategy: Avoiding/Withdrawing
- Both parties know there is a conflict, but they refuse to face it or work toward a resolution.
- Can be appropriate for minor conflicts, when one party holds more power than the other party, or if the issue can work itself out over time.
- Because the conflict remains, it can surface again at a later date and escalate over time.
- This is usually a lose-lose solution.

Strategy: Smoothing
- One party attempts to "smooth" another party by trying to satisfy the other party.
- Often used to preserve or maintain a peaceful work environment.
- The focus can be on what is agreed upon, leaving conflict largely unresolved.
- This is usually a lose-lose solution.

Strategy: Competing/Coercing
- One party pursues a desired solution at the expense of others.
- Managers can use this when a quick or unpopular decision must be made.
- The party who loses something can experience anger, aggravation, and a desire for retribution.
- This is usually a win-lose solution.

Strategy: Cooperating/Accommodating
- One party sacrifices something, allowing the other party to get what it wants. This is the opposite of competing. Q℗
- The original problem might not actually be resolved.
- The solution can contribute to future conflict.
- This is a lose-win solution.

Strategy: Compromising/Negotiating
- Each party gives up something.
- To consider this a win/lose-win/lose solution, both parties must give up something equally important. If one party gives up more than the other, it can become a win-lose solution.

Strategy: Collaborating
- Both parties set aside their original individual goals and work together to achieve a new common goal.
- Requires mutual respect, positive communication, and shared decision-making between parties.
- This is a win-win solution.

ASSERTIVE COMMUNICATION

- Use of assertive communication can be necessary during conflict negotiation.
- Assertive communication allows expression in direct, honest, and nonthreatening ways that do not infringe upon the rights of others.
- It is a communication style that acknowledges and deals with conflict, recognizes others as equals, and provides a direct statement of feelings. Q℗

Elements of Assertive Communication

- Selecting an appropriate location for verbal exchange
- Maintaining eye contact
- Establishing trust
- Being sensitive to cultural needs
- Using "I" statements and including affective elements of the situation
- Avoiding "you" statements that can indicate blame
- Stating concerns using open, honest, direct statements
- Conveying empathy
- Focusing on the behavior or issue of conflict and avoiding personal attacks
- Concluding with a statement that describes a fair solution

GRIEVANCES

- A grievance is a wrong perceived by an employee based on a feeling of unfair treatment that is considered grounds for a formal complaint.
- Grievances that cannot be satisfactorily resolved between the parties involved can require management by a third party.
- Facilities have a formal grievance policy that should be followed when a conflict cannot be resolved.
- The steps of an institution's grievance procedure should be outlined in the grievance policy.

Typical Steps of the Grievance Process

- Started at the first level of management and continued up the chain of command as needed
- Formal hearing if the issue is not resolved at a lower level
- Professional mediation if a solution is not reached during a formal hearing

Resource management

Resource management includes budgeting and resource allocation. Human, financial, and material resources must be considered.
- Budgeting is usually the responsibility of the unit manager, but staff nurses can be asked to provide input.
- Resource allocation is a responsibility of the unit manager as well as every practicing nurse.
- Providing cost-effective client care should not compromise quality of care.

Resources (supplies, equipment, personnel) are critical to accomplishing the goals and objectives of a health care facility, so it is essential for nurses to understand how to effectively manage resources. Q℗

COST-EFFECTIVE CARE

Cost-Containment

Strategies that promote efficient and competent client care while also producing needed revenues for the continued productivity of the organization

> Example: The use of managed care strives to provide clients with a plan designed to meet the needs of their individual medical problem while eliminating the unnecessary use of resources or extended hospital stays.

Cost-Effective

Strategies that achieve optimal results in relation to the money spent to achieve those results. In other words, cost-effective means "getting your money's worth."

Example: Spending increased money on staff training for transmission-based precautions, resulting in the increased and effective use of PPE for client care. These actions have the end result of a decrease in infection transmission and an overall savings in the cost of caring for clients who would have acquired these infections.

COST-EFFECTIVE CARE STRATEGIES

Providing clients with needed education to decrease or eliminate future medical costs associated with future complications

Example: Teaching a client who has a new diagnosis of diabetes mellitus how to adjust the dosage of insulin depending on activity level, reducing the risk of hypoglycemia resulting in the need for medical care.

Promoting the use of evidence-based care, resulting in improved client care outcomes Q EBP

Example: Implementing the use of evidence-based techniques to care for clients who have indwelling catheters, resulting in a decreased incidence of catheter-acquired urinary tract infections.

Promoting cost-effective resource management

Example: Using all levels of personnel to their fullest when making assignments. Delegating effectively to members of the nursing care team.

Example: Providing necessary equipment and properly charging clients.

Example: Returning uncontaminated, unused equipment to the appropriate department for credit.

Example: Using equipment properly to prevent wastage.

Example: Providing training to staff unfamiliar with equipment.

Example: Returning equipment (IV pumps) to the proper department (central service, central distribution) as soon as it is no longer needed. This action will prevent further cost to clients.

Active Learning Scenario

A nurse manager is discussing emotional intelligence with the charge nurses within the facility. What information should the manager include in this discussion? Use the Active Learning Template: Basic Concept to complete this item.

RELATED CONTENT: Define emotional intelligence.

UNDERLYING PRINCIPLES: Identify at least three characteristics of an emotionally intelligent leader.

Active Learning Scenario Key

Using the Active Learning Template: Basic Concept
RELATED CONTENT: Emotional intelligence is the ability of an individual to perceive and manage the emotions of self and others.

UNDERLYING PRINCIPLES
- Insight into the emotions of members of the team
- Understands the perspective of others
- Encourages constructive criticism and is open to new ideas
- Able to maintain focus while multitasking
- Manages emotions and channels them in a positive direction, which in turn helps the team accomplish its goals
- Committed to the delivery of high-quality client care
- Refrains from judgment in controversial or emotionally-charged situations until facts are gathered

Ⓝ *NCLEX® Connection: Management of Care, Concepts of Management*

Application Exercises

1. The nurse manager is preparing a presentation on management styles to the board of directors. Match the scenario with the most effective management style: Autocratic/Authoritarian, Democratic, or Laissez-Faire.

   A. Nursing manager and team of nurses collaborating on a policy for trauma informed work environments.

   B. The nurse leading a resuscitation effort on a client who recently experienced an MI.

   C. Charge nurse wanting to implement new policy with a team of RNs who are motivated and work independently.

   D. Unit manager facilitating a care conference with staff nurses working together to make client centered decisions.

2. A nurse is developing a presentation about the Clinical Judgment Measurement Model (CJMM). Which step of the nursing process should the nurse identify as correlating with the two steps of the CJMM, analyze cues and prioritize hypotheses?

   A. Assessment

   B. Analysis

   C. Planning

   D. Implementation

3. A nurse on a medical-surgical unit is making assignments at the beginning of the shift. Which of the following tasks should the nurse delegate to the LPN?

   A. Obtain vital signs for a client who is 2 hr post procedure following a cardiac catheterization.

   B. Administer a unit of packed red blood cells (RBCs) to a client who has cancer.

   C. Instruct a client who is scheduled for discharge in the performance of wound care.

   D. Develop a plan of care for a newly admitted client who has pneumonia.

4. A nurse manager is developing an orientation plan for newly licensed nurses. Which of the following information should the manager include in the plan? (Select all that apply.)

   A. Skill proficiency

   B. Assignment to a preceptor

   C. Budgetary principles

   D. Computerized charting

   E. Socialization into unit culture

   F. Facility policies and procedures

5. A new nurse on a unit notices that the unit manager does not intervene when there is conflict between team members, even when it escalates. Which of the following conflict resolution strategies is the unit manager demonstrating?

   A. Avoidance

   B. Smoothing

   C. Cooperating

   D. Negotiating

6. An experienced nurse on a urology unit arrives to work on the night shift. The unit manager immediately asks the nurse to float to the pediatric intensive care unit to take a client assignment. The nurse has always maintained a positive attitude when asked to work on another medical-surgical unit but states they do not feel comfortable in the pediatric ICU setting. Match the scenario to the appropriate negotiation example.

   A. The unit manager informs the nurse they will risk disciplinary action if they do not accept the assignment.

   B. The nurse agrees to float to the pediatric ICU to work in a supportive role but will not take assigned clients.

   C. The nurse offers to work on another medical-surgical unit if someone from that unit will float to the pediatric ICU.

   D. The nurse agrees to orient to the pediatric ICU to become competent for future assignments and the nurse manager enlists the services of a staffing agency that provides pediatric nurses on an as needed basis.

   1. Compromising/Negotiating
   2. Competing/Coercing
   3. Collaborating
   4. Cooperating/Accommodating

1. **LAISSEZ-FAIRE:** C; **DEMOCRATIC:** A, D; **AUTOCRATIC/AUTHORITARIAN:** B

   The nurse manager should identify that the laissez-faire style is most effective when dealing with professionals who are motivated and can work independently. The democratic style is most effective when including staff in a group decision using collaboration and communication. The autocratic/authoritarian style is most effective when there is a crisis situation.

   Ⓝ *NCLEX® Connection: Management of Care, Concepts of Management*

2. A. Assessment correlates to the CJMM step of recognizing cues.
   B. **CORRECT:** The nurse should identify that the nursing process step of analysis correlates to the CJMM step of analyzing cues and prioritizing hypotheses.
   C. The nursing process step of planning correlates to the CJMM step of generating solutions.
   D. The nursing process step of Implementation correlates to the CJMM step of take action.

   Ⓝ *NCLEX® Connection: Management of Care, Assignment, Establishing Priorities*

3. A. **CORRECT:** When taking actions, the nurse should identify that it is within the scope of practice of the LPN to monitor a client who is 2 hr post procedure for a cardiac catheterization, because this client is considered stable.
   B. The RN is responsible for administering blood components, including packed RBCs, because this is outside of the scope of practice for the LPN.
   C. The RN is responsible for client education. It is within the scope of practice of the LPN to reinforce but not provide initial client education.
   D. The RN is responsible for developing a plan of care for a client. It is within the scope of practice for the LPN to suggest additions, but not develop the plan of care.

   Ⓝ *NCLEX® Connection: Management of Care, Assignment, Delegation and Supervision*

4. A. **CORRECT:** When generating solutions, the nurse manager should identify that the purpose of orientation is to assist the newly licensed nurse to transition from the role of student to the role of employee and licensed nurse. Include evaluation of skill proficiency and provide additional instruction as indicated.
   B. **CORRECT:** The nurse manager should include assignment of a preceptor to ease the transition of the newly licensed nurse.
   C. Budgetary principles are an administrative skill that is usually the responsibility of the unit manager.
   D. **CORRECT:** The nurse manager should include computerized charting, which is an essential skill for the newly licensed nurse.
   E. **CORRECT:** The nurse manager should include socialization to the unit.
   F. **CORRECT:** The nurse manager should include information about facility policies and procedures, which is essential information for the newly licensed nurse.

   Ⓝ *NCLEX® Connection: Management of Care, Collaboration with Multidisciplinary Team*

5. A. **CORRECT:** When analyzing cues, the nurse should identify that the goal in resolving conflict is a win-win situation. The unit manager is using an ineffective strategy, avoidance, to deal with this conflict. Although the unit manager is aware of the conflict, they are not attempting to resolve it.
   B. When smoothing is used, one person attempts to "smooth" the other party and/or point out areas in which the parties agree. This is typically a lose-lose solution.
   C. When cooperating is used, one party allows the other party to win. This is a lose-win solution.
   D. When negotiating is used, each party gives up something. If one party gives up more than the other, this can become a win-lose solution.

   Ⓝ *NCLEX® Connection: Management of Care, Concepts of Management*

6. A, 2; B, 4; C, 1; D, 3

   When compromising is used, each party agrees to give up something to reach a solution. When competing is used, one party pursues a desired solution at the expense of another. When collaborating, both parties set aside their individual goals to work together for a solution. When cooperating is used, one party allows the other party to win. This is a lose-win solution.

   Ⓝ *NCLEX® Connection: Management of Care, Concepts of Management*

When reviewing the following chapter, keep in mind the relevant topics and tasks of the NCLEX outline, in particular:

Management of Care

CASE MANAGEMENT: Explore resources available to assist the client with achieving or maintaining independence.

CLIENT RIGHTS

Recognize the client's right to refuse treatment/procedures.

Advocate for client rights and needs.

COLLABORATION WITH MULTIDISCIPLINARY TEAM

Review plan of care to ensure continuity across disciplines.

Identify significant information to report to other disciplines.

CONCEPTS OF MANAGEMENT: Act as liaison between the client and others.

CONTINUITY OF CARE

Use documents to record and communicate client information.

Provide and receive hand off care (report) on assigned clients.

REFERRALS: Identify community resources for the client.

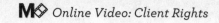

CHAPTER 2 *Coordinating Client Care*

Patient centered care

The 2001 Institute of Medicine (IOM) Quality Chasm report defines patient centered as "providing care that is respectful of and responsive to individual patient preferences, needs, and values, and ensuring that patient values guide all clinical decisions."

In 1987, the Picker Institute created the Eight Principles of Person-Centered Care to put people at the center of health care. People are looked at as individuals who are encouraged to be active in their care with their needs and preferences identified and respected. These eight principles are centered around:
- Access to reliable healthcare advice
- Treatment delivered by trusted healthcare professionals
- Continuity of care
- Involvement in both family and caregivers
- Information and communication that is clear and easy to understand
- Respect for individual preferences and decision-making
- Empathy and respect toward individuals
- Surveying physical needs and environmental concerns of the client

These principles are used to engage clients as consumers of their own care. Client experiences are regulatory and standard of care concerns, which are measured in patient satisfaction surveys. Q**PCC**

Client rights

- Client rights are the legal guarantees that clients have about their health care.
  - Clients using the services of a health care institution retain their rights as individuals and citizens of the United States. The American Hospital Association (AHA) identifies client rights in health care settings in the Patient Care Partnership.
  - Residents in nursing facilities that participate in Medicare programs similarly retain resident rights under statutes that govern the operation of these facilities.
- Nurses are accountable for protecting the rights of clients. Situations that require particular attention include informed consent, refusal of treatment, advance directives, confidentiality, and information security.

NURSING ROLE IN CLIENT RIGHTS

- Nurses must ensure that clients understand their rights while also protecting those rights during the provision of nursing care. Q**PCC**
- Regardless of the client's age, nursing needs, or the setting in which care is provided, the basic tenants are the same. Each client has the right to:
  - Be informed about all aspects of care and take an active role in the decision-making process.
  - Accept, refuse, or request modification to the plan of care.
  - Receive care that is delivered by competent individuals who treat the client with respect.

REFUSAL OF TREATMENT

The Patient Self-Determination Act (PSDA) stipulates that on admission to a health care facility, all clients must be informed of their right to accept or refuse care. Competent adults have the right to refuse treatment, including the right to leave a health care facility without a prescription for discharge from the provider. Q**PCC**

- If the client refuses a treatment or procedure, the client is asked to sign a document indicating that they understand the risk involved with refusing the treatment or procedure, and that they have chosen to refuse it.
- When a client decides to leave the facility without a prescription for discharge, the nurse notifies the provider and discusses with the client the potential risks associated with leaving the facility prior to discharge.
- The nurse carefully documents the information that was provided to the client and that notification of the provider occurred. The client should be informed of the following:
  - Possible complications that could occur without treatment
  - Possibility of permanent physical or mental impairment or disability
  - Possibility of other complications that could lead to death
- The client is asked to sign an Against Medical Advice (AMA) form.
- If the client refuses to sign the form, this is also documented by the nurse.

Advocacy

Advocacy refers to nurses' role in supporting clients by ensuring that they are properly informed, that their rights are respected, and that they are receiving the proper level of care.

- Advocacy is one of the most important roles of the nurse, especially when clients are unable to speak or act for themselves.
- As an advocate, the nurse ensures that the client has the information they need to make decisions about health care.
- Nurses must act as advocates even when they disagree with clients' decisions.
- The complex health care system puts clients in a vulnerable position. Nurses are clients' voice when the system is not acting in their best interest.
- The nursing profession also has a responsibility to support and advocate for legislation that promotes public policies that protect clients as consumers and create a safe environment for their care.

NURSING ROLE IN ADVOCACY

- As advocates, nurses must ensure that clients are informed of their rights and have adequate information on which to base health care decisions.
- Nurses must be careful to assist clients with making health care decisions and not direct or control their decisions.
- Nurses mediate on the client's behalf when the actions of others are not in the client's best interest or changes need to be made in the plan of care.
- Situations in which nurses might need to advocate for clients or assist them to advocate for themselves include the following:
  - End-of-life decisions
  - Access to health care
  - Protection of client privacy
  - Informed consent
  - Substandard practice
- Nurses are accountable for their actions even if they are carrying out a provider's prescription. It is the nurse's responsibility to question a prescription if it could harm a client (i.e., incorrect medication dosage, potential adverse interaction with another prescribed medication, contraindication due to an allergy or medical history). Qs

ESSENTIAL COMPONENTS OF ADVOCACY

SKILLS
- Risk-taking
- Visionary
- Conceptual thinker
- Self-confidence
- Articulate communication
- Assertiveness

VALUES
- Caring
- Autonomy
- Respect
- Empowerment

Informed consent

- Informed consent is a legal process by which a client provides written permission for a procedure or treatment to be performed. Consent is considered to be informed when the client has been provided with and understands the following: Qpcc
  - Reason the treatment or procedure is needed
  - How the treatment or procedure will benefit the client
  - Risks involved if the client chooses to receive the treatment or procedure
  - Other options to treat the problem, including the option of not treating the problem
  - Risk involved if the client chooses no treatment
- The nurse's role in the informed consent process is to witness the client's signature on the informed consent form and to ensure that informed consent has been appropriately obtained.
- The nurse should seek language assistance services if the client does not speak and understand the language used by the provider. Qpcc

INFORMED CONSENT GUIDELINES

Consent is required for all care provided in a health care facility. For most aspects of nursing care, implied consent is adequate. The client provides implied consent when they comply with the instructions provided by the nurse. For example, the nurse is preparing to administer a TB skin test, and the client holds out their arm for the nurse.

- For an invasive procedure or surgery, the client is required to provide written consent.
- State laws regulate who can give informed consent. Laws vary regarding age limitations and emergencies. Nurses are responsible for knowing the laws in their state of practice.
- The nurse must verify that consent is informed and witness the client sign the consent form.

Signing an informed consent form
- The form for informed consent must be signed by a competent adult.
  - Emancipated minors (minors who are independent from their parents [a married minor]) can provide informed consent for themselves.
- The person who signs the form must be capable of understanding the information provided by the health care professional who will be providing the service. The person must be able to fully communicate in return with the health care professional.
- When the person giving the informed consent is unable to communicate due to a language barrier or hearing impairment, a trained medical interpreter must be provided. Many health care agencies contract with professional interpreters who have additional skills in medical terminology to assist with providing information.

Individuals authorized to grant consent for another person

- Parent of a minor
- Legal guardian
- Court–specified representative
- Client's health care surrogate (individual who has the client's durable power of attorney for health care/health care proxy)
- Spouse or closest available relative (state laws vary)

INFORMED CONSENT RESPONSIBILITIES

Provider: Obtains informed content. To do so, the provider must inform the client of the following:

- Complete description of the treatment/procedure
- Description of the professionals who will be performing and participating in the treatment
- Description of the potential harm, pain, and/or discomfort that might occur
- Options for other treatments and the possible consequences of taking other actions
- The right to refuse treatment
- Risk involved if the client chooses no treatment

Client: Gives informed consent. To give informed consent, the client must do the following:

- Give it voluntarily (no coercion involved).
- Be competent and of legal age, or be an emancipated minor. (If the client is unable to provide consent, an authorized person must give consent.)
- Receive sufficient information to decide based on an informed understanding of what is expected.

Nurse

- Witnesses informed consent. The nurse is responsible for the following: **Q**s
  - Ensuring that the provider provided the client the necessary information
  - Ensuring that the client understood the information and is competent to give informed consent
  - Having the client sign the informed consent document
  - Notifying the provider if the client has more questions or does not understand any of the information provided (The provider is then responsible for giving clarification.)
- The nurse documents the following:
  - Reinforcement of information originally given by the provider
  - That questions the client had were forwarded to the provider
  - Use of an language assistance services

2.1 Case study

Scenario introduction

Tiana is an RN in a surgery center. Nathan is a client scheduled for repair of an abdominal hernia. On the morning of the scheduled surgery, Nathan arrives at the surgery center with many questions regarding the upcoming surgery. A consent was signed in the clinic and Tiana proceeds with confirming that Nathan continues to give consent.

Scene 1

Tiana: "Nathan, I'd like you to look at your informed surgical consent form and tell me if it is still your intent to have surgery today."

Nathan: "I do have a few other questions about the surgery. I've been talking to my friend who works in surgery and he brought up some points I hadn't considered before."

Scene 2

Tiana: "Do you feel comfortable addressing your questions with me, and if they're not nursing-related, I will let the surgeon know that she needs to come and talk to you before surgery?"

Nathan: "That's fine. See, I'm in this friend's wedding in two weeks and need to clarify what the recovery period will be like. Am I going to be able to take part in all the wedding activities?"

Tiana: "Certainly, I'll have the surgeon talk to you about that before you're transferred to the operating room."

Scene 3

Tiana: "Dr. Follman, Nathan Yu, your client scheduled for an abdominal hernia repair this morning, has some questions regarding his upcoming surgery."

Dr. Follman: "I don't have time to come up, please proceed with the transfer to the operating room."

Tiana: "I am concerned about the viability of his consent if he still has questions and I feel he needs have those questions addressed by you before he is transferred."

Scenario conclusion

Dr. Follman arrived in the preoperative area and answered all of Nathan's questions. She also thanked Tiana for informing her of the issue. Tiana thought about how difficult it is to question a surgeon in the hierarchy of the surgical environment. She felt that advocating for the client was worth the fear she had to overcome to question Dr. Follman.

Case study exercise

1. Related to the case study above, Tiana knows that consent is considered to be informed when the client has been provided with and understands which of the following? Select all that apply.

   A. Reason the treatment or procedure is needed

   B. How the treatment or procedure will benefit the client

   C. Documented evidence related to the procedure in written form

   D. Risks involved if the client chooses to receive the treatment or procedure

   E. Other options to treat the problem, including the option of not treating the problem

   F. Risk involved if the client chooses no treatment

INTERFACILITY TRANSER FORM

Health Care Providers

1234 Main Street
Shermer, IL 12345
1.800.555.1234

TRANSFER FROM: _____

Client condition: ☐ Stable ☐ Unstable

Reason for transfer and Benefits and Risks of transfer:
☐ Client/responsible person's request
☐ Need for higher level of care not available at this facility
☐ Need for diagnostic equipment not available at this facility
☐ Transfer request by:
☐ Other: _____

Benefits of Transfer: _____

_____

Risks of Transfer:
☐ Death
☐ Vehicular accident
☐ Bleeding
☐ Pulmonary Decompensation
☐ Cardiac Decompensation
☐ Delivery in route
☐ Deterioration of medical condition:
☐ Additional delay in receiving appropriate treatment
☐ Other

_____ I certify that based upon the information available at the time of transfer, the medical benefits and treatment at the accepting facility, outweigh the increased risks to the client in the case of pregnancy, the unborn infant.

_____ After client assessment, I certify that I have discussed the risks and benefits to the client that were known to me at the time of transfer.

Medical Diagnosis: _____

_____

Provider's Name: _____

Signature: _____

Date: _____ Time: _____

I acknowledge by my signature that I agree to my transfer to the receiving facility and the transferring provider has discussed with me the risks and benefits of transfer.

Client Signature: _____

Client unable to sign, signature
of responsible person: _____

Relationship: _____

Approval of Transfer

_____ The receiving facility has agreed to accept the client, provide appropriate medical treatment and has available and qualified personnel for the treatment of this client.

Name/title of transferring facility
contact receiving above approval: _____

Name/title of receiving facility
contact granting above approval: _____

Name of receiving facility: _____

Name of provider receiving client
from transferring provider: _____

Name of transferring nursing
personnel giving report: _____

Name of receiving nursing
personnel receiving report: _____

Available space confirmed by: _____

Time: _____

Method of Transfer

Name of transferring facility:

Time of arrival: Time of transfer:

Qualified personnel with appropriate medical equipment which will be able to use all necessary and appropriate life support measures will transfer the client:

☐ BLS ☐ ALS ☐ Air transport ☐ Other: _____

Treatment

_____ The transferring facility has within its capacity provided medical treatment to minimize the risk to the client's health (and in the case of pregnancy, the unborn infant).

Treatment rendered included:
☐ IV:
☐ Medications:
☐ Oxygen:
☐ Procedures:

Vital signs at the time of transfer:
T _____ P _____ R _____ BP _____

Records sent with client:
☐ Laboratory findings:
☐ Radiographs:
☐ EKG   Valuables
☐ Medical record   ☐ To the family

Discharge client assessment: _____

Name of Transferring Nurse: _____

Signature: _____ Date: _____

TRANSFER REPORT

H Health Care Providers

1234 Main Street
Shermer, IL 12345
1.800.555.1234

Name: _____
Admission date: _____

DOB: _____
Medical record #: _____

Transfer date: _____
Transfer from: _____
Transfer to: _____

Attending provider: _____
Address: _____
Phone: _____

Contact: _____
Address: _____
Phone: _____
Relationship: _____

Notify ☐ Yes ☐ No

Reason for transfer

Vital signs:
T _____ P _____ R _____ BP _____ WT _____
Diagnosis: _____
Prognosis/rehab potential: _____
Allergies: _____
Diet: _____
Activity level: _____
Precautions: _____

ADLs

	No assistance needed	Assistance/ supervision	Total care
Walking			
Transfers			
Bathing			
Eating			
Oral hygiene			
Dressing			

Medication:

Date/time of last dose:

Treatment:

Date/time:

Prosthesis: _____
Hearing: _____
Speech: _____
Vision: _____
Bowel/bladder: _____
Mental status: _____
Emotional status: _____
Additional information: _____

Provider signature: _____
Date: _____

Nurse signature: _____
Date: _____

Health Care Providers

1234 Main Street
Shermer, IL 12345
1.800.555.1234

Patient Discharge Summary

Name: _____

Address: _____

Email address: _____

SSN: _____

DOB: _____

Sex: ☐ Male   ☐ Female

Reason for admittance: _____

Diagnosis at admittance: _____

Treatment summary: _____

Discharge reason:

☐ Needs met
☐ Patient deceased
☐ Hospital admission
☐ Moved away
☐ Refused services
☐ Discharge to outpatient therapy
☐ Transferred: hospice services
☐ Transferred: other home health services
☐ Transferred: nursing home

Discharge state:

☐ Independent
☐ Assistance required: minimal
☐ Assistance required: moderate
☐ Assistance required: maximal
☐ Assistance required: total

Date discharged: _____

Physician approved: ☐ Yes   ☐ No

Diagnosis at discharge: _____

Further treatment plan: _____

Follow up with provider? ☐ Yes   ☐ No

Follow-up date: _____

Notes: _____

Medication information:
(include name, dose and route)

Frequency

Instructions/adverse effects

Signature: _____

Date: _____

Advance directives

- The purpose of advance directives is to communicate a client's wishes regarding end-of-life care should the client become unable to do so.
- The PSDA requires that all clients admitted to a health care facility be asked if they have advance directives.
  - A client who does not have advance directives must be given written information that outlines their rights related to health care decisions and how to formulate advance directives. Qᴘᴄᴄ
  - A health care representative should be available to help with this process.

COMPONENTS OF ADVANCE DIRECTIVES

Two components of an advance directive are the living will and the durable power of attorney for health care.

LIVING WILL

- A living will is a legal document that expresses the client's wishes regarding medical treatment in the event the client becomes incapacitated and is facing end-of-life issues. Types of treatments that are often addressed in a living will are those that have the capacity to prolong life. Examples of treatments that are addressed are cardiopulmonary resuscitation, mechanical ventilation, and feeding by artificial means.
- Living wills are legal in all states. However, state statutes and individual health care facility policies can vary. Nurses need to be familiar with their state statute and facility policies.
- Most state laws include provisions that health care providers who follow the health care directive in a living will are protected from liability.

DURABLE POWER OF ATTORNEY FOR HEALTH CARE

A durable power of attorney for health care/health care proxy is a legal document that designates a health care surrogate, who is an individual authorized to make health care decisions for a client who is unable.

- The person who serves in the role of health care surrogate to make decisions for the client should be very familiar with the client's wishes.
- Living wills can be difficult to interpret, especially in the face of unexpected circumstances. A durable power of attorney for health care, as an adjunct to a living will, can be a more effective way of ensuring that the client's decisions about health care are honored.

PROVIDER'S PRESCRIPTIONS

- Unless a do not resuscitate (DNR) or allow natural death (AND) prescription is written, the nurse should initiate CPR when a client has no pulse or respirations. The written prescription for a DNR or AND must be placed in the client's medical record. The provider consults the client and the family prior to administering a DNR or AND.
- Additional prescriptions by the provider are based on the client's individual needs and decisions and provide for comfort measures. The client's decision is respected in regard to the use of antibiotics, initiation of diagnostic tests, and provision of nutrition by artificial means.

NURSING ROLE IN ADVANCE DIRECTIVES

- Providing written information regarding advance directives
- Documenting the client's advance directives status
- Ensuring that advance directives are current and reflective of the client's current decisions
- Recognizing that the client's choice takes priority when there is a conflict between the client and family, or between the client and the provider
- Informing all members of the health care team of the client's advance directives Qᴘᴄᴄ

Confidentiality and information security

Clients have the right to privacy and confidentiality in relation to their health care information and medical recommendations.

- Nurses who disclose client information to an unauthorized person can be liable for invasion of privacy, defamation, or slander.
- The security and privacy rules of the Health Insurance Portability and Accountability Act (HIPAA) were enacted to protect the confidentiality of health care information and to give the client the right to control the release of information. Specific rights provided by the legislation include:
  - The rights of clients to obtain a copy of their medical record and to submit requests to amend erroneous or incomplete information
  - A requirement for health care and insurance providers to provide written information about how medical information is used and how it is shared with other entities (permission must be obtained before information is shared)
  - The rights of clients to privacy and confidentiality

NURSING ROLE IN CONFIDENTIALITY

It is essential for nurses to be aware of the rights of clients regarding privacy and confidentiality. Facility policies and procedures are established to ensure compliance with HIPAA regulations. It is essential that nurses know and adhere to the policies and procedures. HIPAA regulations also provide for penalties in the event of noncompliance with the regulations. Qs

PRIVACY RULE

The Privacy Rule of HIPAA requires that nurses protect all written and verbal communication about clients.

Components of the Privacy Rule

- Planned change might be a proactive way to improve care quality. Change might also be required by a regulatory board.
- Only health care team members directly responsible for the client's care are allowed access to the client's records. Nurses cannot share information with other clients or staff not involved in the care of the client.
- Clients have a right to read and obtain a copy of their medical record, and agency policy should be followed when the client requests to read or have a copy of their record.
- No part of the client record can be copied except for authorized exchange of documents between health care institutions. For example,
  ○ Transfer from a hospital to an extended care facility
  ○ Exchange of documents between a general practitioner and a specialist during a consult
- Client medical records must be kept in a secure area to prevent inappropriate access to the information. Using public display boards to list client names and diagnoses is restricted.
- Electronic records should be password-protected, and care must be taken to prevent public viewing of the information. Health care workers should use only their own passwords to access information.
- Client information cannot be disclosed to unauthorized individuals, including family members who request it and individuals who call on the phone.
  ○ Many hospitals use a code system in which information is only disclosed to individuals who can provide the code.
  ○ Nurses should ask any individual inquiring about a client's status for the code and disclose information only when an individual can give the code.
- Communication about a client should only take place in a private setting where it cannot be overheard by unauthorized individuals. The practice of "walking rounds," where other clients and visitors can hear what is being said, is no longer sanctioned. Taped rounds also are discouraged because nurses should not receive information about clients for whom they are not responsible. Change-of-shift reports can be done at the bedside as long as the client does not have a roommate and no unsolicited visitors are present. Qpcc

Information technology

- Informatics is the use of computers to systematically resolve issues in nursing. The use of technology in health care is increasing and most forms of communication are in electronic format. Qι
- Examples of how a nurse can use the electronic format while providing client care include laptops for documentation and the use of an automated medication dispensing system to dispense medications.
- Databases on diseases and medications are available for the nurse to review. These databases can also be used as a teaching tool when nurses are educating clients.
- The nurse can review medications, diseases, procedures, and treatments using an electronic format.
- Computers can be beneficial for use with clients who have visual impairments.
- The Internet is a valuable tool for clients to review current medications and health questions. This is especially true for clients who have chronic illnesses.
- Nurses should instruct clients to only review valid and credible websites by verifying the author, institution, credentials, and how current the article is. A disclaimer will be presented if information is not medical advice.
- Clients can access their electronic health record (EHR) which is part of e-health. E-health enables the client to make appointments online, review laboratory results, refill an electronic prescription, and review billing information. The goal of e-health is improved health care outcomes due to 24 hr access by the client and provider to the client's health care information.
- Telehealth, a technology-aided option for client assessment and communication, will change client and provider interactions. Telehealth can bring efficiencies into a system where decreased reimbursement and the nursing shortage are becoming more common.
- Other technologies being looked at are robotics in the form of nursebots, biomechatronics, biometrics, smart cards, and point-of-care testing.

INFORMATION SECURITY

- Health information systems (HIS) are used to manage administrative functions and clinical functions. The clinical portion of the system is often referred to as the clinical information systems (CIS). The CIS can be used to coordinate essential aspects of client care. Qι
- In order to comply with HIPAA regulations, each health care facility has specific policies and procedures designed to monitor staff adherence, technical protocols, computer privacy, and data safety.

INFORMATION SECURITY PROTOCOLS

- Log off from the computer before leaving the workstation to ensure that others cannot view protected health information (PHI) on the monitor.
- Never share a user ID or password with anyone.
- Never leave a client's chart or other printed or written PHI where others can access it.
- Shred any printed or written client information used for reporting or client care after it is no longer needed.

USE OF SOCIAL MEDIA

- The use of social media by members of the nursing profession is common practice. The benefits to using social media are numerous. It provides a mechanism for nurses to access current information about health care and enhances communication among nurses, colleagues, and clients and families. It also provides an opportunity for nurses to express concerns and seek support from others. However, nurses must be cautious about the risk of intentional or inadvertent breaches of confidentiality via social media.
- The right to privacy is a fundamental component of client care. Invasion of privacy as it relates to health care is the release of client health information to others without the client's consent. Confidentiality is the duty of the nurse to protect a client's private information.
- The inappropriate use of social media can result in a breach of client confidentiality. Depending on the circumstances, the consequences can include termination of employment by the employer, discipline by the board of nursing, charges of defamation or invasion of privacy, and in the most serious of circumstances, federal charges for violation of HIPAA.

PROTECTING YOURSELF AND OTHERS

- Become familiar with facility policies about the use of social media and adhere to them.
- Avoid disclosing any client health information online. Be sure no one can overhear conversations about a client when speaking on the telephone.
- Do not take or share photos or videos of a client.
- Remember to maintain professional boundaries when interacting with clients online.
- Never post a belittling or offensive remark about a client, employer, or coworker.
- Report any violations of facility social media policies to the nurse manager.

COLLABORATION WITH THE INTERPROFESSIONAL TEAM

- One of the primary roles of nursing is the coordination and management of client care in collaboration with the health care team. In so doing, high-quality health care is provided as clients move through the health care system in a cost-effective and time-efficient manner. Qrc
- To effectively coordinate client care, a nurse must understand collaboration with the interprofessional team, principles of case management, continuity of care (including consultations, referrals, transfers, and discharge planning), and motivational principles to encourage and empower self, staff, colleagues, and other members of the interprofessional team.

- An interprofessional team is a group of health care professionals from various disciplines. Collaboration involves discussion of client care issues in making health care decisions, especially for clients who have multiple problems. The specialized knowledge and skills of each discipline are used in the development of an interprofessional plan of care that addresses multiple problems. Nurses should recognize that the collaborative efforts of the interprofessional team allow the achievement of results that a team member would be incapable of accomplishing alone.
  - Nurse-provider collaboration should be fostered to create a climate of mutual respect and collaborative practice.
  - Collaboration occurs among different levels of nurses and nurses with different areas of expertise.
  - Collaboration should also occur between the interprofessional team, the client, and the client's family/significant others when an interprofessional plan of care is being developed.
  - Collaboration is a form of conflict resolution that results in a win-win solution for both the client and health care team.

NURSE QUALITIES FOR EFFECTIVE COLLABORATION

- Good communication skills
- Assertiveness
- Conflict negotiation skills
- Leadership skills
- Professional presence
- Decision-making and critical thinking skills

THE NURSE'S ROLE

- Coordinate the interprofessional team. Qrc
- Have a holistic understanding of the client, the client's health care needs, and the health care system.
- Provide the opportunity for care to be provided with continuity over time and across disciplines.
- Provide the client with the opportunity to be a partner in the development of the plan of care.
- Provide information during rounds and interprofessional team meetings regarding the status of the client's health.
- Provide an avenue for the initiation of a consultation related to a specific health care issue.
- Provide a link to post discharge resources that might need a referral.

VARIABLES THAT AFFECT COLLABORATION

Decision-making is also influenced by the facility hierarchy.

- In a centralized hierarchy, nurses at the top of the organizational chart make most of the decisions.
- In a decentralized hierarchy, staff nurses who provide direct client care are included in the decision-making process. Large organizations benefit from the use of decentralized decision-making because managers at the top of the hierarchy do not have firsthand knowledge of unit-level challenges or problems. Decentralized decision-making promotes job satisfaction among staff nurses.

BEHAVIORAL CHANGE STRATEGY AND THEORY

Although bombarded with constant change, members of the interprofessional team can be resistant to change. Three strategies a manager can use to promote change are the rational-empirical, normative-re-educative, and the power-coercive. Often the manager uses a combination of these strategies.

Rational-empirical: The manager provides factual information to support the change. Used when resistance to change is minimal.

Normative-reeducative: The manager focuses on interpersonal relationships to promote change.

Power-coercive: The manager uses rewards to promote change. Used when individuals are highly resistant to change.

PLANNED CHANGE

Planned change is important in health care because it enables the interprofessional team to replace unproven methods with evidence-based ones.

- Planned change might be a proactive way to improve care quality. Change might also be required by a regulatory board.
- Variables that affect whether change can fully take place include individual and organizational willingness, competing demands, and whether the change is meaningful.
- Changes in technology are more readily accepted than social change.
- Include people who will be affected by the change in the planning process to decrease resistance. Qᴛᴄ

LEWIN'S CHANGE THEORY

Lewin's change theory is a common model for promoting planned change, which has three stages.
- Unfreezing: Need for change is identified or created.
- Change/Movement: Strategies (driving forces) that overcome resistance to change (restraining forces) are identified and implemented.
- Refreezing: The change is integrated and the system is re-stabilized.

Lewin's theory has been adapted into a stages of change model for individual change, with five stages:
- Precontemplation: No intent to change is present or has been considered.
- Contemplation: The individual considers adopting a change.
- Preparation: The individual intends to implement the change in the near future.
- Action: The individual implements the change.
- Maintenance: The individual continues the new behavior without relapse.

STAGES OF TEAM FORMATION

Teams typically work through a group formation process before reaching peak performance.

Forming: Members of the team get to know each other. The leader defines tasks for the team and offers direction.

Storming: Conflict arises, and team members begin to express polarized views. The team establishes rules, and members begin to take on various roles.

Norming: The team establishes rules. Members show respect for one another and begin to accomplish some of the tasks.

Performing: The team focuses on accomplishment of tasks.

GENERATIONAL DIFFERENCES TEAM MEMBERS

Generational differences influence the value system of the members of an interprofessional team and can affect how members function within the team. Generational differences can be challenging for members of a team, but working with individuals from different generations also can bring strength to the team.

- Veterans (Silent Generation, Traditionals): Born 1925 to 1942
- Baby Boomers: Born 1942 to early 1960s
- Generation X: Born mid-1960s to early 1980s
- Generation Y (Millennial): Born mid-1980s to 2000
- Generation Z (Homelanders): Born after 2001

CASE MANAGEMENT

Case management is the coordination of care provided by an interprofessional team from the time a client starts receiving care until they no longer receive services. Qᴛᴄ

PRINCIPLES OF CASE MANAGEMENT

- Case management focuses on managed care of the client through collaboration of the health care team in acute and post-acute settings.
- The goal of case management is to avoid fragmentation of care and control cost.
- A case manager collaborates with the interprofessional health care team during the assessment of a client's needs and subsequent care planning, and follows up by monitoring the achievement of desired client outcomes within established time parameters.

- A case manager can be a nurse, social worker, or other designated health care professional. A case manager's role and knowledge expectations are extensive. Therefore, case managers are required to have advanced practice degrees or advanced training in this area.
- Case manager nurses do not usually provide direct client care.
- Case managers usually oversee a caseload of clients who have similar disorders or treatment regimens.
- Case managers in the community coordinate resources and services for clients whose care is based in a residential setting.

NURSING ROLE IN CASE MANAGEMENT

- Coordinating care, particularly for clients who have complex health care needs
- Facilitating continuity of care
- Improving efficiency of care and utilization of resources Qᴛᴄ
- Enhancing quality of care provided
- Limiting unnecessary costs and lengthy stays
- Advocating for the client and family

CRITICAL PATHWAYS

A critical or clinical pathway or care map can be used to support the implementation of clinical guidelines and protocols. These tools are usually based on cost and length of stay parameters mandated by prospective payment systems (Medicare and insurance companies).

- Case managers often initiate critical pathways, but they are used by many members of the interprofessional team.
- Critical pathways are often specific to a diagnosis type and outline the typical length of stay and treatments.
- When a client requires treatment other than what is typical or requires a longer length of stay, it is documented as a variance, along with information describing why the variance occurred.

CONTINUITY OF CARE: CONSULTATIONS, REFERRALS, TRANSFERS, AND DISCHARGE PLANNING

Continuity of care refers to the consistency of care provided as clients move through the health care system. It enhances the quality of client care and facilitates the achievement of positive client outcomes. Qᴘᴄᴄ

- Continuity of care is desired as clients move from one:
  ○ Level of care to another (from the ICU to a medical unit).
  ○ Facility to another (from an acute care facility to a skilled facility).
  ○ Unit/department to another (from the PACU to the postsurgical unit).
- Nurses are responsible for facilitating continuity of care and coordinating care through documentation, reporting, and collaboration.
- A formal, written plan of care enhances coordination of care between nurses, interprofessional team members, and providers.

NURSING ROLE IN CONTINUITY OF CARE

THE NURSE'S ROLE AS COORDINATOR OF CARE INCLUDES:

- Facilitating the continuity of care provided by members of the health care team
- Acting as a representative of the client and as a liaison when collaborating with the provider and other members of the health care team. When acting as a liaison, the nurse serves in the role of client advocate by protecting the rights of clients and ensuring that client needs are met

AS THE COORDINATOR OF CARE, THE NURSE IS RESPONSIBLE FOR:

- Admission, transfer, discharge, and postdischarge prescriptions
- Initiation, revision, and evaluation of the plan of care
- Reporting the client's status to other nurses and the provider
- Coordinating the discharge plan
- Facilitating referrals and the use of community resources

CONSULTATIONS

- A consultant is a professional who provides expert advice in a particular area. A consultation is requested to help determine what treatment/services the client requires.
- Consultants provide expertise for clients who require a specific type of knowledge or service (a cardiologist for a client who had a myocardial infarction, a psychiatrist for a client whose risk for suicide must be assessed).

THE NURSE'S ROLE REGARDING CONSULTATIONS

- Initiate necessary consults or notify the provider of the client's needs so the consult can be initiated.
- Provide the consultant with all pertinent information about the problem (information from the client/family, the client's medical records).
- Incorporate the consultant's recommendations into the client's plan of care.

REFERRALS

A referral is a formal request for a service by another care provider. It is made so that the client can access the care identified by the provider or the consultant. Qᴘᴄᴄ

- The care can be provided in the acute setting or outside the facility.
- Clients being discharged from health care facilities to their home can still require nursing care.
- Discharge referrals are based on client needs in relation to actual and potential problems and can be facilitated with the assistance of social services, especially if there is a need for:
  ○ Specialized equipment (cane, walker, wheelchair, grab bars in bathroom)
  ○ Specialized therapists (physical, occupational, speech)
  ○ Care providers (home health nurse, hospice nurse, home health aide)
- Knowledge of community and online resources is necessary to appropriately link the client with needed services.

THE NURSE'S ROLE REGARDING REFERRALS

- Begin discharge planning upon the client's admission.
- Evaluate client/family competencies in relation to home care prior to discharge.
- Involve the client and family in care planning.
- Collaborate with other health care professionals to ensure all health care needs are met and necessary referrals are made.
- Complete referral forms to ensure proper reimbursement for prescribed services.

TRANSFERS

Clients can be transferred from one unit, department, or one facility to another. Continuity of care must be maintained as the client moves from one setting to another.

- The use of communication hand-off tools (I PASS the BATON, PACE) promotes continuity of care and client safety. Qs
- The nurse's role regarding transfers is to provide written and verbal report of the client's status and care needs.
  - Client medical diagnosis and care providers
  - Client demographic information
  - Overview of health status, plan of care, and recent progress
  - Alterations that can precipitate an immediate concern
  - Most recent vital signs and medications, including when a PRN was given
  - Notification of assessments or client care needed within the next few hours
  - Allergies
  - Diet and activity prescriptions
  - Presence of or need for specific equipment or adaptive devices (oxygen, suction, wheelchair)
  - Advance directives and whether a client is to be resuscitated in the event of cardiac or respiratory arrest
  - Family involvement in care and health care proxy, if applicable

DISCHARGE PLANNING

Discharge planning is an interprofessional process that is started by the nurse at the time of the client's admission. Qтc

- The nurse conducts discharge planning with both the client and client's family for optimal results.
- Discharge planning serves as a starting point for continuity of care. As client care needs are identified, measures can be taken to prepare for the provision of needed support.
- A comprehensive discharge plan includes a review of the following client information.
  - Current health and prognosis
  - Religious or cultural beliefs
  - Ability to perform ADLs
  - Mobility status and goals
  - Sensory, motor, physical, or cognitive impairments
  - Support systems and caregivers
  - Financial resources and limitations
  - Potential supports and resources in the community
  - Internal and external home environment
  - Need for assistance with transportation or home maintenance
  - Need for therapy, wound care, or other services
  - Need for medical equipment
- The need for additional services (home health, physical therapy, and respite care) can be addressed before the client is discharged so the service is in place when the client arrives home.
- A client who leaves a facility without a prescription for discharge from the provider is considered leaving against medical advice (AMA). A client who is legally competent has the legal right to leave the facility at any time. The nurse should immediately notify the provider. If the client is at risk for harm, it is imperative that the nurse explain the risk involved in leaving the facility. The individual should sign a form relinquishing responsibility for any complications that arise from discontinuing prescribed care. The nurse should document all communication, as well as the specific advice that was provided for the client. A nurse who tries to prevent the client from leaving the facility can face legal charges of assault, battery, and false imprisonment.

DISCHARGE INSTRUCTIONS INCLUDE

- Step-by-step instructions for procedures to be done at home. Clients should be given the opportunity to provide a return demonstration of these procedures to validate learning
- Medication regimen instructions for home, including adverse effects and actions to take to minimize them
- Precautions to take when performing procedures or administering medications
- Indications of medication adverse effects or medical complications that the client should report to the provider
- Names and numbers of providers and community services the client or family can contact
- Plans for follow-up care and therapies

THE NURSE'S ROLE WITH REGARD TO DISCHARGE IS TO PROVIDE A WRITTEN SUMMARY:

- Type of discharge (prescribed by provider, AMA)
- Date and time of discharge, who accompanied the client, and how the client was transported (wheelchair to a private car, stretcher to an ambulance)
- Discharge destination (home, long-term care facility)
- A summary of the client's condition at discharge (gait, dietary intake, use of assistive devices, blood glucose)
- A description of any unresolved problems and plans for follow-up
- Disposition of valuables, medications brought from home, and prescriptions
- A copy of the client's discharge instructions

COMMUNICATION

- Poor communication can lead to adverse outcomes, including sentinel events (unexpected death or serious injury of a client).
- Communication regarding the client's status and needs is required anytime there is a transfer of care, whether from one unit or facility to another, or at change-of-shift, as the nurse hands off the care of the client to another health care professional.

COMMUNICATION TOOLS

- A number of communication hand-off tools are available to improve communication and promote client safety (I-SBAR, PACE, I PASS the BATON, Five P's). Qs
- Nurses might also communicate interprofessionally through electronic means (through electronic medical record systems and e-mail). Qʟ
  - E-mail communication can be informal but should maintain a professional tone. Don't use text abbreviations. Make the message concise yet thorough so the reader has clear understanding of the intent.
  - Read messages before sending to ensure there is not a negative or rude tone.
- Some facilities permit text messaging. Check the facility policy regarding this type of communication, and never send confidential information through text.

HAND-OFF OR CHANGE-OF-SHIFT REPORT

- Performed with the nurse who is assuming responsibility for the client's care
- Describes the current health status of the client
- Informs the next shift of pertinent client care information
- Provides the oncoming nurse the opportunity to ask questions and clarify the plan of care
- Should be given in a private area (a conference room or at the bedside) to protect client confidentiality

REPORT TO THE PROVIDER Qᴛᴄ

- Assessment data integral to changes in client status
- Recommendations for changes in the plan of care
- Clarification of prescriptions

DOCUMENTATION

The ANA Scope and Standards for Nurse Administrators suggests that the nurse administrator analyzes data from documentation to identify trends and possible problems regarding client care.

Documentation to facilitate continuity of care includes the following:

- Graphic records that illustrate trending of assessment data (vital signs)
- Flow sheets that reflect routine care completed and other care-related data
- Nurses' notes that describe changes in client status or unusual circumstances
- Client care summaries that serve as quick references for client care information
- Nursing care plans that set the standard for care provided
  - Standardized nursing care plans provide a starting point for the nurse responsible for care plan development.
  - Standardized plans must be individualized to each client.
  - All documentation should reflect the plan of care.

Active Learning Scenario

A nurse is explaining the role of a case manager to a newly licensed nurse. What should the case manager include in the discussion? Use the *ATI Active Learning Template: Basic Concept* to complete this item.

UNDERLYING PRINCIPLES: Identify three roles of a case manager.

Active Learning Scenario Key

Using the ATI Active Learning Template: Basic Concept
UNDERLYING PRINCIPLES: Roles of a case manager
- Coordinating care of clients who have complex health care needs
- Facilitating continuity of care
- Improving efficiency of care
- Enhancing quality of care provided
- Limiting cost and lengthy stays
- Advocating for the client and family

Ⓝ *NCLEX® Connection: Management of Care, Concepts of Management*

Case Study Exercise Key

1. A. **CORRECT:** The nurse should identify that informed consent occurs when the client understands the reason the treatment or procedure is needed.
   B. **CORRECT:** The nurse should identify that informed consent occurs when the client understands how the treatment or procedure will benefit the client.
   C. The nurse should document evidence related to the procedure in written form.
   D. **CORRECT:** The nurse should identify that informed consent occurs when the client understands the risks involved if the client chooses to receive the treatment or procedure.
   E. **CORRECT:** The nurse should identify that informed consent occurs when the client understands the other options to treat the problem, including the option of not treating the problem.
   F. **CORRECT:** The nurse should identify that informed consent occurs when the client understands the risk involved if the client chooses no treatment.

Ⓝ *NCLEX® Connection: Management of Care, Informed Consent*

Application Exercises

1. A nurse is caring for a client who has chest pain. The client says, "I am going home immediately." Which of the following actions should the nurse take? (Select all that apply.)

   A. Notify the client's family of their intent to leave the facility.

   B. Document the client's intent to leave the facility against medical advice (AMA).

   C. Explain to the client the risks involved if they choose to leave.

   D. Ask the client to sign a form relinquishing responsibility of the facility.

   E. Prevent the client from leaving the facility until the provider arrives.

2. A nurse is serving as a preceptor to a newly licensed nurse and is explaining the role of a nurse advocate. Which of the following situations illustrates the advocacy role? (Select all that apply).

   A. Verifying that a client understands what is done during a cardiac catheterization

   B. Discussing treatment options for a terminal diagnosis

   C. Informing members of the health care team that a client has do-not-resuscitate status

   D. Reporting that a health team member on the previous shift did not provide care as prescribed

   E. Assisting a client to make a decision about their care based on the nurse's recommendations

3. A nurse is caring for a client who is scheduled for surgery. The client hands the nurse information about advance directives and states, "Here, I don't need this. I am too young to worry about life-sustaining measures and what I want done for me." Which of the following actions should the nurse take?

   A. Return the papers to the admitting department with a note stating that the client does not wish to address the issue at this time.

   B. Explain to the client that you never know what can happen during surgery and to fill the papers out just in case.

   C. Contact a representative to talk with the client and offer additional information about the purpose of advance directives.

   D. Inform the client that surgery cannot be conducted unless the advance directives forms are completed.

4. A nurse who has just assumed the role of unit manager is examining the skills necessary for interprofessional collaboration. Which of the following actions support the nurse's interprofessional collaboration during a care team meeting? (Select all that apply.)

   A. Use aggressive communication when addressing the team.

   B. Recognize the knowledge and skills of each member of the team.

   C. Ensure that a nurse is assigned to serve as the group facilitator for all interprofessional meetings.

   D. Encourage the client and family to participate in the team meeting.

   E. Support team member requests for referral.

5. A case manager is discussing critical pathways with a group of newly hired nurses. Which of the following statements made by the newly licensed nurse indicates understanding?

   A. "The time to fill out the pathways often increases the cost of care."

   B. "The pathway shows an estimate of the number of days the client will be hospitalized."

   C. "Deviance from the pathway is a sign of improved care quality."

   D. "The pathway includes information about the client's history."

1. A. Notifying the client's family without the client's permission violates the client's right to confidentiality. The nurse should notify the client's provider.
   B. **CORRECT:** When taking actions, the nurse should document the type of discharge, including an AMA discharge.
   C. **CORRECT:** When taking action, the nurse should warn the client of the risks involved in leaving the hospital against medical advice.
   D. **CORRECT:** When taking actions, the nurse should ask the client to sign an AMA form to provide legal protection for the hospital.
   E. The nurse should identify that trying to prevent a client from leaving the hospital by any action (threatening them or refusing to give them their clothes) can be charged with assault, battery, and false imprisonment.

   Ⓝ *NCLEX® Connection: Management of Care, Legal Rights and Responsibilities*

2. A. **CORRECT:** When taking actions, the nurse should identify that the role of a nurse advocate includes ensuring that the client has given informed consent.
   B. Discussing treatment options is not within the scope of practice of the nurse.
   C. **CORRECT:** When taking actions, the nurse should identify that the role of a nurse advocate includes ensuring that the client's care is consistent with their DNR status.
   D. **CORRECT:** When taking actions, the nurse should identify that the role of a nurse advocate includes ensuring that all clients receive proper care.
   E. Assisting a client to make decisions about their care based on nurse recommendations is inappropriate. The nurse should support the client in making their own decisions.

   Ⓝ *NCLEX® Connection: Management of Care, Advocacy*

3. A. The nurse should advocate for the client by ensuring that the client understands the purpose of advance directives.
   B. Explaining to the client about uncertainties that can occur during surgery is nontherapeutic and can cause the client to be anxious about the surgery.
   C. **CORRECT:** When taking actions, the nurse should advocate for the client by ensuring that the client understands the purpose of advance directives. Seeking the assistance of a client representative to provide information to the client is an appropriate action.
   D. Telling the client that the surgery cannot be conducted unless an advance directive is completed is untrue and is a barrier to therapeutic communication.

   Ⓝ *NCLEX® Connection: Management of Care, Advance Directives/Self–Determination/Life Planning*

4. A. The nurse should use assertive skills when communicating with the interprofessional team.
   B. **CORRECT:** When taking actions, the nurse should recognize that each member of the team has specific skills to contribute to the collaboration process.
   C. A nurse can serve as the facilitator. However, this role can be assumed by any member of the team.
   D. **CORRECT:** Collaboration should occur among the client, family, and interprofessional team.
   E. **CORRECT:** The nurse should support suggestions for referrals to link clients to appropriate resources.

   Ⓝ *NCLEX® Connection: Management of Care, Collaboration with Multidisciplinary Team*

5. A. Critical pathways often reduce the cost of care by streamlining care services.
   B. **CORRECT:** When evaluating outcomes, the nurse should identify that the newly licensed nurse understands the teaching when the nurse states that Critical pathways are specific to a client diagnosis and show the average length of stay a client with the diagnosis type will have.
   C. Deviances from the pathway require documentation of explanation because it usually indicates the client is not progressing at the expected rate.
   D. Critical pathways include a projection of treatments the client will receive.

   Ⓝ *NCLEX® Connection: Management of Care, Concepts of Managements*

When reviewing the following chapter, keep in mind the relevant topics and tasks of the NCLEX outline, in particular:

Management of Care

ADVANCE DIRECTIVES/SELF-DETERMINATION/LIFE PLANNING: Integrate advance directives into client plan of care.

ADVOCACY: Discuss identified treatment options with client and respect their decisions.

CLIENT RIGHTS: Provide education to clients and staff about client rights and responsibilities.

CONFIDENTIALITY/INFORMATION SECURITY: Assess staff member and client understanding of confidentiality requirements.

ETHICAL PRACTICE: Recognize ethical dilemmas and take appropriate action.

INFORMED CONSENT: Verify the client receives appropriate education and consents to care and procedures.

INFORMATION TECHNOLOGY: Apply knowledge of facility regulations when accessing client records.

LEGAL RIGHTS AND RESPONSIBILITIES: Educate the client/staff on legal issues.

Safety and Infection Control

REPORTING OF INCIDENT/EVENT/IRREGULAR OCCURRENCE/ VARIANCE: Report unsafe practice of health care personnel and intervene as appropriate (e.g., substance abuse, improper care, staffing practices).

STANDARD PRECAUTIONS/TRANSMISSION-BASED PRECAUTIONS/SURGICAL ASEPSIS: Educate client and staff regarding infection control measures.

CHAPTER 3 *Professional Practice*

Professional responsibilities are the obligations that nurses have to their clients. To meet professional practice responsibilities, nurses must be knowledgeable in the following areas: professional role accountability; role qualifications and competence; nursing licensure; personal, professional, and leadership development; nursing organizations; professional advocacy; business skills; legal practice; disruptive behavior; and ethical practice.

ROLE ACCOUNTABILITY

Accountability means that nurses are answerable to themselves and others for their actions and impact on others. Regardless of the specific setting, a nurse administrator has accountabilities that are basic to the role. The ANA Nursing Administration Scope and Standards of Practice (2016) notes the following areas of core accountabilities:

- Safety, Quality, and Risk Management: working to create an environment that supports the nurses' ethical and social obligations to deliver safe and effective care while working to protect the organization from liability.
- Health Advocacy: supporting self-determination of care and advocate for protection and rights of all involved in healthcare, including clients, nurses, providers, populations, and systems.
- Clinical Care Delivery: requires a knowledge of the healthcare environment, supports and role models a safe and effective model of care.
- Healthy Work Environment: establishment and maintenance of a place of optimal well-being where the staff feel supported, safe, and respected.
- Accountability for Resource Management: having and employing knowledge and strategic management of fiscal and human resources.
- Legal and Regulatory Compliance: implementing and maintaining a compliance program that meets the legal and regulatory requirements of the many different approval and accreditation processes of the local, state, and federal entities.
- Networking, Partnering, and Collaborating: meeting the expectation of collaborating and building alliances across a wide span of influence.

ROLE QUALIFICATIONS AND COMPETENCE

EDUCATION

Licensed practical nurses (LPN) obtain nursing education in either certificate, diploma, or associate degree programs. Registered nurses (RN) obtain nursing education in either associate degree, diploma, or baccalaureate degree programs. Baccalaureate education for nurses continues to be seen as important as nursing practice has become more complex. Associate degree programs are essential for bringing many students who are place or time bound or prefer to access community college programs to gain a nursing education. The Institute of Medicine (IOM) also noted in their 2010 report that there needs to be a nursing education system that supports seamless academic progression. The increase in RN–BSN programs, mobility programs, and distance learning programs show there is progress in promoting academic progression.

When the associate degree or diploma nurse is a licensed RN, they are frequently encouraged by their employer to obtain a BSN. In 2010, the IOM recommended that at least 80 percent of RNs have a BSN by 2020. In 2016, the IOM reported that this goal was ambitious. The percentage of employed nurse with a BSN or higher increased from 49 percent to 51 percent. The report noted findings related to the goal and drew several conclusions:

- Hospitals are increasingly hiring baccalaureate-prepared nurses.
  - AD degree nurses may not have the same earning potential and responsibilities as nurses with higher degrees.
  - AD nurses may be more hireable in nonhospital locations.
- New partnerships between community colleges and universities using a model of education that streamlines articulation to BSN education are occurring.

The National Council of State Boards of Nursing's 2020 National Nursing Workforce Survey showed that more than 60 percent of RNs had a baccalaureate degree or higher. For first-time licensure applicants, the most common educational preparation was a baccalaureate degree, the second most common was an associate degree, followed by a diploma as the third most common.

The ANA Nursing Administration Scope and Standards of Practice states that nurse administrators must at minimum have a baccalaureate degree, hold an active RN license, and meet all state requirements. Nurse administrators who are responsible for large system and organization-wide leadership are recommended to have a master's degree or doctoral degree in management, nursing leadership, policy, or administration.

QUALIFICATIONS AND RULES RELATED TO NURSING LICENSURE AND PRACTICE

- The core of nursing practice is regulated by state law.
- Each state has enacted statutes that define the parameters of nursing education, licensure, and practice and give the authority to regulate the practice of nursing to its state board of nursing.
  - Boards of nursing have the authority to adopt rules and regulations that further regulate nursing practice. Although the practice of nursing is similar among states, it is critical that nurses know the laws and rules governing nursing in the state in which they practice.
  - The laws and rules governing nursing practice in a specific state can be accessed at the state board's website.
  - Boards of nursing have the authority to both issue and revoke a nursing license. Boards can revoke or suspend a nurse's license for various offenses, including practicing without a valid license, substance use disorders, conviction of a felony, professional negligence, and providing care beyond the scope of practice. Nurses should review the practice act in their states. Qı
  - Boards set standards for nursing education programs and further delineate the scope of practice for registered nurses, licensed practical nurses, and advanced practice nurses.
- State laws vary as to when an individual can begin practicing nursing. Some states allow graduates of nursing programs to practice under a limited license, whereas some states require licensure by passing the NCLEX® before working.

NURSE LICENSURE COMPACT (NLC)

Until the year 2000, nurses were required to hold a current license in every state in which they practiced. This became problematic with the increase in the electronic practice of nursing. For example, a nurse in one state interprets the reading of a cardiac monitor and provides intervention for a client who is physically located in another state. Additionally, many nurses cross state lines to provide direct care. It is not unusual for a nurse who is located near a state border to make home visits on both sides of the state line.

- To address these issues, the mutual recognition model of nurse licensure (the Nurse Licensure Compact [NLC]) has been adopted by many states. This model allows nurses who reside in a NLC state to practice in another NLC state. Nurses must practice in accordance with the statues and rules of the state in which the care is provided. State boards can prohibit a nurse from practicing under the NLC if the license of the nurse has been restricted by a board of nursing.
- Nurses who do not reside in a NLC state must practice under the state-based practice model. In other words, if a nurse resides in a non-NLC state, the nurse must maintain a current license in every state in which they practice. Some states now require background checks with licensure renewal. It is illegal to practice nursing with an expired license.
- The Enhanced Nurse Licensure Compact (eNLC) was revised in 2017. It aligned licensing standards (criminal history background checks) in an effort to bring more states into the compact. Nurses in eNLC states have one multistate license, with the ability to practice in-person or via telehealth in both their home state and other eNLC states.

PROFESSIONAL AND LEADERSHIP DEVELOPMENT

The science of nursing has progressed through practice, theory, and research. Nursing continues to be a profession of life-long learners who are motivated to expand their roles, practice, and leadership. Opportunities for professional development and advancement contribute to nurses' job satisfaction.

Nurse licensure protects the public from fraudulent, unsafe, and ineffective nursing practice. There are mandatory requirements to show continued competency for renewal of licensure that vary from state to state. These requirements include continuing education, designated numbers of clinical practice hours, clinical practice portfolios, and other activities.

MAGNET RECOGNITION PROGRAM

The American Nurses Credentialing Center awards Magnet Recognition to health care facilities that provide high-quality client care and attract and retain well-qualified nurses. The term magnet is used to recognize the facility's power to draw nurses to the facility and to retain them. Qı

- Facilities must create a culture that uses 14 foundational forces of magnetism and model five key components:
  - Empirical data showing quality care results
  - Development of innovation, improvements, or generation of new knowledge
  - Exemplary nursing practice
  - A culture of empowerment
  - Transformational leadership
- The facility must submit documentation to the American Nurses Credentialing Center (ANCC) that demonstrates adherence to ANA nurse administrator standards.
- After documentation that the standards have been met, an on-site appraisal is conducted. A facility that meets the standards is awarded magnet status for a 4-year period.

PATHWAY TO EXCELLENCE RECOGNITION

A program of practice standards to promote a positive practice environment using evidence-based standards Qı

- Acute or long-term care facilities can apply for recognition with this program.
- The Pathway to Excellence designation process includes an application process and adherence to 12 standards of practice, along with an independent survey of the facility.

CERTIFICATION OF ADVANCED PRACTICE NURSES (APRN)

The state legislation governs licensure which is the minimal accepted level of practice. Certification is awarded by nongovernmental agencies and represents excellence in practice. The American Nurses Credentialing Center (ANCC) was formed by many nursing specialty organizations who supported the formation of a central organization to certify nurses. Protection of the public drives certification. There are education and practice requirements for nurses to practice in this expanded nursing role. The APRN scope of practice is regulated by the states.

A list of ANCC certifications can be found at https://www.nursingworld.org/our-certifications/

THE CONSENSUS MODEL FOR APRN REGULATION

The National Council of State Boards of Nursing (NCSBN) created the Consensus Model for APRN Regulation to provide guidance to state boards to form more consistent regulatory rules for APRNs. During the COVID-19 pandemic, the increased need for nurses moved some states to lift unnecessary restrictions on APRNs, which then allowed nurses to move more freely across state lines and assist in surge areas. The Consensus Model for APRN Regulation outlines regulatory requirements that should be adopted by every state. For a better understanding of the Consensus Model, visit https://ncsbn.org/739.htm.

CONTINUING EDUCATION

A nurse leader assesses needs and implements continuing education opportunities for the employees they supervise. To support new policies, work duties, or responsibilities, staff need appropriate instruction to understand what is expected of them. The effective nurse leader role models effective clinical decision making. The leader helps staff enhance their professional and personal development. Finally, the leader is often a mentor for new nurses and essential for developing future nurse leaders. Role modeling enthusiasm and collegiality and addressing bullying and incivility creates a positive workplace.

DEVELOPING AN EDUCATIONAL PROGRAM

- Identify the knowledge or skills needed by staff.
- Find the current level of knowledge or skills held by staff.
- Determine the gap between what staff knows and the desired knowledge.
- Assess the resources you can use to educate staff.
- Use the available resources effectively.
- Measure outcomes during the evaluation phase. Ql

3.1 Advanced Practice Certification ANCC Certifying Exams

Nurse Practitioner Certifications
- Family Nurse Practitioner (FNP-BC)
- Adult-Gerontology Primary Care Nurse Practitioner (AGPCNP-BC)
- Adult-Gerontology Acute Care Nurse Practitioner (AGACNP-BC)
- Psychiatric-Mental Health Nurse Practitioner (PMHNP-BC)

Clinical Nurse Specialist Certification
Adult-Gerontology Clinical Nurse Specialist

Specialty Certifications
- Ambulatory Care Nursing (AMB-BC)
- Cardiac Vascular Nursing (CV-BC)
- Gerontological Nursing (GERO-BC)
- Informatics Nursing (RN-BC)
- Medical-Surgical Nursing (MEDSURG-BC)
- Nurse Executive (NE-BC)
- Pain Management Nursing (PMGT-BC)
- Pediatric Nursing (PED-BC)
- Psychiatric-Mental Health Nursing (PMH-BC)

PROFESSIONAL PRACTICE EVALUATION

Standard 15 of the American Nurses Association (ANA) Nursing Administration Scope and Standards of Practice states a nurse administrator evaluates their own and other nurses' practice. To do this, the nurse administrator...
- Self-reflects on practice on a regular basis and recognizes areas they need to develop.
- Reviews practice to see if it is consistent with regulatory requirements. Ql
- Complies with organizational policies and procedures.
- Revises or maintains organizational policies to support interprofessional evidence-based practice.
- Uses constructive feedback to assist peers and others in their practice.
- Asks for feedback from colleagues, supervisors, and others on their own practice and leadership abilities.
- Uses evaluation information to initiate positive change in their own practice.

SELF-CARE AND PERSONAL DEVELOPMENT

The American Nurses Association Enterprise created Healthy Nurse Health Nation (HNHN) to inspire nurses to improve their health and be role models for others. Areas of concern include more nurses experiencing preventable health conditions, such as being overweight, having higher stress levels, and not getting the recommended amount of sleep. Shift work is one culprit in causing these issues. Other healthcare workforce concerns are workplace violence and musculoskeletal injuries. The Bureau of Labor Statistics report that RNs have among the highest rates of injuries and illnesses compared to all other healthcare employment. It is vitally important that nurses improve their health. Ql

HNHN is implemented by engaging nurses to be educators and advocates for health on three levels:

- Individual
- Organizational
- Interpersonal

The six key HNHN action areas are:

- Physical activity
- Rest
- Nutrition
- Quality of life
- Safety
- Mental health

Creating a healthy nurse population can create:

- A healthier workforce
- Effective, safe, and sustainable health care
- Role models of health

Provision Five of the ANA Code of Ethics states that a nurse "owes the same duties to self as to others." Areas within this provision include:

- Promotion of personal health, safety, and well-being
- Preservation of wholeness of character and integrity
- Maintenance of competence
- Continuation of personal and professional growth

PROFESSIONAL ADVOCACY AND HEALTH POLICY

It is a responsibility for nurse leaders to advocate for professional nursing. Nurses have a history of advocating for accountability in nursing by requiring nursing licensure. Licensure helps to protect the public by licensing those nurses who meet requirements for safe and effective patient care. Nurses have an obligation to take on difficult problems by questioning and raising awareness of the issues. Qᴘᴄᴄ

Participating in the political process is a way to influence policy making by lawmakers. Nurses can impact policy decisions by:

- Maintaining active membership in a nursing organization to add power to the collective voice of nursing.
- Lobbying legislators in person or in writing to make concerns known to policy makers.
- Interacting knowledgeably with the media to educate the public and influence policy.
- Joining political action committees (PACs) created to persuade legislators to vote a certain way.

Nurses have not historically had a strong political voice. For a stronger presence, the nurse needs to be willing to be politically active and join with other nurses to collectively impact policy. Currently, nurses are lobbying to impact legislation on the following:

- Quality of care
- Access to care
- Workplace safety, including workplace violence issues
- Healthcare restructuring
- Reimbursement for APRNs
- Funding for the education of nurses

Nurses have power to impact changes in policy by participating in drafting legislation. There are several factors that nurses must realize to rally their power:

- The time is right for nurses to advocate for a better healthcare system. The current limitations in the system create an opportunity for positive change.
- The United States has around 3 million nurses. This is a powerful voting alliance.
- The public trusts nurses, as noted by the Gallup poll annual survey placing nurses first almost every year in honesty and ethics. The one exception since nurses were added to the poll in 1999 was 2001, when firefighters led the poll.
- Nurses have an increasing knowledge base with more nurses with advanced degrees and prelicensure programs teaching more leadership, management, and political processes.
- The art and science of nursing blends caring, clinical judgment, and science to give nurses a unique perspective in any arena.
- More nurses who are willing to use their expertise and speak out on issues in healthcare should be encouraged to step up to educate and influence consumers about desired changes.

BUSINESS SKILLS

Nurse administrators are expected to participate in the budget process and determine how to allocate resources, including personnel. Involving staff in this process increases the cost-consciousness of the department. Qʟ

3.2 ANA's Political Action Committee (PAC) Top Federal Legislative Priorities 2022

- Health System Transformation
- Safe Staffing
- Nursing Workforce Development
- Home Health
- Opioid Epidemic
- Workplace Violence
- COVID-19

3.3 ANA Guide for Engagement with Legislators

- First, build a relationship. Get to know who they are by researching their interests, background, and voting record.
- Second, meet with them, preferably while at home in their district. This first meeting is best as an introduction and not an "asking for something" meeting.
- When you have an "ask" (seeking support of an initiative or bill), do your homework and be prepared for the meeting.

FINANCIAL RESOURCES

Budget planning is a learned process and gets better with experience. An interesting way to look at the steps in the budgetary process is to compare them to the nursing process:

- Assess what should be included in the budget.
- Diagnose what needs to be done in creating a budget that effectively uses resources.
- Develop the plan using the determined budget cycle. This is frequently a 12-month fiscal year budget cycle.
- Implement the budget and monitor according to the policy of the organization. Healthcare institutions often use monthly statements to see where deviations from the budget may be occurring.
- Evaluate the budget and modify as needed throughout the fiscal year.

The three most common types of budgets are:

- Personnel budget: cost of staff needed for the patient census. Difficulties arise with census fluctuations and personnel shortages which may require higher payments to staff.
- Operating budget: cost of running the hospital including electricity, maintenance, and supplies.
- Capital budget: large equipment costs, generally those over $5,000 and plans for purchases of buildings.

HUMAN RESOURCES

Healthcare facilities have many employees, which is necessary because many of the organizations are open 24 hours a day, seven days a week, every day of the year. There is a mix of highly skilled professionals and ancillary support staff to work with clients who have complex needs and to maintain a safe environment.

The nurse manager's role in human resources is related to staffing their unit or department. Steps in staffing are:

- Analyzing the staff mix of nurses and unlicensed personnel necessary to meet fiscal plans and carry out a safe and effective client care delivery system.
- Based on the job description, recruiting, interviewing, and selecting nursing staff.
- Orientating and mentoring new staff using established organizational resources.
- Socializing the new staff to the organization and unit norms.
- Scheduling staff creatively to increase productivity and to retain staff.

Legal practice and professional liability

To be safe practitioners, nurses must understand the legal aspects of the nursing profession. Qs

- Understanding the laws governing nursing practice allows nurses to protect client rights and reduce the risk of nursing liability.
- Nurses are accountable for practicing nursing in accordance with the various sources of law affecting nursing practice. It is important that nurses know and comply with these laws. By practicing nursing within the confines of the law, nurses function by...
  - Providing safe, competent care
  - Advocating for clients' rights
  - Providing care that is within the nurse's scope of practice
  - Discerning the responsibilities of nursing in relation to the responsibilities of other members of the health care team
  - Providing care that is consistent with established standards of care
  - Shielding themselves from liability

FEDERAL REGULATIONS

Federal regulations have a great impact on nursing practice. Some of the federal laws affecting nursing practice include the following.

- Health Insurance Portability and Accountability Act (HIPAA)
- Americans with Disabilities Act (ADA)
- Mental Health Parity Act (MHPA)
- Patient Self-Determination Act (PSDA)
- Uniform Anatomical Gift Act (UAGA)
- National Organ Transplant Act (NOTA)
- Emergency Medical Treatment and Active Labor Act (EMTALA)

CRIMINAL AND CIVIL LAWS

Criminal law is a subsection of public law and relates to the relationship of an individual with the government. Violations of criminal law can be categorized as either a felony (a serious crime [e.g., homicide]) or misdemeanor (e.g., a less serious crime [petty theft]). A nurse who falsifies a record to cover up a serious mistake can be found guilty of breaking a criminal law.

Civil laws protect the individual rights of people. One type of civil law that relates to the provision of nursing care is tort law. Torts can be classified as unintentional, quasi-intentional, or intentional.

Unintentional Torts

- Negligence: Practice or misconduct that does not meet expected standards of care and places the client at risk for injury (e.g., a nurse fails to implement safety measures for a client who has been identified as at risk for falls). Qpcc
- Malpractice: Professional negligence (e.g., a nurse administers a large dose of medication due to a calculation error. The client has a cardiac arrest and dies).

Quasi-Intentional Torts

- Invasion of privacy: Intrusion into a client's private affairs or a breach of confidentiality (e.g., a nurse releases the medical diagnosis of a client to a member of the press).
- Defamation: False communication or communication with careless disregard for the truth with the intent to injure an individual's reputation.
  - Libel: Defamation with the written word or photographs (e.g., a nurse documents in a client's health record that a provider is incompetent).
  - Slander: Defamation with the spoken word (e.g., a nurse tells a coworker that she believes a client has been unfaithful to the spouse).

Intentional Torts

- Assault: The conduct of one person makes another person fearful and apprehensive (e.g., threatening to place a nasogastric tube in a client who is refusing to eat).
- Battery: Intentional and wrongful physical contact with a person that involves an injury or offensive contact (e.g., restraining a client and administering an injection against their wishes).
- False imprisonment: A competent person not at risk for injury to self or others is confined or restrained against their will (e.g., using restraints on a competent client to prevent their leaving the health care facility).

STATE LAWS

State laws concerning nursing practice noted in **QUALIFICATIONS AND RULES RELATED TO NURSING LICENSURE AND PRACTICE** area in this chapter

GOOD SAMARITAN LAWS

Good Samaritan laws, which vary from state to state, protect nurses who provide emergency assistance outside of the employment location. The nurse must provide a standard of care that is reasonable and prudent. Qpcc

MALPRACTICE (PROFESSIONAL NEGLIGENCE)

- Malpractice is the failure of a person with professional training to act in a reasonable and prudent manner. The terms "reasonable and prudent" are generally used to describe a person who has the average judgment, foresight, intelligence, and skill that would be expected of a person with similar training and experience. (3.4)
- Professional negligence issues that prompt most malpractice suits include failure to do the following:
  - Follow either professional or facility established standards of care.
  - Use equipment in a responsible and knowledgeable manner.
  - Communicate effectively and thoroughly with the client.
  - Document care that was provided.
- Nurses can avoid being liable for negligence by doing the following:
  - Following standards of care
  - Giving competent care
  - Communicating with other health team members
  - Developing a caring rapport with clients
  - Fully documenting assessments, interventions, and evaluations

3.4 Elements necessary to prove negligence

		EXAMPLE: CLIENT WHO IS A FALL RISK
1.	*Duty to provide care as defined by a standard* Care that should be given or what a reasonably prudent nurse would do	The nurse should complete a fall risk assessment for all clients upon admission, per facility protocol.
2.	*Breach of duty by failure to meet standard* Failure to give the standard of care that should have been given	The nurse does not perform a fall risk assessment during admission.
3.	*Foreseeability of harm* Knowledge that failing to give the proper standard of care can cause harm to the client	The nurse should know that failure to take fall-risk precautions can endanger a client at risk for falls.
4.	*Breach of duty has potential to cause harm (combines elements 2 and 3)* Failure to meet the standard had potential to cause harm; relationship must be provable	If a fall risk assessment is not performed, the client's risk for falls is not determined and the proper precautions are not put in place.
5.	*Harm occurs* Occurrence of actual harm to the client	The client falls out of bed and breaks their hip.

STANDARDS OF CARE (PRACTICE)

- Nurses base practice on established standards of care or legal guidelines for care. These standards of care can be found in the following: Qᴘᴄᴄ
  - The nurse practice act of each state
    - These acts govern nursing practice, and legal guidelines for practice are established and enforced through a state board of nursing or other government agency.
    - Nurse practice acts vary from state to state, making it obligatory for the nurse to be informed about their state's nurse practice act as it defines the legal parameters of practice.
  - Published standards of nursing practice, which are developed by professional organizations (e.g., the American Nurses Association, National Association of Practical Nurse Education and Services, Inc.) and specialty organizations (e.g., the American Association of Critical Care Nurses; Wound, Ostomy and Continence Nurses Society; and Oncology Nurses Society)
  - Accrediting bodies (The Joint Commission)
  - Originally mandated quality assurance programs, which have evolved into quality improvement
  - Sentinel event reporting: "An unexpected occurrence involving death or serious or psychological injury, or the risk thereof"
  - Failure mode and effects analysis, which examines all potential failures in a design, including event sequencing risks, vulnerabilities, and improvement areas
  - National Patient Safety Goals, which augments core measures and promotes client safety through client identification, effective staff communication, safe medication use, infection prevention, safety risk identification, and preventing wrong-site surgery
  - Health care facility policies and procedures
    - Policies and procedures, maintained in the facility's policy and procedure manual, establish the standard of practice for employees of that institution.
    - These manuals provide detailed information about how the nurse should respond to or provide care in specific situations and while performing client care procedures.
    - Nurses who practice according to institutional policy are legally protected if that standard of care still results in an injury. For example, if a client files a complaint with the board of nursing or seeks legal counsel, the nurse who has followed the facility's policies will not usually be charged with misconduct.
    - It is very important that nurses are familiar with their institution's policies and procedures and provide client care in accordance with these policies. For example:
      □ Assess and document findings postoperatively according to institutional policy.
      □ Change IV tubing and flush saline locks according to institutional policy.

- Standards of care guide, define, and direct the level of care that should be given by practicing nurses. They also are used in malpractice lawsuits to determine if that level was maintained.
- Nurses should refuse to practice beyond the legal scope of practice and/or outside of their areas of competence regardless of reason (e.g., staffing shortage, lack of appropriate personnel). Qᴘᴄᴄ
- Nurses should use the formal chain of command to verbalize concerns related to assignment considering current legal scope of practice, job description, and area of competence.

IMPAIRED COWORKERS

- Impaired health care providers pose a significant risk to client safety. Qs
- A nurse who suspects a coworker of using alcohol or other substances while working has a duty to report the coworker to appropriate management personnel as specified by institutional policy. At the time of the infraction, the report should be made to the immediate supervisor (the charge nurse, to ensure client safety).
- Health care facility policies should provide guidelines for handling employees who have a substance use disorder. Many facilities provide peer assistance programs that facilitate entry into a treatment program.
- Each state board of nursing has laws and regulations that govern the disposition of nurses who have been reported secondary to substance use. Depending on the individual case, the boards have the option to require the nurse to enter a treatment program, during which time the nurse's license can be retained, suspended, or revoked. If a nurse is allowed to maintain licensure, there usually are work restrictions put in place (e.g., working in noncritical care areas and being restricted from administering controlled medications QᴘᴄᴄC
- Health care providers who are found guilty of misappropriation of controlled substances also can be charged with a criminal offense consistent with the infraction.
- Behaviors can be difficult to detect if the impaired nurse is experienced at masking the substance use disorder.

BEHAVIORS CONSISTENT WITH A SUBSTANCE USE DISORDER

- Smell of alcohol on breath or frequent use of strong mouthwash or mints
- Impaired coordination, sleepiness, shakiness, and/or slurred speech
- Bloodshot eyes
- Mood swings and memory loss
- Neglect of personal appearance
- Excessive use of sick leave, tardiness, or absences after a weekend off, holiday, or payday
- Frequent requests to leave the unit for short periods of time or to leave the shift early
- Frequently "forgetting" to have another nurse witness wasting of a controlled substance

- Frequent involvement in incidences where a client assigned to the nurse reports not receiving pain medication or adequate pain relief (impaired nurse provides questionable explanations)
- Documenting administration of pain medication to a client who did not receive it or documenting a higher dosage than has been given by other nurses
- Preferring to work the night shift where supervision is less or on units where controlled substances are more frequently given

MANDATORY REPORTING

In certain situations, health care providers have a legal obligation to report their findings in accordance with state law.

ABUSE

- All 51 jurisdictions (50 states and the District of Colombia) have statutes requiring report of suspicion of child abuse. The statutes set out which occupations are mandatory reporters. In many states, nurses are mandatory reporters.
- A number of states also mandate that health care providers, including nurses, report suspected violence of neglect against vulnerable persons (older or dependent adults).
- Nurses are mandated to report any suspicion of mistreatment following facility policy.

COMMUNICABLE DISEASES

- Nurses are also mandated to report to the proper agency (local health department, state health department) when a client is diagnosed with a communicable disease. Qs
- A complete list of reportable diseases and a description of the reporting system are available through the Centers for Disease Control and Prevention Web site. Each state mandates which diseases must be reported in that state. There are more than 60 communicable diseases that must be reported to public health departments to allow officials to do the following.
  - Ensure appropriate medical treatment of diseases (e.g., tuberculosis).
  - Monitor for common-source outbreaks (e.g., foodborne: hepatitis A).
  - Plan and evaluate control and prevention plans (e.g., immunizations for preventable diseases).
  - Identify outbreaks and epidemics.
  - Determine public health priorities based on trends.
  - Educate the community on prevention and treatment of these diseases.

ORGAN DONATION

- Organ and tissue donation is regulated by federal and state laws. Health care facilities have policies and procedures to guide health care workers involved with organ donation.
- Donations can be stipulated in a will or designated on an official card.
- Federal law requires health care facilities to provide access to qualified specialists who make the request to clients and/or family members and provide information regarding consent, organ and tissues that can be donated, and how burial or cremation will be affected by donation.
- Nurses are responsible for answering questions regarding the donation process and for providing emotional support to family members.

TRANSCRIBING MEDICAL PRESCRIPTIONS

- Nurses might need to receive new prescriptions for client care or medications by verbal or telephone prescription.
- When transcribing a prescription into a paper or electronic chart, nurses must do the following:
  - Be sure to include all necessary elements of a prescription: date and time prescription was written; new client care prescription or medication including dosage, frequency, route of administration; and signature of nurse transcribing the prescription as well as the provider who verbally gave the prescription.
  - Follow institutional policy regarding the time frame within which the provider must sign the prescription (usually within 24 hr).
  - Use strategies to prevent errors when taking a medical prescription that is given verbally or over the phone by the provider.
    - Repeat back the prescription given, making sure to include the medication name (spell if necessary), dosage, time, and route. Qs
    - Question any prescription that seems contraindicated due to a previous or concurrent prescription or client condition.

Disruptive behavior

- Nurses experience incivility, lateral violence, and bullying at an alarming rate. The perpetrator can be a provider or a nursing colleague. Consequences of disruptive behavior include poor communication, which can negatively affect client safety and productivity, resulting in absenteeism, decreased job satisfaction, and staff turnover. Some nurses can choose to leave the profession due to these counterproductive behaviors.
- If disruptive behavior is allowed to continue, it is likely to escalate. Over time, it can be viewed as acceptable in that unit's or department's culture.

TYPES OF DISRUPTIVE BEHAVIOR

- Incivility is defined as an action that is rude, intimidating, and insulting. It includes teasing, joking, dirty looks, and uninvited touching.
- Lateral violence is also known as horizontal abuse or horizontal hostility. It occurs between individuals who are at the same level within the organization. For example, a more experienced staff nurse can be abusive to a newly licensed nurse. Common behaviors include verbal abuse, undermining activities, sabotage, gossip, withholding information, and ostracism.
- Bullying behavior is persistent and relentless and is aimed at an individual who has limited ability to defend themselves. Bullying occurs when the perpetrator is at a higher level than the victim (for example, a nurse manager to a staff nurse). It is abuse of power that makes the recipient feel threatened, disgraced, and vulnerable. For example, a nurse manager can demonstrate disfavor for another nurse by making unfair assignments or refusing a promotion.
- Cyberbullying is a type of disruptive behavior using the Internet or other electronic means.

INTERVENTIONS TO DETER DISRUPTIVE BEHAVIORS

- Create an environment of mutual respect among staff.
- Model appropriate behavior.
- Increase staff awareness about disruptive behavior.
- Make staff aware that offensive online remarks about employers and coworkers are a form of bullying and are prohibited even if the nurse is off-duty and it is posted off-site from the facility.
- Avoid making excuses for disruptive behavior.
- Support zero tolerance for disruptive behavior.
- Establish mechanisms for open communication between staff nurses and nurse managers.
- Adopt policies that limit the risk of retaliation when disruptive behavior is reported.

Ethical practice

- Ethics has several definitions, but the foundation of ethics is based on an expected behavior of a certain group in relation to what is considered right and wrong.
- Morals are the values and beliefs held by a person that guide behavior and decision-making.
- Ethical theory analyzes varying philosophies, systems, ideas, and principles used to make judgments about what is right and wrong, good and bad. Two common types of ethical theory are utilitarianism and deontology.
  - Utilitarianism (teleological theory): Decision-making based on what provides the greatest good for the greatest number of individuals
  - Deontological theory: Decision-making based on obligations, duty, and what one considers to be right or wrong
- Unusual or complex ethical issues might need to be dealt with by a facility's ethics committee.

Ethical principles are standards of what is right or wrong regarding important social values and norms. Ethical principles pertaining to the treatment of clients include the following. Qpcc

- Autonomy: The ability of the client to make personal decisions, even when those decisions might not be in the client's own best interest
- Beneficence: Care that is in the best interest of the client
- Fidelity: Keeping one's promise to the client about care that was offered
- Justice: Fair treatment in matters related to physical and psychosocial care and use of resources
- Nonmaleficence: The nurse's obligation to avoid causing harm to the client
- Veracity: The nurse's duty to tell the truth

3.5 The nurse's role in ethical decision-making

	EXAMPLES
An agent for the client facing an ethical decision	Caring for an adolescent client who is deciding whether to undergo an elective abortion even though their parents believe it is wrong
	Discussing options with parents who have to decide whether to consent to a blood transfusion for a child when their religion prohibits such treatment
A decision-maker in regard to nursing practice	Assigning staff nurses a higher client load than recommended because administration has cut the number of nurses per shift
	Witnessing a surgeon discuss only surgical options with a client without informing the client about more conservative measures available

ETHICAL DECISION MAKING FOR NURSING

Ethical dilemmas are problems for which more than one choice can be made, and the choice is influenced by the values and beliefs of the decision-makers. These are common in health care, and nurses must be prepared to apply ethical theory and decision-making.

- A problem is an ethical dilemma if:
  - It cannot be solved solely by a review of scientific data.
  - It involves a conflict between two moral imperatives.
  - The answer will have a profound effect on the situation/client.
- Nurses have a responsibility to be advocates and to identify and report ethical situations. Qpcc
  - Doing so through the chain of command offers some protection against retribution.
  - Some state nurse associations offer protection for nurses who report substandard or unethical practice.
- Ethical decision-making is the process by which a decision is made about an ethical issue. Frequently, this requires a balance between science and morality. There are several steps in ethical decision-making:
  - Identify whether the issue is an ethical dilemma.
  - State the ethical dilemma, including all surrounding issues and individuals involved.
  - List and analyze all possible options for resolving the dilemma and review implications of each option.
  - Select the option that aligns with the ethical principle applicable to this situation, the decision maker's values and beliefs, and the profession's values set forth for client care. Justify why that one option was selected.
  - Apply this decision to the dilemma and evaluate the outcomes.

- The American Nurses Association Code of Ethics for Nurses and the International Council of Nurses' Code of Ethics for Nurses are commonly used by professional nurses. The Code of Ethics for Licensed Practical/ Vocational Nurses issued by the National Association for Practical Nurse Education and Services also serves as a set of standards for Nursing Practice. Codes of ethics are available at the organizations' websites. Qpcc
- The Uniform Determination of Death Act (UDDA) can be used to assist with end-of-life and organ donor issues.
  - The UDDA provides two formal definitions of death that were developed by the National Conference of Commissioners on Uniform State Laws. Death is determined by one of two criteria:
    - Irreversible cessation of circulatory and respiratory functions
    - Irreversible cessation of all functions of the entire brain, including the brain stem
  - A determination of death must be made in accordance with accepted medical standards.

Active Learning Scenario

A nurse is preparing to serve on a committee that will review the policy on disruptive behavior. Use the ATI Active Learning Template: Basic Concept to complete this item.

RELATED CONTENT: Describe another term used for lateral violence.

NURSING INTERVENTIONS: Describe at least four interventions to deter disruptive behavior.

Active Learning Scenario Key

Using the ATI Active Learning Template: Basic Concept

RELATED CONTENT: Lateral violence is also known as horizontal abuse or horizontal hostility.

NURSING INTERVENTIONS
- Create an environment of mutual respect among staff.
- Model appropriate behavior.
- Increase staff awareness about disruptive behavior.
- Make staff aware that offensive online remarks about employers and coworkers are a form of bullying and is prohibited even if the nurse is off-duty and it is posted off-site of the facility.
- Avoid making excuses for disruptive behavior.
- Support zero tolerance for disruptive behavior.
- Establish mechanisms for open communication between staff nurses and nurse managers.
- Adopt policies that limit the risk of retaliation when disruptive behavior is reported.

Ⓝ *NCLEX® Connection: Management of Care, Concepts of Management*

Application Exercises

1. A nurse administrator is creating a presentation about developing an educational program. Place the steps for developing an educational program in the correct order.

   A. Find the current level of knowledge or skills held by staff.

   B. Access the resources you can use to educate staff.

   C. Measure outcomes during the evaluation phase.

   D. Identify the knowledge or skills needed by staff.

   E. Determine the gap between what staff knows and the desired knowledge.

   F. Use the available resources effectively.

2. Match the professional development to the correct definition.

   1. Seek responsibilities
   2. Effective communicator
   3. Feedback from colleagues
   4. Advanced education
   5. Transition to positive positions
   6. Experienced mentors
   7. Proficient in technology
   8. Business knowledge
   9. Engaged learner

   A. Be an engaged learner; keep up with current literature, leadership podcasts, and books; and take courses in leadership topics (business, communication, interprofessional).

   B. Complete a graduate program in nursing administration.

   C. Develop business knowledge.

   D. Seek feedback from your colleagues and supervisors on how you can improve your leadership skills.

   E. Become proficient in technology, software, and informatics.

   F. Become an effective communicator and negotiator and know how to resolve conflict.

   G. Find an experienced nurse leader to be your mentor.

   H. Seek responsibilities in committee and governance leadership and in state and national committee experience.

   I. As you advance to a nurse leader role, look for positions with structure in place to help you transition to that new role.

3. Think about a legislative priority affecting healthcare. Use the space below to construct a practice letter to a senator detailing the influence this issue has on the consumer and the type of change needed to provide safe, quality, patient-centered care to the client.

4. A nurse witnesses an assistive personnel (AP) reprimand a client for not using the urinal properly. The AP threatens to put a diaper on the client if the urinal is not used more carefully next time. Which of the following torts is the AP committing?

   A. Assault

   B. Battery

   C. False imprisonment

   D. Invasion of privacy

5. A newly licensed nurse is preparing to insert an IV catheter in a client. Which of the following sources is most important for the nurse to utilize when reviewing the procedure and the standard at which it should be performed?

   A. Website

   B. Institutional policy and procedure manual

   C. More experienced nurse

   D. State nurse practice act

6. A nurse manager is preparing a presentation on ethical principles. Match the following examples to their respective ethical principles.

   A. A client refuses their scheduled morning medications.

   B. A nurse administers a PRN topical anesthetic prior to inserting a peripheral IV catheter.

   C. A nurse reports their own medication error to the charge nurse.

   D. A nurse reviews with a client their prescribed medications prior to their discharge home.

   E. A nurse manager ensures all personnel receive scheduled breaks.

   F. A nurse manager attends a scheduled appointment with a client's family to discuss end-of-life care.

   1. Autonomy
   2. Beneficence
   3. Fidelity
   4. Justice
   5. Nonmaleficence
   6. Veracity

1. D, A, E, B, F, C

   When taking actions, the nurse should identify that strategically planning faculty development uses steps like the nursing process and NCSBN Clinical Judgment Measurement Model (NCJMM). The nurse should use the following sequence when developing the educational program: 1. Assessing, Recognizing Cues (identifying knowledge) 2. Analysis, Analyze Cues (Find the current level of knowledge) 3. Analysis, Prioritize Hypotheses (Determine the gap) 4. Planning Generate Solutions (Assess resources) 5. Implementation, Take Actions (Use the resources) 6. Evaluation, Evaluate Outcomes (Measure outcomes).

   (N) *NCLEX® Connection: Management of Care,*
   Concepts of Management

2. A, 9; B, 4; C, 8; D, 3; E, 7; F, 2; G, 6; H, 1; I, 5

   (N) *NCLEX® Connection: Management of Care,*
   Concepts of Management

3. When constructing your letter, include a return address, date, the senator's address, and a salutation. Introduce yourself as a constituent of your state and identify your profession (Registered Nurse). Include information about why you are writing your senator. Ask for a response and thank your senator for their time. Close with your name.

   (N) *NCLEX® Connection: Management of Care,*
   Concepts of Management

4. A. **CORRECT:** When recognizing cues, the nurse should identify that assault is conduct that makes a person fear they will be harmed.
   B. Battery is physical contact without a person's consent.
   C. False imprisonment is restraining a person against their will. It includes the use of physical or chemical restraints and refusing to allow a client to leave a facility.
   D. Invasion of privacy is the unauthorized release of a client's private information.

   (N) *NCLEX® Connection: Management of Care,*
   Concepts of Management

5. A. A website might not provide information that is consistent with institutional policy.
   B. **CORRECT:** When generating solutions, the nurse should identify that the institutional policy and procedure manual will provide instructions on how to perform the procedure that is consistent with established standards. This is the resource that should be used.
   C. A more experienced nurse on the unit might not perform the procedure according to the policy and procedure manual.
   D. The nurse practice act identifies scope of practice and other aspects of the law, but it does not set standards for performance of a procedure.

   (N) *NCLEX® Connection: Management of Care,*
   Advance Directives/Self-Determination/Life Planning

6. A, 1; B, 5; C, 6; D, 2; E, 4; F, 3

   When generating solutions, the nurse should identify that autonomy involves respecting the client's wishes and decisions, such as when a client refuses their scheduled medication. Beneficence is the duty to promote goodness when caring for the client. When a nurse reviews with a client their prescribed medications prior to their discharge home, they are promoting goodness and kindness. Fidelity is the agreement to keep a commitment to someone. A nurse who attends a scheduled appointment with a client's family is practicing fidelity. Justice is equal distribution of resource, such as when a nurse manager ensures all personnel receive their scheduled breaks. Nonmaleficence is the duty to not cause harm to the client. When the nurse administers a topical anesthetic prior to inserting an IV, they are promoting nonmaleficence by attempting to minimize pain during a potential painful procedure. Veracity is being truthful when communicating. When the nurse reports their own medication error to the nurse manager, they are practicing the principle of veracity.

   (N) *NCLEX® Connection: Management of Care,*
   Concepts of Management

When reviewing the following chapter, keep in mind the relevant topics and tasks of the NCLEX outline, in particular:

Management of Care

CASE MANAGEMENT: Initiate, evaluate, and update client plan of care.

CONTINUITY OF CARE

Perform procedures necessary to safely admit, transfer and/or discharge a client.

Follow up on unresolved issues regarding client care (e.g., laboratory results, client requests).

Safety and Infection Control

ACCIDENT/ERROR/INJURY PREVENTION: Determine client/staff member knowledge of safety procedures.

Inclusive and Evidence-Based Care Environment

A caring and inclusive environment provides equal access to resources for people who might not have that opportunity because of disability, ethnicity, gender, geographical location, or financial situation. This chapter recognizes aspects of caring, culture, equity, diversity, inclusivity, and evidence-based practice in providing a safe and effective care environment that respects and values clients and healthcare personnel.

PROMOTING EQUITY AND INCLUSIVITY

CARING

Caring is a core concept of nursing. It is an understanding and connection between nurse and client. The ANA Code of Ethics Provision 1 notes that the nurse "practices with compassion and respect for the inherent dignity, worth, and unique attributes of every person."

The National Council of State Boards of Nurses (NCSBN) includes caring as one of the integrated processes described as fundamental to the practice of nursing. Caring is integrated throughout the NCLEX test plans. It is defined as the nurse and client interacting with respect and trust with the nurse providing support and compassion. Qpcc

What does caring look like? The attributes of caring according to Sister Simone Roach illustrate how a caring nurse appears in the Seven Cs of Caring.

CULTURALLY CONGRUENT PRACTICE

The ANA included culturally congruent practice for the first time in the 2015 Scope and Standards of Practice. Standard 8 states, "The registered nurse practices in a manner that is congruent with cultural diversity and inclusion principles." Culturally congruent practice is further described as applying evidence-based practice with the clients' cultural values and practices for the goal of reducing health disparities.

Nurses practicing culturally congruent practice have a level of cultural humility demonstrated by incorporating self-evaluation throughout one's life of personal bias, addressing inequities in healthcare, and developing partnerships that work with communities in a mutually beneficial way to support defined populations. Qpcc

POPULATION TRENDS

The United States population has experienced an increase in minority and older populations as seen in the 2019 projections by the U.S. Census Bureau. In some cities, minorities now comprise over half of the population. Currently, minorities encompass 37% of the U.S. population, but that is expected to rise to 57% of the population in 2060. Persons 65 and older are projected to rise from 16% to 23% in 2060. In addition, older adults are working longer.

Federally defined minority groups:

- Asian American
- Black or African American
- Hispanic or Latino
- Native Hawaiian and other Pacific Islander
- Indigenous Peoples and Alaska Native

ECONOMIC AND SOCIAL CHANGES

Problems such as increased unemployment, homelessness, and poverty, as well as decreased access to health insurance and healthcare, can be linked to changing world economics. The anxiety and depression that are linked to these problems are associated with increased mental health illnesses such as anxiety/depression, substance abuse, and violence.

The opportunities for education, employment, and property ownership that are accessible to upper- and middle-class Americans are often unattainable for people of minority groups who are more frequently in a lower socioeconomic class. In the U.S., the percentage of those living in poverty in 2019 was greater than 12%.

The environment of minority populations can be consistent with poverty. Housing, schools, and recreational facilities are different for people in the suburbs versus those in the inner city. Substandard environments lead to a continuation of the cycle of poverty for many people.

Economic and social change is increasing acts of violence in schools, churches, and playgrounds. Young men in poverty are more prone to high unemployment rates and high rates of violence. Young women ages 15 to 24 are subject to intimate partner violence, which is not specific to any ethnic, racial, socioeconomic, or educational group. Attitudes toward culturally diverse groups range from hate and violence to respect and celebration. Ignorance tends to cause fear and prejudice, while an attempt to learn about others is integral to achieving culturally competent care.

The 2019 ANA Position Statement: Nursing Advocacy for LGBTQ+ Populations sets forth its position on delivering culturally congruent care to lesbian, gay, bisexual, transgender, queer, and other sexual orientations (LGBTQ+). Discrimination against LGBTQ+ individuals remains an issue in society and in healthcare environments. Types of discrimination, societal stigma, and disrespect for human rights cause decreased access to healthcare for the LGBTQ+ population.

SOCIAL DETERMINANTS OF HEALTH

Social determinants of health are circumstances that can result in health inequities. Typically, the lower the socioeconomic level, the worse the health consequences. Social determinants of health are the conditions in which people live, work, play, and worship. Q SDoH

The U.S. Department of Health and Human Services categorizes the social determinants of health into five domains: 1. Neighborhood and built environment; 2. Healthcare access and quality; 3. Social and community context; 4. Education access and quality; and 5. Economic stability.

The list below compiled by the World Health Organization (WHO) contains examples of the social determinants of health that can influence health equity.

- Employment and income or unemployment and job insecurity
- Education adequate for employment or low level of education
- Positive or negative working life environment
- Adequate food or food insecurity
- Good or poor housing, basic amenities, and the environment
- Good or poor early childhood development
- Social inclusion and non-discrimination or social exclusion and discrimination
- Good access or poor access to affordable health services of decent quality

To reduce inequities in health and improve health along all social sectors, society needs to address social determinants of health. Systemic change needs to occur. Identifying disparities involves research at many levels, including local levels, to determine where the gaps in healthcare are located. Lack of data is often identified as an obstacle in understanding healthcare inequalities. Some examples of the negative side of the social determinants of health are lack of insurance coverage and disparities in outcome data, such as chronic conditions, infant mortality, and mental health risks. Nurses are responsible for assessing for possible negative consequences of social determinants of health and implementing strategies to promote health. Q SDoH

4.1 Case Study – Social Determinants of Health – Healthcare access and quality

Scenario Introduction

Mabel is a sixteen-year-old client living in a rural area of the country who has been diagnosed with stage II uterine cancer. The operation to remove Mabel's ovaries and uterus was done seven days ago. Emily is a nurse at the local rural clinic who is caring for Mabel. Anne is Mabel's mother. Emily is discussing treatment plans with both Mabel and Anne.

Scene 1

Emily: "Mabel, your chemotherapy appointments will be at the Metropolis Medical Center (located 155 miles to the east) on Tuesdays, and then your oncologist will see you there on Thursdays for six weeks."

Anne: "I don't know how we are going to be able to make that trip twice each week. Can Mabel get the chemotherapy here at the clinic?"

Emily: "Currently, the local facility that administers chemotherapy has temporarily stopped services because of a staffing shortage. Can you tell me your concerns about making the trip for Mabel's chemotherapy?"

Anne: "I have to work, and it's going to be hard for me to take off twice per week. I really don't have reliable transportation to drive long distances."

Emily: "I understand this is going to be difficult for you. Do you have any friends or relatives who can assist with driving?"

Anne: "No, I don't have anyone who can assist with driving; most of our friends and relatives live about 30 miles from here. I am really frustrated at the lack of available services here. I've checked into several resources, and most don't service this area. There are no rides or support groups."

Emily: "I can understand your frustration, and I hear this from many people. I have contacted Metropolis Medical Center, and they don't provide transportation or support groups in this area. I will do all that I can to help you get the services you need."

Scene 2

Mabel: "Mom, I know how hard it is getting me to all of these out-of-town appointments while trying to work and keep your job too. I feel so guilty."

Anne: "Mabel, it's not your fault. We will work this out; don't worry. I just wish there were more options here."

Scene 3

Mabel: "Emily, I would like to talk to someone about what this means for my future and how to deal with my feelings about never being able to get pregnant."

Anne: "Is there a mental health provider who does this type of counseling locally?"

Emily: "No, I'm sorry. There is no one here that does that. I will see if I can set this up when you are at Metropolis for your other treatment."

Scenario Conclusion

- Nurse Emily consulted with Mabel's oncologist about Anne's concerns and was able to get the chemotherapy scheduled for once weekly, which was better for Anne.
- What other options are there for specialists to provide healthcare in rural areas? What difficulty may there be in finding a support group? Where may the client find one? What other information could the nurse gather related to social determinants of health? Q SDoH

Case Study Exercise

1. Which of the following social determinants of health (SDOH) domains should Nurse Emily address with Mabel and Anne?

   A. Neighborhood and built environment

   B. Healthcare access and quality

   C. Social and community context

   D. Economic stability

   E. Education access and quality

Promoting equity in education

Nursing education program leaders are working to identify minority faculty recruitment strategies. Some of these strategies are same culture mentoring and consultants to promote culturally competent care.

The report from the National Academy of Medicine, The Future of Nursing 2020-2030: Charting a Path to Health Equity summarizes that nurse educators should do the following to empower the next generation of nurses to address health equity:

- Content on social determinants of health and health equity should not be taught in just a few of the courses but rather throughout the nursing program.
- Extend learning opportunities on the social determinants of health to community clinical opportunities.
- Identify racism in the classroom and provide inclusive learning opportunities.
- Recruit, support, and mentor faculty and students from diverse backgrounds. ◯PCC

RECRUITING AND RETAINING A DIVERSE WORKFORCE

The AACN Fact Sheet Enhancing Diversity in the Nursing Workforce notes a link between a diverse nursing workforce and the ability to provide culturally competent care. More underrepresented groups in nursing need to be recruited into the profession. The U.S. Census Bureau is projecting that minority populations will become the majority in the next 30 years. There were only 19.2% of nurses from minority backgrounds in the nursing workforce in 2017. Men accounted for only 9.1% of nurses. Recruiting more diverse nurses can also help to alleviate the nursing shortage.

Aging Workforce and Retention: To support age diversity in nursing practice, some things that may keep the older nurse practicing longer are:

- Flexible scheduling
- Preceptor positions
- Positive relations between nurses of all ages
- Better ergonomics
- Improved environmental design of the workplace to decrease time walking
- Strategic placement of aids such as mechanical lifts, decentralized supply storage, and better lighting

To support recruitment and retention for all nurses, the following areas need to be attractive:

- Nursing salaries
- Work environment
- Safe staffing with no floating or mandatory overtime

Specific areas to address for diversity in the nursing workforce are:

- Education of anyone associated with the hiring process about implicit bias.
- Following a standard process in the hiring process that levels the playing field.
- Advertisement in new areas with diverse audiences to increase the diversity of your applicants.
- Encouraging minorities to pursue careers in healthcare.

EVIDENCE-BASED PRACTICE AND RESEARCH

Evidence-based practice (EBP) is the use of current knowledge from research and other credible sources, on which to base clinical judgment and client care. ◯EBP

OVERVIEW OF EBP

The ANA Code of Ethics for Nurses states in Provision 7, "The nurse, in all roles and settings, advances the profession through research and scholarly inquiry, professional standards development, and the generation of both nursing and health policy."

The Essentials of Nursing: Core Competencies for Nursing Education (2021) includes Domain 4: Scholarship for the Nursing Discipline. The basic critical key for nurses is to be able to critique current research and understand how it is applied or can be applied to nursing knowledge.

Entry-level professional nursing competencies are:

- 4.1: Advance the scholarship of nursing
- 4.2: Integrate best evidence into nursing practice
- 4.3: Promote the ethical conduct of scholarly activities
- The term "evidence-based" can be used alternatively with "research-based."
- Nurses need to understand how best practices and EBP are used to improve the quality of care.
- Administrative support is key in making changes in policy for EBP and accessing resources.
- Organizational support is important in creating a climate where long-standing practices may be uprooted with new evidence.
- Accrediting bodies are starting to see EBP as a standard.

STRATEGIES FOR THE NEW NURSE TO USE TO PROMOTE EBP

- Use data gathering resources to stay current with new evidence – professional journal, textbooks, experts in the field, and colleagues. ◯EBP
- Use multiple resources to gather evidence on a topic.
- Support clinical interventions and teaching strategies with evidence.
- Use resources that have already been established in your area of specialty to find current evidence.
- Use nationally sanctioned clinical practice guidelines when implementing and evaluating your practice.
- Promote spirits of inquiry and risk-taking in questioning and then challenging longstanding nursing traditions.

- Do not subscribe to myths or traditions that are not supported by evidence.
- Widen your network and collaborate with nurses on a local and global level.
- Practice interdisciplinary collaboration to bring nursing evidence to play in decision-making.

POSITIVE CONSEQUENCES OF USING EBP

- Client outcomes are improved.
- Cost of care is lower.
- Delivery of high-quality care

COMPETENCIES OF THE NURSE ADMINISTRATOR IN INTEGRATING EVIDENCE AND RESEARCH INTO PRACTICE

ANA Nursing Administration Scope and Standards of Practice lists the following:
- Use EBP to guide administrative practice; incorporate evidence when making change.
- Encourage and enable staff and colleagues to engage in research; provide available resources.
- Program a positive climate for collaborative research and clinical inquiry.
- Achieve better client outcomes by promoting use of evidence at the consumer level.
- Advocate for the use of ethical principles of research.
- Evaluate outcome evidence to improve quality of care.
- Disseminate research findings.

USE OF THE EVIDENCE-BASED APPROACH

- Cultivate a spirit of inquiry.
- Ask a clinical question – A PICOT format is commonly used to search for the evidence needed to solve a problem. Q EBP
  - P – Patient or population
  - I – Intervention or interest area
  - C – Comparison
  - O – Outcome
  - T – Time
- Search for the best evidence for your question.
- Evaluate the evidence—look at validity, reliability, and applicability.
- Use the evidence, your clinical expertise and patient preferences and values in making a decision on whether to change practice.
- Use an evaluation process to measure outcomes of the change—did the change positively or negatively affect practice?
- Disseminate the outcomes.

RESEARCH-BASED ETHICAL ISSUE
- To protect the ethical rights of participants in a research study, a committee called an institutional review board (IRB) is consulted.
- An informed consent must be obtained for most studies that explains the study and assures participants of their rights.

All nurses should have a basic understanding of EBP and a willingness to utilize current evidence in their practice. Facilitation of an environment that supports EBP is a role for nurse administrators. Nurses that conduct the research should be supported by collaborative arrangements with healthcare agencies and academia. Policy makers need to be informed so health policy can be changed or created as applicable. Finally, the healthcare consumer must be educated so evidence becomes part of a system where the client is able to more knowledgeably self-direct their care. Q EBP

4.3 Evidence-based practice blockers

- Lack of knowledge about EBP
- Not empowered to make changes to practice
- Lack of time and resources to research and analyze
- Lack of support from administration

4.4 Evidence-based practice promoters

- Knowledge of how to incorporate EBP
- Time and resources needed to research and analyze
- Support from administration
- Presence of EBP policies and procedures

Active Learning Scenario

A nurse manager is preparing to discuss social determinants of health with a group of newly licensed nurses. List the information that should be included in the discussion for social determinants of health. Use the ATI Active Learning Template: Basic Concept to complete this item.

UNDERLYING PRINCIPLES

- Identify 5 social determinants of health that can influence a client's health status.
- List 2 characteristics or behaviors within each health determinant.

Application Exercises

1. Match the examples of the caring nurse to the Seven Cs of Caring.

   1. Creative thinking
   2. Competent
   3. Compassionate
   4. Commitment
   5. Confident
   6. Conscientious
   7. Comportment

   A. Committed to assuring the delivery of excellent care

   B. Comportment in communicating a caring presence through professional behaviors and appearance

   C. Compassionate care in being with another in their suffering; understanding and empathy

   D. Conscientiousness in adhering to the standards of practice as an accountable and responsible nurse

   E. Competence in the knowledge, skill, and attitude a nurse exhibits in their role

   F. Confidence in self and ability to understand another person's life

   G. Creativity in critically thinking and using the imagination to gain new insights in how to provide care

2. A nurse manager is developing a presentation about delivering culturally congruent care. Which of the following are consistent with the practice of culturally congruent care? (Select all that apply.)

   A. Critiquing the biases of others
   B. Addressing inequities in healthcare
   C. Partnering with a majority population to make community decisions
   D. Promoting shared decision-making healthcare solutions
   E. Assessing own personal biases

3. A nurse manager is providing education to a newly licensed nurse. What strategies should the nurse manager include when educating about the use of evidence-based practice (EBP) in the workplace?

4. A nurse manager is providing education about the use of evidence-based practice (EBP) in the workplace to a newly licensed nurse. What are three positive outcomes the nurse manager should identify when using EBP?

Case Study Exercise Key

1. B. **CORRECT:** Nurse Emily should address the SDOH domain of healthcare access and quality with Mabel and their mother. The nurse should identify that individuals who live in rural locations have difficulty accessing quality healthcare. Anne reported concerns about the inability of getting their child to their appointments and decrease of local health care resources. Therefore, it is important for Nurse Emily to listen to their concerns, be supportive, and try to find resources to assist with meeting their needs.

   (N) *NCLEX® Connection: Management of Care, Advocacy*

Application Exercises Key

1. A, 4; B, 7; C, 3; D, 6; E, 2; F, 5; G, 1

   (N) *NCLEX® Connection: Management of Care, Concepts of Management*

2. A. Nurses practicing culturally congruent care have a level of cultural humility demonstrated by incorporating self-evaluation throughout one's life of personal bias.
   B. **CORRECT:** Nurses practicing culturally congruent care have a level of cultural humility demonstrated by addressing inequities in healthcare.
   C. Nurses practicing culturally congruent care have a level of cultural humility demonstrated by developing partnerships that work with communities in a mutually beneficial way to support defined populations.
   D. **CORRECT:** Nurses practicing culturally congruent care have a level of cultural humility demonstrated by promoting shared healthcare-making decisions.
   E. **CORRECT:** Nurses practicing culturally congruent care have a level of cultural humility demonstrated by incorporating self-evaluation throughout one's life of personal bias.

   (N) *NCLEX® Connection: Management of Care, Concepts of Management*

3. When taking actions, the nurse manager should encourage the newly licensed nurse to use multiple data gathering resources to stay current and gather evidence on a topic. Use evidence to support clinical interventions. Use nationally sanctioned clinical practice guidelines. Network and collaborate with local and global nurses to support the use of EBP.

   (N) *NCLEX® Connection: Management of Care, Information Technology*

4. When taking actions, the nurse manager should identify that the use of EBP leads to improved client outcomes, lower cost of care, and high-quality care.

   (N) *NCLEX® Connection: Management of Care, Information Technology*

Active Learning Scenario Key

Using the ATI Active Learning Template: Basic Concept

UNDERLYING PRINCIPLES

- Social determinants of health factors include:
  ○ Neighborhood and built environment: Safe air quality, safe living environment, and crime rate.
  ○ Healthcare access and quality: Access to health services and use of health-related services, and delivery of quality healthcare.
  ○ Social and community context: a high social standing within the community, a low social standing within the community, access to community events, and family; friends, and community that support culture, values, and beliefs of the client.
  ○ Education access and quality: No education, low education, high education, and availability of quality schools.
  ○ Economic stability: Jobs/occupations that provide a low income, jobs/occupations that provide a high income, and jobs/occupations that provide dependable work hours.

   (N) *NCLEX® Connection: Management of Care, Concepts of Management*

When reviewing the following chapter, keep in mind the relevant topics and tasks of the NCLEX outline, in particular:

Safety and Infection Control

EMERGENCY RESPONSE PLAN

Use clinical decision–making/critical thinking for emergency response plan.

Determine which client(s) to recommend for discharge in a disaster situation.

REPORTING OF INCIDENT/EVENT/IRREGULAR OCCURRENCE/ VARIANCE

Evaluate response to error/event/occurrence.

Identify need/situation where reporting of incident/event/irregular occurrence/variance is appropriate.

SECURITY PLAN

Apply principles of triage and evacuation procedures/protocols.

Follow security plan and procedures (e.g., newborn nursery security, violence, controlled access).

CHAPTER 5 Culture of Safety in Delivering Care

Maintaining a safe environment refers to the precautions and considerations required to ensure that physical environments are safe for clients and staff. Qs

Knowing how to maintain client safety has been identified by the Institute of Medicine as a competency that graduates of nursing programs must possess.

Common errors in health care are related to medication errors, errors related to diagnostic testing, surgical errors, health care-acquired infection, and errors in hand-off reporting and care.

Quality and Safety Education for Nurses (QSEN) faculty propose that nursing education focus not only on the knowledge needed to provide safe care but also on the skills and attitudes that accompany this competency.

To maintain a safe environment, nurses must have knowledge, skills, and attitudes about QSEN competencies, handling infectious and hazardous materials, safe use of equipment, accident and injury prevention, home safety, and ergonomic principles.

Culture of safety

- A culture of safety is one that promotes openness and error reporting. Developing a culture of safety often results in a lower number of adverse events.
- Facilities should have a risk management department to help identify hazards, prevent adverse events, track the occurrence of negative client incidents, and manage hazards.
- There are several types of events that are reported and tracked under risk management programs.

Service occurrences relate to client services, and can include a slight delay in service or an unsatisfactory service.

Near misses are situations where a negative outcome almost occurs (an accident, illness, or injury).

Serious incidents reported include minor injuries, loss of equipment or property, or a significant service interrupted.

Sentinel events refer to unexpected death, major physical or psychological injury, or situations where there was a direct risk of either of these. Major investigation is required in the case of sentinel events. Sentinel events are classified as one of the following occurring within the facility.

- Major loss of function or death that was not expected with the client's medical condition
- Client attempted suicide during round-the-clock care, a hemolytic transfusion reaction, wrong site or wrong client surgical procedures, rape, infant abduction, or discharge to the wrong family.

Failure to rescue is the most severe, and describes a situation where the client develops a complication that leads to death. In failure to rescue situations, there were client indicators that were missed by one or more health care personnel that indicated that a complication was occurring.

QSEN competencies in nursing programs

Concern about the quality and safety of health care in the U.S. has prompted numerous reports and initiatives designed to address this issue. Data from the Joint Commission identify poor communication as a key factor in the majority of sentinel events. The Institute of Medicine (IOM) report *To Err is Human: Building a Safer Health System* (1999) spoke to the frequency of unnecessary deaths and preventable medical errors, and identified system failure as a major factor. Subsequent publications pointed to the need to redesign the provision of client care and improve education of students in health care programs.

The QSEN project identified specific competencies to include in each prelicensure nursing curriculum. These six competencies are now integral components of the curriculum of many nursing programs in the United States.

Q**pcc** PATIENT-CENTERED CARE: The provision of caring, compassionate, and culturally sensitive care that addresses clients' physiological, psychological, sociological, spiritual, and cultural needs, preferences, and values

Q**tc** TEAMWORK AND COLLABORATION: The delivery of client care in partnership with multidisciplinary members of the health care team to achieve continuity of care and positive client outcomes

Q**ebp** EVIDENCE-BASED PRACTICE: The use of current knowledge from research and other credible sources on which to base clinical judgment and client care

Q**qi** QUALITY IMPROVEMENT: Care-related and organizational processes that involve the development and implementation of a plan to improve health care services and better meet clients' needs

Q**s** SAFETY: The minimization of risk factors that could cause injury or harm while promoting quality care and maintaining a secure environment for clients, self, and others

Q**i** INFORMATICS: The use of information technology as a communication and information-gathering tool that supports clinical decision-making and scientifically-based nursing practice

Handling infectious and hazardous materials

- Handling infectious and hazardous materials refers to infection control procedures and precautions for handling toxic, radioactive, or other hazardous materials. Q**s**
- Safety measures are taken to protect the client, nurse, and other personnel and individuals from harmful materials and organisms.

INFECTION CONTROL

Infection control is extremely important to prevent cross-contamination of communicable organisms and health care-associated infections.

- Staff education on infection prevention and control is a responsibility of the nurse.
- Facility policies and procedures should serve as resources for proper implementation of infection prevention and control.
- Any client who is suspected of having or is known to have a communicable disease should be placed in the appropriate type of isolation.
- The nurse should ensure that appropriate equipment is available and that isolation procedures are properly carried out by all health care team members.
- Use of standard precautions by all members of the health care team should be enforced. Employees should have non-latex gloves (nitrile or vinyl) made available to them. Facilities avoid the use of latex products to eliminate the risk of allergic reactions related to latex allergies.

- Facilities should provide resources for employees to perform hand hygiene in client care areas.
- Health care team members should use securely tied, moisture-resistant bags for disposing of soiled items. To remain cost-effective, items should only be double-bagged if the outside of a bag becomes contaminated.
- The nurse should use safety needles or needle-less IV systems to prevent client and staff injuries from improper manipulation. Q**s**
- The nurse should dispose of biomedical waste in sharps containers immediately after use.
- If a needlestick occurs, the nurse should report it to facility risk management in accordance with facility policy and state law. An incident or occurrence report should also be filed. Most policies include testing of the client and nurse for bloodborne illnesses (e.g., hepatitis and human immunodeficiency virus [HIV]).
- Four levels of precautions (standard, airborne, droplet, and contact) are recommended for individuals who come into contact with clients carrying infectious organisms. Precautions consistent with the infectious organism should be followed as indicated.
- Members of the health care team must clean and maintain equipment that is shared by clients on a unit (e.g., blood pressure cuffs, thermometers, pulse oximeters).
- The health care team should keep designated equipment in the rooms of clients who are on contact precautions.

HAZARDOUS MATERIALS

- Nurses and other members of the health care team are at risk for exposure to hazardous materials.
- Employees have the right to refuse to work in hazardous working conditions if there is a clear threat to their health.
- Health care team members should follow occupational safety and health guidelines as set by the Occupational Safety and Health Administration (OSHA).
  - Provide each employee a work environment that is free from recognized hazards that can cause or are likely to cause death or serious physical harm.
  - Make protective gear accessible to employees working under hazardous conditions or with hazardous materials (e.g., antineoplastic medications, sterilization chemicals).
  - Provide measurement devices, and keep records that document an employee's level of exposure over time to hazardous materials (e.g., radiation from x-rays).
  - Provide education and recertification opportunities to each employee regarding these rules and regulations for handling hazardous materials.
  - Provide a manual containing safety data sheets (SDSs) to every workplace and provide safety information (level of toxicity, handling and storage guidelines, and first aid and containment measures to take in case of accidental release of toxic, radioactive, or other dangerous materials). This manual should be available to all employees and can be housed in a location such as the emergency department of a hospital.
  - Designate an institutional hazardous materials (HAZMAT) response team that responds to hazardous events.

5.1 Example incident report

H | Health Care Providers

INCIDENT REPORT
This form should not be placed in the medical record or copied

1234 Main Street
Shermer, IL 12345
1.800.555.1234

Name of person completing form: _____

Provider(s): _____
_____

Date of incident: _____

Time of incident: _____

Date form completed: _____

Location (select one)
Floor/Unit: _____   Room #: _____

- [ ] Administrative Office
- [ ] Ambulatory
- [ ] Birthing Suite
- [ ] Blood Bank
- [ ] Cafeteria
- [ ] Cardiac Cath
- [ ] Central Supply
- [ ] Client's Restroom
- [ ] Client's Room
- [ ] Dialysis
- [ ] EEG
- [ ] Elevator
- [ ] Other: _____

- [ ] Emergency Department
- [ ] Extended Care Facility
- [ ] Home
- [ ] ICU
- [ ] Labor & Delivery
- [ ] Laboratory
- [ ] Lobby
- [ ] Medical Records
- [ ] Medication Room
- [ ] Mental Health
- [ ] Nuclear Medicine
- [ ] Nursery

- [ ] Nurses Station
- [ ] Obstetrics
- [ ] Operating Room
- [ ] Parking Areas
- [ ] Pathology
- [ ] Pharmacy
- [ ] Public Restroom
- [ ] Radiology
- [ ] Recovery Room
- [ ] Rehab/Therapy
- [ ] Same Day Surgery
- [ ] Stairs

Person affected by incident (select one)

- [ ] Employee
- [ ] Home patient
- [ ] In-patient
- [ ] Out-patient
- [ ] Provider

- [ ] Visitor
- [ ] Volunteer
- [ ] Not applicable
- [ ] Other:

List below information if not a client
Last name: _____
First name: _____
Sex: _____
Age, DOB: _____

Staff most closely involved in event (select one)

- [ ] Intern
- [ ] Practical Nurse
- [ ] Medical Student
- [ ] Patient Care Assistant
- [ ] Pharmacist
- [ ] Physician
- [ ] Registered Nurse
- [ ] Resident Physician

- [ ] Security
- [ ] Student Nurse
- [ ] Surgical Assistant
- [ ] Technician
- [ ] Therapist
- [ ] Volunteer
- [ ] Administrative
- [ ] Environmental

- [ ] EMS
- [ ] Physician Assistant
- [ ] Certified Registered Nurse Anesthetist
- [ ] Certified Registered Nurse Practitioner
- [ ] Not applicable
- [ ] Other: _____

Site of injury (select one)

- [ ] Abdomen
- [ ] Ankle(s)
- [ ] Arm(s)
- [ ] Back
- [ ] Buttocks
- [ ] Chest

- [ ] Ear(s)
- [ ] Elbow(s)
- [ ] Eye(s)
- [ ] Face
- [ ] Foot (Feet)
- [ ] Hand(s)

- [ ] Head
- [ ] Hip(s)
- [ ] Internal Injury
- [ ] Knee(s)
- [ ] Leg(s)
- [ ] Mouth

- [ ] Neck
- [ ] Nose
- [ ] Shoulder(s)
- [ ] Wrist(s)
- [ ] Not applicable
- [ ] Other: _____

Condition of the client prior to incident (select one)

- [ ] Agitated
- [ ] Alert
- [ ] Confused
- [ ] Disoriented

- [ ] Dizzy
- [ ] Faint
- [ ] Medicated
- [ ] Unconscious

- [ ] Uncooperative
- [ ] Weak
- [ ] Not applicable
- [ ] Other: _____

Incident report   **1**

Health Care Providers · INCIDENT REPORT

Description of incident (select one)

- ☐ Abrasion
- ☐ Abscess
- ☐ Amputation
- ☐ Birth injury
- ☐ Brain damage
- ☐ Burn - chemical
- ☐ Burn - electrical
- ☐ Burn - other
- ☐ Circulatory impairment
- ☐ Coma
- ☐ Concussion
- ☐ Contracture
- ☐ Contusion
- ☐ Damage to property

- ☐ Death
- ☐ Decubitus
- ☐ Dislocation
- ☐ Edema
- ☐ Foreign body
- ☐ Fracture
- ☐ Hematoma
- ☐ Hemorrhage
- ☐ Hives
- ☐ Hyperthermia
- ☐ Hypothermia
- ☐ Infection
- ☐ Inflammation
- ☐ Injury to teeth

- ☐ Laceration
- ☐ Loss of property
- ☐ Miscarriage
- ☐ Necrosis
- ☐ Obstruction
- ☐ Pain
- ☐ Paralysis
- ☐ Perforation
- ☐ Permanent disfigurement
- ☐ Poisoning
- ☐ Rape
- ☐ Rash
- ☐ Redness
- ☐ Self-inflicted injury

- ☐ Sensory impairment
- ☐ Skin puncture
- ☐ Skin tear
- ☐ Spinal damage
- ☐ Sprain
- ☐ Strain
- ☐ Suicide
- ☐ Wound disruption

- ☐ Not applicable
- ☐ Other: _____

Seen/treated by (select one)

- ☐ Attending provider
- ☐ Emergency department
- ☐ Nurse (provider notified - no prescription received)

- ☐ On-call provider
- ☐ Not applicable
- ☐ Other: _____

Treatment after incident (select one)

- ☐ Received
- ☐ Refused
- ☐ Unknown
- ☐ Not applicable

Quality information (select all that apply)

Transcription error involved?   ☐ Yes   ☐ No

- ☐ **Procedure**
- ☐ Adverse outcome
- ☐ Application/removal of cast/sprint
- ☐ Break in sterile technique
- ☐ Client tolerance
- ☐ Client refusal
- ☐ Consent - improper
- ☐ Consent - lack of
- ☐ Delay in reporting results
- ☐ Delay in treatment
- ☐ Error in reporting result
- ☐ Other: _____

- ☐ **Diagnostic test**
- ☐ Foreign object left in patient
- ☐ Hemorrhage
- ☐ Inappropriate operation
- ☐ Inappropriate time/sequence
- ☐ Incorrect utensil count
- ☐ Lost/mishandled specimen
- ☐ Monitoring
- ☐ Not prescribed
- ☐ Omitted
- ☐ Perforation

- ☐ **Treatment related**
- ☐ Positioning
- ☐ Return to OR during same admission
- ☐ Surgical checklist not completed
- ☐ Transfer/moving of client
- ☐ Wrong client
- ☐ Wrong procedure
- ☐ Wrong site
- ☐ Wrong test
- ☐ Wrong treatment
- ☐ Unknown

- ☐ **Medication**
- ☐ Break in sterile technique
- ☐ Client refusal
- ☐ Consent - improper
- ☐ Consent - lack of
- ☐ Contaminated
- ☐ Contraindicated
- ☐ Cross-match/typing error
- ☐ Delay in administration
- ☐ Discontinued by client
- ☐ Drug interaction
- ☐ Duplicated
- ☐ Food interaction
- ☐ Given after discontinued
- ☐ Given without Prescription
- ☐ Inappropriate anesthetic
- ☐ Inappropriate site

- ☐ **Blood**
- ☐ Incomplete additives
- ☐ Incompatible blood
- ☐ Incorrect narcotic count
- ☐ Infiltration requiring treatment
- ☐ IV conscious sedation with reversal agent given
- ☐ Medication given before culture
- ☐ Mislabeled
- ☐ Out of date
- ☐ Omission
- ☐ Reaction - blood
- ☐ Reaction - correct medication
- ☐ Reaction - incorrect medication
- ☐ Repeated attempts to start IV
- ☐ Tubing not changed
- ☐ Wrong client

- ☐ Wrong Dose
- ☐ Wrong Flow Rate
- ☐ Wrong Medication (see below)
- ☐ Wrong Route
- ☐ Wrong Solution
- ☐ Wrong Time
- ☐ Other: _____

Medication:
Name:
Dosage:
Given:
Route:

Incident report   2

⊞ Health Care Providers   INCIDENT REPORT

Fall section

Surface condition (select one if applicable)   □ Wet   □ Unknown
                                                   □ Dry   □ Other:_____

Circumstances related to fall (select one if applicable)

□ Ambulating - with permission   □ From toilet   □ Slipped
□ Ambulating - without permission   □ From wheelchair   □ Tripped
□ Dizzy   □ Improper footwear   □ Unable to follow instructions
□ During assistance by staff   □ In shower   □ Visitor assisted client in ambulation
□ Equipment   □ In tub   without staff assistance
□ Fainted   □ Incontinent   □ Unknown
□ Found on floor   □ Lost balance   □ Other:_____
□ From bed   □ Off stretcher
□ From chair   □ Off table

Client status prior to fall (complete all)

Call light on: □ Yes   □ No   □ N/A   Risk for fall assessed before incident?   □ Yes   □ No   □ N/A
Restraints: □ Yes   □ No   □ N/A   Medication?   □ Yes   □ No
                □ Refused □ Removed   Name:_____
Side rails: □ Yes   □ No   □ N/A   Dosage:_____
                □ Refused   Was restraint policy followed?   □ Yes   □ No   □ N/A
Bed position: □ Yes   □ No   □ N/A   Was client on fall precautions?   □ Yes   □ No   □ N/A

Environmental component (select one if applicable) – Equipment

□ Disconnected   □ Preventive maintenance   □ Unknown
□ Dislodged   □ Not available   □ Other:_____
□ Equipment failure   □ Tampered with
□ Equipment malfunction □ User error

Device type:_____   Model #:_____   Serial #:_____

Hazardous materials and waste

□ Spill/leak   □ Exposure to hazardous   □ Other:_____
Utilities management   material (specify):_____
□ Medical gasses   □ Sewage problem   □ Other:_____
□ Medical vacuum   □ Telephone problem
□ Power failure   □ Water problem

Security

□ Assult   □ Breach of confidentiality □ Property loss   □ Weapon
□ Altercation   □ Gun   □ Property damage   □
□ Other:

Miscellaneous component (select all that apply)

□ Blood borne exposure   □ Provider complaint   □ Unknown
□ Client/visitor/family complain □ Readmission in 72 hours   □ Other:_____
□ Client refused treatment   □ Staff complaint
□ Elopement   □ Unauthorized alcohol
□ Fire   □ Unauthorized drugs
□ Left AMA   □ Unplanned transfer to critical care
□ Needle stick

Detailed description of the incident:

_____
_____
_____
_____
_____
_____

Incident report   **3**

Safe use of equipment

Safe use of equipment refers to the appropriate operation of health care-related equipment by educated staff. Equipment-related injuries can occur as a result of malfunction, disrepair, or mishandling of mechanical equipment. Qs

Nurses' responsibilities related to equipment safety

- Learning how to use and maintaining competency in the use of equipment
- Checking that equipment is accurately set and functioning properly (oxygen, nasogastric suction) at the beginning of and during each shift
- Ensuring that electrical equipment is grounded (three-pronged plug and grounded outlet) to decrease the risk for electrical shock
- Ensuring that outlet covers are used in environments with individuals at risk for sticking items into them
- Unplugging equipment using the plug, not the cord, to prevent bending the plug prongs, which increases the risk for electrical shock
- Ensuring that life-support equipment is plugged into outlets designated to be powered by a backup generator during power outages
- Disconnecting all electrical equipment prior to cleaning
- Ensuring that all pumps (general and PCA) have free-flow protection to prevent an overdose of fluids or medications
- Ensuring that outlets are not overcrowded and that extension cords are used only when absolutely necessary (if they must be used in an open area, tape the cords to the floor)
- Using all equipment only as it is intended
- Ensuring that equipment is regularly inspected by the engineering or maintenance department and by the user prior to use. Faulty equipment (e.g., frayed cords, disrepair) can start a fire or cause an electrical shock and should be removed from use and reported immediately per agency policy.

Specific risk areas

- Preventing injury is a major nursing responsibility.
- Many factors affect a client's ability to protect themselves. Qs
  - Age (pediatric and older adult clients are at greater risk)
  - Mobility
  - Cognitive and sensory awareness
  - Emotional state
  - Lifestyle and safety awareness
- Review facility protocol for managing specific high-risk situations.

FALLS

Prevention of client falls is a major nursing priority. Screen all clients for risk factors related to falls.

- Physiological changes associated with aging (decreased strength, impaired mobility and balance, endurance limitations, decreased sensory perception) can increase the risk of injury for some older adults. Ⓖ
- Other risk factors include decreased visual acuity, generalized weakness, orthopedic problems (diabetic neuropathy), urinary frequency, gait and balance problems (Parkinson's disease, osteoporosis, arthritis), and cognitive dysfunction. Adverse effects of medications (orthostatic hypotension, drowsiness) also can increase the risk for falls.
- Clients are at greater risk for falls when multiple risk factors are present, and clients who have fallen previously are at risk for falling again.
- To evaluate incidence of client falls, a formula based on 1,000 client days can be used. Using this formula, a facility can compare its fall rates to other facilities.

(Number of client falls ÷ number of client days) × 1,000 = fall rate per 1,000 client days

PREVENTION OF FALLS Qs

The plan for each client is individualized based on the fall risk assessment findings.

GENERAL MEASURES TO PREVENT FALLS

- Ensure that the client understands how to use all assistive devices and can locate necessary items.
- Place clients at risk for falls near the nursing station.
- Ensure that bedside tables, overbed tables, and frequently used items (telephone, water, tissues, and call light) are within the client's reach.
- Maintain the bed in low position.
- Keep bed rails up for clients who are sedated, unconscious, or otherwise compromised, and partly up for other clients.
- Avoid using full side bed rails for clients who get out of bed or attempt to get out of bed without assistance.
- Provide clients with nonskid footwear.
- Keep the floor free from clutter with a clear path to the bathroom (no scatter rugs, cords, or furniture).
- Ensure adequate lighting.
- Lock wheels on beds, wheelchairs, and carts to prevent the device from rolling during transfers or stops.
- Use chair or bed sensors to alert staff of independent ambulation for clients at risk for getting up unattended.

SEIZURES

Seizures can occur at any time during a person's life and can be due to epilepsy, fever, or a variety of medical conditions.

SEIZURE PRECAUTIONS

Seizure precautions (measures to protect the client from injury should a seizure occur) are taken for clients who have a history of seizures that involve the entire body or result in unconsciousness. Qs

Protective measures for clients who are at high risk for a seizure include the following.

- Assign the client a room close to the nurses' station and insert a peripheral IV.
- Ensure that rescue equipment, including oxygen, an oral airway, and suction equipment, is at the bedside. A saline lock can be placed for intravenous access if the client is at high risk for experiencing a generalized seizure.
- Instruct the client to use precautions such as avoiding possible seizure triggers when out of bed.
- If a seizure occurs, provide monitoring and treatment as indicated. **SEE FUNDAMENTALS CHAPTER 12: CLIENT SAFETY.**

SECLUSION AND RESTRAINTS

Seclusion and restraints are used to prevent clients from injuring themselves or others. For more about restraints, see **FUNDAMENTALS CHAPTER 12: CLIENT SAFETY.**

- Seclusion is the placement of a client in a private and safe room. Seclusion is used for clients who are at risk for injuring themselves or others.
- Physical restraint involves the application of a device that limits the client's movement. A restraint can limit the movement of the entire body or a body part.
- Chemical restraints are medications given to a client whose behavior poses a safety risk to themselves or others.

RISKS ASSOCIATED WITH RESTRAINTS Qs

- Deaths by asphyxiation and strangulation have occurred with restraints. Many facilities no longer use a vest restraint for that reason.
- The client can also experience complications related to immobility (pressure injuries, urinary and fecal incontinence, pneumonia).

LEGAL CONSIDERATIONS

- Nurses should understand agency polices as well as federal and state laws that govern the use of restraints and seclusion.
- False imprisonment means the confinement of a person without their consent. Improper use of restraints can subject the nurse to charges of false imprisonment.

GUIDELINES

- Use restraints according to the prescription parameters for the shortest time necessary. Attempt early release if the client's behavior is calm.
- Restraints are for the protection of clients or others, after all other less restrictive methods of behavior modification have been tried.
- The client or family might have a range of emotions surrounding the use of restraints. Explain the purpose of the restraint and that the restraint is only temporary.
- PRN prescriptions for restraints are not permitted.
- The treatment must be prescribed by the provider based on a face-to-face assessment of the client. In an emergency in which there is immediate risk to the client or others, the nurse can place a client in restraints. The nurse must obtain a prescription from the provider as soon as possible in accordance with agency policy (usually within 1 hr).
- The prescription must specify the reason for the restraint, the type of restraint, the location of the restraint, how long the restraint can be used, and the behaviors demonstrated by the client that warrant use of the restraint.
- In medical facilities, the prescription should be limited to 4 hr of restraints for an adult, 2 hr for clients between the ages of 9 to 17 years, and 1 hr for clients younger than 9 years of age. For adult clients who have violent or self-destructive behavior, the prescription should be for 4 hr. Providers can renew these prescriptions with a maximum of 24 consecutive hours.

NURSING RESPONSIBILITIES

Obtain a prescription from the provider for the restraint. If the client is at risk for harming self or others and a restraint is applied prior to consulting the provider, ensure that notification of the provider occurs in accordance with facility protocol. Qs

- Conduct neurosensory checks every 2 hr or according to facility policy to include:
  - Circulation
  - Sensation
  - Mobility
- Offer food and fluids.
- Provide with means for hygiene and elimination.
- Monitor vital signs.
- Provide range of motion of extremities.
- Follow agency polices regarding restraints, including the need for signed consent from the client or guardian.
- Review the manufacturer's instructions for correct application.
- Remove or replace restraints frequently.
- Pad bony prominences.
- Secure restraints (according to facility policy and procedure) to a part of the bed frame that can raise or lower when the bed controls are used. Do not secure restraints to the siderails of the bed.
- If restraints with a buckle strap are not available, use a quick-release knot to tie the strap.

- Ensure that the restraint is loose enough for range of motion and has enough room to fit two fingers between the device and the client.
- Regularly assess the need for continued use of restraints.
- Never leave the client unattended without the restraints.
- Document client data before, during, and after restraint use, as well as behavioral interventions and care measures.

FIRE SAFETY

Fires in health care facilities are usually due to problems related to electrical or anesthetic equipment. Unauthorized smoking can also be the cause of a fire.

All staff must meet the following requirements:
- Know the location of exits, alarms, fire extinguishers, and oxygen turnoff valves.
- Make sure equipment does not block fire doors.
- Know the evacuation plan for the unit and the facility.

Fire response follows the RACE sequence

R: Rescue and protect clients in close proximity to the fire by moving them to a safer location. Clients who are ambulatory can walk independently to a safe location.

A: Activate the facility's alarm system and then report the fire's details and location.

C: Confine the fire by closing doors and windows and turning off any sources of oxygen and any electrical devices. Ventilate clients who are on life support with bag-valve masks.

E: Extinguish the fire if possible using the appropriate fire extinguisher.

FIRE EXTINGUISHERS

To use a fire extinguisher, use the PASS sequence.

P: Pull the pin.

A: Aim at the base of the fire.

S: Squeeze the handle.

S: Sweep the extinguisher from side to side, covering the area of the fire.

Classes of fire extinguishers

Class A is for combustibles (paper, wood, upholstery, rags, and other types of trash fires).

Class B is for flammable liquids and gas fires.

Class C is for electrical fires.

Environmental safety

Nurses play a pivotal role in promoting safety in the client's home and community. Nurses often collaborate with the client, family, and members of the interprofessional team (social workers, occupational therapists, physical therapists) to promote client safety. QTC

When the client demonstrates factors that increase the risk for injury (regardless of age), a home hazard evaluation should be conducted by a nurse, physical therapist, and/or occupational therapist. The client is made aware of the environmental factors that can pose a risk to safety and suggested modifications to be made.

Many factors contribute to the client's risk for injury.
- Age and developmental status
- Mobility and balance
- Knowledge about safety hazards
- Sensory and cognitive awareness
- Communication skills
- Home and work environment
- Community
- Medical and pharmacological status

To initiate a plan of care, the nurse must identify risk factors using a risk assessment tool and complete a nursing history, physical examination, and home hazard appraisal.

SAFETY RISKS BASED ON AGE AND DEVELOPMENTAL STATUS

- The age and developmental status of the client create specific safety risks. QPCC
- Infants and toddlers are at risk for injury due to a tendency to put objects in their mouth and from hazards encountered while exploring their environment.
- Preschool- and school-age children often face injury from limited or underdeveloped motor coordination.
- Adolescents' risks for injury can stem from increased desire to make independent decisions and relying on peers for guidance rather than family.
- Some of the accident prevention measures for specific age groups are found below. See **FUNDAMENTALS CHAPTER 13: HOME SAFETY FOR AGE-SPECIFIC SAFETY RECOMMENDATIONS.**

INFANTS AND TODDLERS

Aspiration
- Keep all small objects out of reach.
- Cut or break food that is age-appropriate into small, bite-sized pieces.
- Do not place the infant in the supine position while feeding or to prop the infant's bottle.

Water safety

- Never leave an infant or toddler unattended in the bathtub.
- Block access to bathrooms, pools, and other standing water.
- Begin teaching water safety when developmentally appropriate.

Suffocation

- Follow recommendations for safe sleep environment and positioning for infants.
- Keep latex balloons and plastic bags away from infants and toddlers.
- Teach caregivers CPR and Heimlich maneuver.

Poisoning

- Keep houseplants and cleaning agents locked away and out of reach.
- Inspect for and remove hazardous chemicals, medications, and sources of lead from the infant's or toddler's environment.

Falls

- Prevent falls from cribs, high beds, diaper changing surfaces, stairs, and windows.
- Supervise when in a highchair, swing, stroller, or similar device, and restrain according to manufacturer's recommendations. Discontinue use when the infant or toddler outgrows size limits.

Motor vehicle injury

- Follow car seat requirements based on height, weight, and age.
- Follow recommendations for choosing a safe car seat, and always place it in the back seat.

Burns

- Supervise the use of faucets and test water temperature.
- Keep matches, lighters, and electrical equipment and sources out of reach.

PRESCHOOLERS AND SCHOOL-AGE CHILDREN

Drowning

- Be sure the child has learned to swim and knows rules of water safety.
- Prevent unsupervised access to pools or other bodies of water.
- Teach the child to wear a life jacket in boats.

Motor vehicle injury

- Follow recommendations for car seat use and placement.
- Use seat belts properly after booster seats are no longer necessary.
- Use protective equipment when participating in sports, riding a bike, or riding as a passenger on a bike.
- Teach the child safety rules of the road.

Firearms

- Keep firearms unloaded, locked up, and out of reach.
- Teach the child to never touch a gun or stay at a friend's house where a gun is accessible.
- Store bullets in a different location from guns.

Play injury

- Ensure that play equipment is the appropriate size for the child.
- Teach the child to play in safe areas and avoid heavy machinery, railroad tracks, excavation areas, quarries, trunks, vacant buildings, and empty refrigerators.
- Teach the child to avoid strangers and keep parents informed of strangers.

Burns

- Teach the child about the dangers of playing with matches, fireworks, and firearms.
- Teach school-age child how to properly use a microwave and other cooking instruments.

Poison

- Teach the child about the hazards of alcohol, cigarettes, and prescription, non-prescription, and illegal substances.
- Keep potentially dangerous substances out of reach.
- Teach parents to have the nationwide poison control number near every phone in the home and programmed in each cell phone (1-800-222-1222). Qs

ADOLESCENTS

Motor vehicle and injury

- Ensure that the teen has completed a driver's education course.
- Set rules on seat belt use, the number of people allowed to ride in a car, and calling for a ride home if a driver is impaired.
- Reinforce safety precautions for sports and hobbies.
- Teach water safety.

Burns

- Instruct the teen to use sunblock and protective clothing.
- Discuss the dangers of sunbathing and tanning beds.

Other risks

- Be alert to indications of depression, anxiety, or other behavioral changes.
- Educate the teen on the hazards of smoking, alcohol, legal and illegal substances, and unprotected sex.
- Discuss dangers of social networking and the internet.

YOUNG AND MIDDLE-AGE ADULTS

Motor vehicle crashes are a leading cause of death and injury to adults. Occupational injuries contribute to the injury and death rate of adults. High consumption of alcohol and suicide are also major concerns for adults.

CLIENT EDUCATION

- Follow recommendations for safe alcohol consumption.
- Be attuned to behaviors that suggest the presence of depression or thoughts of suicide. Seek counseling or contact a provider.
- Be proactive about safety in the workplace and in the home.
- Be aware of hazards associated with networking and the internet.
- Protect skin with the use of sun-blocking agents and protective clothing.

OLDER ADULTS

- Many older adults are able to maintain a lifestyle that promotes independence and the ability to protect themselves from safety hazards.
- Prevention is important because older adult clients can have longer recovery times from injuries and are at an increased risk for complications from injuries.

Risk factors for falls

- The rate at which age-related changes occur varies greatly among older adults. Ⓖ
- Physical, cognitive, and sensory changes
- Changes in the musculoskeletal and neurologic systems
- Impaired vision and/or hearing
- Ambulating frequently at night because of nocturia and incontinence.
- History of a previous fall

Modifications to improve home safety

- Remove items that could cause the client to trip (e.g., throw rugs).
- Provide assistive devices and safety equipment.
- Ensure that lighting is adequate inside and outside the home.

HOME SAFETY PLAN

- Keep emergency numbers near the phone for prompt use in the event of an emergency of any type.
- Develop a family plan for evacuating the home and practice it regularly.

5.4 Categories of triage during mass casualty

Emergent or immediate
(CLASS I, RED TAG)

Highest priority is given to clients who have life-threatening injuries but also have a high possibility of survival once they are stabilized.

Urgent or delayed
(CLASS II, YELLOW TAG)

Second-highest priority is given to clients who have major injuries that are not yet life-threatening and usually require treatment in 30 min to 2 hr.

Nonurgent or minimal
(CLASS III, GREEN TAG)

The next highest priority is given to clients who have minor injuries that are not life-threatening and can wait hours to days for treatment.

Expectant
(CLASS IV, BLACK TAG)

The lowest priority is given to clients who are not expected to live and will be allowed to die naturally. Comfort measures can be provided, but restorative care will not.

ADDITIONAL RISKS IN THE HOME AND COMMUNITY

Additional risks in the home and community include fires, passive smoking, carbon monoxide poisoning, and food poisoning. Natural and human-made disasters are a threat to homes and communities. Nurses should teach clients about the dangers of these additional risks.

Fire

Home fires continue to be a major cause of death and injury for people of all ages. Nurses should educate clients about the importance of a home safety plan.

- Ensure that the number and placement of fire extinguishers and smoke alarms are adequate and that they are operable.
- Be sure to close windows and doors if able.
- Exit a smoke-filled area by covering the mouth and nose with a damp cloth and getting down as close to the floor as possible.
- In the event that the clothing or skin is on fire, "stop, drop, and roll" to extinguish the fire.

Safe use of oxygen in the home

If oxygen is used in the home, oxygen safety measures should be reviewed. Oxygen can cause materials to combust more easily and burn more rapidly, so the client and family must be provided with information on use of the oxygen delivery equipment and the dangers of combustion.

- Use and store oxygen equipment according to the manufacturer's recommendations.
- Place a "No Smoking" sign in a conspicuous place near the front door of the home. A sign can also be placed on the door to the client's bedroom. Ⓠs
- Inform the client and family of the danger of smoking in the presence of oxygen. Family members and visitors who smoke should do so outside the home.
- Ensure that electrical equipment is in good repair and well grounded.
- Replace bedding that generates static electricity (wool, nylon, synthetics) with items made from cotton.
- Keep flammable materials (e.g., heating oil, nail polish remover) away from the client when oxygen is in use.
- Follow general measures for fire safety in the home (having a fire extinguisher readily available and an established exit route) should a fire occur.

Passive smoking

Passive smoking (secondhand smoke) is the unintentional inhalation of tobacco smoke.

- Exposure to nicotine and other toxins places people at risk for numerous diseases, including cancer, heart disease, and lung infections.
- Low birth weight, prematurity, stillbirths, and sudden unexpected infant death (SUID) have been associated with maternal smoking.
- Passive smoking is associated with childhood development of bronchitis, pneumonia, and middle ear infections.
- For children who have asthma, exposure to passive smoke can result in an increase in the frequency and severity of asthma attacks.

NURSING ACTIONS

- Inform clients about the hazards of smoking and exposure to smoke from cigarettes, cigars, and pipes. The effects of vapors from electronic cigarettes is unclear. ⓆEBP
- Discuss resources to stop smoking (smoking-cessation programs, medication support, self-help groups).

Carbon monoxide

- Carbon monoxide is a very dangerous gas because it binds with hemoglobin and ultimately reduces the oxygen supplied to tissues in the body.
- Carbon monoxide cannot be seen, smelled, or tasted.
- Indications of carbon monoxide poisoning include nausea, vomiting, headache, weakness, and unconsciousness.

CLIENT EDUCATION

- Ensure proper ventilation when using fuel-burning devices (lawn mowers, wood-burning and gas fireplaces, charcoal grills).
- Have gas-burning furnaces, water heaters, chimneys, flues, and appliances inspected annually.
- Flues and chimneys should be unobstructed.
- Install and maintain carbon monoxide detectors.

Food poisoning

- Most food poisoning is caused by bacteria (*Escherichia coli*, *Listeria monocytogenes*, *salmonella*).
- Very young, very old, pregnant, and immunocompromised individuals are at risk for complications.
- Clients who are especially at risk are instructed to follow a low-microbial diet.

MEASURES TO PREVENT FOOD POISONING

- Proper hand hygiene
- Ensuring that eggs, meat, and fish are cooked to the correct temperature
- Handling raw and cooked food separately to avoid cross-contamination
- Not using the same container, cutting board, or utensils for raw and cooked foods
- Refrigerating perishable items
- Washing raw fruits and vegetables before peeling, cutting, or eating
- Not consuming unpasteurized dairy products or untreated water

---

5.5 Biological incidents and their treatment and prevention

Inhalational anthrax

MANIFESTATIONS
- Fever
- Cough
- Shortness of breath
- Muscle aches
- Mild chest pain
- Meningitis
- Shock

PREVENTION: Anthrax vaccine for high-risk; ciprofloxacin & doxycycline IV/PO following exposure

TREATMENT: Includes one or two additional antibiotics (vancomycin, penicillin, and anthrax antitoxin)

Cutaneous anthrax

MANIFESTATIONS
- Starts as a lesion that can be itchy
- Develops into a vesicular lesion that later becomes necrotic with the formation of black eschar
- Fever, chills

PREVENTION: Anthrax vaccine for high-risk

TREATMENT: Ciprofloxacin, doxycycline

Botulism

MANIFESTATIONS
- Difficulty swallowing
- Double vision
- Slurred speech
- Descending progressive weakness
- Nausea, vomiting, abdominal cramps
- Difficulty breathing

PREVENTION/TREATMENT
- Airway management
- Antitoxin
- Elimination of toxin

Smallpox

MANIFESTATIONS
- High fever
- Fatigue
- Severe headache
- Rash
- Chills
- Vomiting
- Delirium

PREVENTION: Vaccine; can vaccinate within 3 days of exposure; contact and airborne precautions

TREATMENT: Supportive care (prevent dehydration, provide skin care, medications for pain and fever); antibiotics for secondary infections

Tularemia

MANIFESTATIONS
- Sudden fever, chills, headache, diarrhea, muscle aches, joint pain, dry cough, progressive weakness
- If airborne, life-threatening pneumonia and systemic infection

PREVENTION: Vaccine under review by the FDA

TREATMENT: Streptomycin or gentamicin are drugs of choice; in mass causality, use doxycycline or ciprofloxacin

Viral hemorrhagic fevers

Examples: Ebola, yellow fever

MANIFESTATIONS
- Sore throat
- Headache
- High temperature
- Nausea, vomiting, diarrhea
- Internal and external bleeding
- Shock

PREVENTION: Vaccination available for yellow fever, Argentine hemorrhagic fever; barrier protection from infected person, isolation precautions specific to disease

TREATMENT: No cure, supportive care only; minimize invasive procedures

Plague

MANIFESTATIONS
- Forms can occur separately or in combination
- Pneumonic: fever, headache, weakness, pneumonia with shortness of breath, chest pain, cough, bloody or watery sputum
- Bubonic: swollen, tender lymph glands, fever, headache, chills, weakness
- Septicemic: fever, chills, prostration, abdominal pain, shock, disseminated intravascular coagulation, gangrene of nose and digits

PREVENTION: Contact precautions until decontaminated; droplet precautions until 72 hr after antibiotics

TREATMENT: Streptomycin/gentamicin or tetracycline/doxycycline

Disasters

- Natural disasters, such a tornadoes and floods, and human-made events (forest fires or explosions) can occur without warning.
- Encourage personal emergency preparedness for clients and families, which includes gathering supplies (food, water, clothing, communication devices, extra medications, and personal documents).

Ergonomic principles

Ergonomics are the factors or qualities in an object's design and/or use that contribute to comfort, safety, efficiency, and ease of use. Qs

- Body mechanics is the proper use of muscles to maintain balance, posture, and body alignment when performing a physical task. Nurses use body mechanics when providing care to clients by lifting, bending, and carrying out the activities of daily living.
- The risk of injury to the client and the nurse is reduced with the use of good body mechanics. Whenever possible, mechanical lift devices should be used to lift and transfer clients. Many health care agencies have "no manual lift" and "no solo lift" policies.
- **SEE FUNDAMENTALS CHAPTER 14: ERGONOMIC PRINCIPLES AND CLIENT POSITIONING FOR MORE INFORMATION.**

GUIDELINES TO PREVENT INJURY

- Know your agency's policies regarding lifting.
- Plan for activities that require lifting, transfer, or ambulation of a client, and ask other staff members to be ready to assist at the time planned.
- Maintain good posture and exercise regularly to increase the strength of arm, leg, back, and abdominal muscles so these activities require less energy.
- Use smooth movements when lifting and moving clients to prevent injury through sudden or jerky muscle movements.
- When standing for long periods of time, flex the hip and knee through use of a footrest. When sitting for long periods of time, keep the knees slightly higher than the hips.
- Avoid repetitive movements of the hands, wrists, and shoulders. Take a break every 15 to 20 min to flex and stretch joints and muscles.
- Maintain good posture (head and neck in straight line with pelvis) to avoid neck flexion and hunched shoulders, which can cause impingement of nerves in the neck.
- Avoid twisting the spine or bending at the waist (flexion) to minimize the risk for injury.
- Keep objects close to the body core when lifting and bend the knees to keep the center of gravity closer to the ground.
- When lifting an object from the floor, flex the hips, knees, and back. Get the object to thigh level, keeping the knees bent and straightening the back. Stand up while holding the object as close as possible to the body, bringing the load to the center of gravity to increase stability and decrease back strain.

- Use assistive devices whenever possible and seek assistance whenever it is needed.
- Face the direction of movement when moving a client.
- Use your own body as a counterweight when pushing or pulling, which makes the movement easier. Qs
- Use sliding, rolling, and pushing movements when possible because these require less energy than lifting and have less risk for injury.
- Avoid twisting the thoracic spine and bending the back while the hips and knees are straight.
- Assess the client's ability to help with repositioning and mobility (balance, muscle strength, endurance).
- Determine the need for additional personnel or assistive devices (transfer belt, hydraulic lift, sliding board, gait belt).

Reporting incidents

Facility protocols refer to the plans and procedures in place to address specific issues that health care institutions face.

Nurses must understand their role in relation to development and implementation of facility protocols, including reporting incidents, disaster planning, emergency response, and security plans.

Incident reports are records of unexpected or unusual incidents that affected a client, employee, volunteer, or visitor in a health care facility.

- Facilities can also refer to incident reports as unusual occurrence or quality variance reports.
- In most states, if proper safeguards are employed, incident reports cannot be subpoenaed by clients or used as evidence in lawsuits.

EXAMPLES OF WHEN AN INCIDENT REPORT SHOULD BE FILED:

- Medication errors
- Procedure/treatment errors
- Equipment-related injuries/errors
- Needlestick injuries
- Client falls/injuries
- Visitor/volunteer injuries
- Threats made to clients or staff
- Loss of property (dentures, jewelry, personal wheelchair)

Nurses must ensure the safety of clients' valuables. If a client is admitted to the facility and does not have a family member present, secure the client's valuables in accordance with facility policy. If an individual requests the client's valuables, the client must identify the person and give that person permission to be in possession of the valuables.

NURSING ROLE IN REPORTING INCIDENTS

In the event of an incident that involves a client, employee, volunteer, or visitor, the nurse's priority is to assess the individual for injuries and institute any immediate care measures necessary to decrease further injury. If the incident was client-related, notify the provider and implement additional tests or treatment as prescribed. Qs

INCIDENT REPORTS

- Should be completed by the person who identifies that an unexpected event has occurred (This might not be the individual most directly involved in the incident.)
- Should be completed as soon as possible and within 24 hr of the incident
- Considered confidential and are not shared with the client (it is not acknowledged to the client that one was completed.)
- Not placed nor mentioned in the client's health care record (However, a description of the incident should be documented factually in the client's record.)
- Include an objective description of the incident and actions taken to safeguard the client, as well as assessment and treatment of any injuries sustained
- Forwarded to the risk management department or officer (varies by facility), possibly after being reviewed by the nurse manager
- Provide data for performance improvement studies regarding the incidence of client injuries and care-related errors Qⁱ

WHEN COMPLETING AN INCIDENT REPORT, INCLUDE:

- Client's name and hospital number (or visitor's name and address if visitor is injured), along with the date, time, and location of the incident
- Factual description of the incident and injuries incurred, avoiding assumptions as to the incident's cause
- Names of witnesses to the incident and client or witness comments regarding the incident
- Corrective actions that were taken, including notification of the provider and referrals
- Name and dose of any medication or identification number of any equipment involved in the incident

Disaster planning and emergency response

A disaster is an event that can cause serious damage, destruction, injuries, and death. In many situations, a hospital can manage the event with the support of local resources.

A mass casualty incident (MCI) is a catastrophic event that overwhelms local resources. Multiple resources (federal and state) are necessary to handle the crisis.

EMERGENCY OPERATING PLAN

Each facility must have an emergency operating plan (EOP). An essential component of the plan is the provision of training all personnel regarding each component of the EOP. Nurses should understand their responsibilities in the EOP.
- Facilities accredited by The Joint Commission must have an EOP and are mandated to test the plan at least twice a year. Qs
- The EOP should interface with local, state, and federal resources.

INTERNAL AND EXTERNAL EMERGENCIES

Disasters that health care facilities face include internal and external emergencies.

Internal emergencies occur within a facility and include loss of electric power or potable (drinkable) water and severe damage or casualties related to fire, weather (e.g., tornado, hurricane), explosion, or terrorist act. Readiness includes safety and hazardous materials protocols and infection control policies and practices.

External emergencies affect a facility indirectly and include weather (e.g., tornado, hurricane), volcanic eruptions, earthquakes, pandemics, chemical plant explosions, industrial accidents, building collapses, major transportation accidents, and terrorist acts (including biological and chemical warfare). Readiness includes a plan for participation in community-wide emergencies and disasters.

DISASTER RESPONSE AGENCIES

Various agencies, governmental and nongovernmental, are responsible for different levels of disaster response. Agencies that have a role in disaster response include the Federal Emergency Management Agency (FEMA), Centers for Disease Control and Prevention (CDC), U.S. Department of Homeland Security (DHS), American Red Cross, Office of Emergency Management (OEM), and the public health system.

To receive assistance with an MCI, a state must request assistance. Federal programs include the National Incident Management System, National Domestic Preparedness Organization, and Strategic National Stockpile.

NURSING ROLE IN DISASTER PLANNING AND EMERGENCY RESPONSE

EMERGENCY RESPONSE PLANS

- Health care institutions use a planning committee to develop emergency preparedness plans. The committee reviews information regarding the potential for various types of natural and human-made emergencies based on the characteristics of the community. The committee should also determine what resources are necessary to meet potential emergencies and include this information in the plan. Qs
- The Hospital Incident Command System (HICS) for disaster management offers a clear structure for disaster management at the facility level. QEBP
- Nurses and other members of the health care team should be involved in the development of an EOP for such emergencies. Criteria under which the EOP are activated should be clear. Roles for each employee should be outlined and administrative control determined. A designated area should be established for the area command center, as well as a person to serve as the incident control manager/commander.
- Key roles in the EOP include a provider to manage client numbers and resources (medical command physician), an individual to prioritize treatment (triage officer), and a media liaison (community relations/public information officer). Further information and training is available through FEMA (http://training.fema.gov).
- The nurse should create an action plan for personal family needs.
- All-hazards preparedness for human-made events includes plans for disasters of chemical, biological, radiological, nuclear, and explosive (CBRNE) nature.

MASS CASUALTY TRIAGE

Principles of mass casualty triage should be followed in health care institutions involved in a mass casualty event. Qs
- These differ from the principles of triage typically followed during provision of day-to-day services in an emergency or urgent care setting.
- During mass casualty events, casualties are separated based on their potential for survival, and treatment is allocated accordingly. This type of triage is based on doing the greatest good for the greatest number of people.
- Nurses can find this situation very stressful because clients who are not expected to survive are cared for last.

DISCHARGE/RELOCATION OF CLIENTS

During an emergency (a fire or a mass casualty event), nurses help make decisions regarding discharging clients or relocating them so their beds can be used for clients who have higher priority needs.

Nurses can use the following criteria when identifying which clients are stable enough to discharge.
- First, discharge or relocate ambulatory clients requiring minimal care.
- Next, plan for continuation of care for clients who require some assistance, which could be provided in the home or tertiary care facility.
- Do not discharge or relocate clients who are unstable or require continued nursing care and assessment unless they are in imminent danger.

TYPES OF EMERGENCIES

Biological incidents

- Be alert to indications of a possible bioterrorism attack because early detection and management is key. Often, the manifestations are similar to other illnesses.
- Be alert for the appearance of a disease that does not normally occur at a specific time or place, has atypical manifestations, or occurs in a specific community or group of people.
- In most instances, infection from biological agents is not spread from one client to another. Management of the incident includes recognition of the occurrence, directing personnel in the proper use of personal protective equipment, and, in some situations, decontamination and isolation.
- Use appropriate isolation measures.
- Transport or move clients only if needed for treatment and care.
- Take measures to protect self and others.
- Recognize indications of infection/poisoning and identify appropriate treatment interventions.

Chemical incidents

- Chemical incidents can occur as result of an accident or due to a purposeful action (terrorism).
- Take measures to protect self and avoid contact.
- Assess client and intervene to maintain airway, breathing, and circulation. Administer first aid as needed.
- Remove the offending chemical by undressing the client and removing all identifiable particulate matter. Provide immediate and prolonged irrigations of contaminated areas. Irrigate skin with running water, except for dry chemicals (lye or white phosphorus). In the case of exposure to a dry chemical, brush the agent off of clothing and skin. QEBP
- Gather a specific history of the injury, if possible (name and concentration of the chemical, duration of exposure).
- Know which facilities are open to exposed clients and which are open only to unexposed clients.
- Follow the facility's emergency response plans (personal protection measures, handling and disposal of wastes, use of space and equipment, reporting).

Hazardous material incidents

- Take measures to protect self and avoid contact.
- Approach the scene with caution.
- Identify the hazardous material with available resources (emergency response guidebook, poison control centers).
- Know the location of the Safety Data Sheet (SDS) manual.
- Try to contain the material in one place prior to the arrival of the hazardous materials team.
- Decontaminate affected individuals as much as possible at or as close as possible to the scene.
  - Don gloves, gown, mask, and shoe covers to protect self from contamination.
  - Carefully and slowly remove contaminated clothing so that deposited material does not become airborne.
  - With few exceptions, water is the universal antidote. For biological hazardous materials, wash skin with copious amounts of water and antibacterial soap.
  - Place contaminated materials into large plastic bags and seal them.

Nuclear incidents

- Damage can occur from radiation, radioactive fallout, or from the force of the blast.
- Decontamination is required.
- Treatment is symptomatic for burns and puncture injuries. Some clients can remain contaminated for years.

Explosive incidents

- Explosive incidents are the most common method used for terrorist activity. These incidents can cause injury from the heat (decomposition), airborne metal or fragments, and temperature changes.
- Treatment depends on injury type, with burns being the most common.

Radiological incidents

- The amount of exposure is related to the duration of exposure, distance from the source, and amount of shielding.
- The facility where victims are treated should activate interventions to prevent contamination of treatment areas. Floors, furniture, air vents, and ducts should be covered, and radiation-contaminated waste should be disposed of according to procedural guidelines.
- Wear water-resistant gowns, double-glove, and fully cover bodies with caps, booties, masks, and goggles.
- Wear radiation or dosimetry badges to monitor the amount of radiation exposure.
- Survey clients initially with a radiation meter to determine the amount of contamination.
- Decontamination with soap, water, and disposable towels should occur prior to the client entering the facility. Water runoff will be contaminated and should be contained.
- After decontamination, resurvey clients for residual contamination, and continue irrigation of the skin until the client is free of all contamination.

Security plans

- All facilities should have security plans in place that include preventive, protective, and response measures designed for identified security needs.
- Security issues faced by health care facilities include admission of potentially dangerous individuals, vandalism, infant abduction, and information theft.
- The International Association for Healthcare Security and Safety (IAHSS) provides recommendations for the development of security plans.

NURSING ROLE IN SECURITY PLANS

- Nurses should be prepared to take immediate action when breaches in security occur. Time is of the essence in preventing a breach in security. Qs

SECURITY MEASURES

- An identification system that identifies employees, volunteers, physicians, students, and regularly scheduled contract services staff as authorized personnel of the facility
- Electronic security systems in high-risk areas (e.g., the maternal newborn unit to prevent infant abductions, the emergency department to prevent unauthorized entrance)
  - Key code access into and out of high-risk areas
  - Wrist bands that electronically link parents and their infants
  - Alarms integrated with closed-circuit television cameras

Emergency designations

Health care facilities have color code designations for emergencies. These vary between institutions but may include any of the following examples.

- Code Red: fire
- Code Pink: newborn/infant/child abduction
- Code Orange: chemical spill
- Code Blue: medical emergency
- Code Gray: tornado
- Code Black: bomb threat

In addition, some hospitals use plain language descriptions for significant alerts, such as violent situations or evacuations (e.g., "Facility Alert: active shooter, main lobby.")

Nurses should be familiar with procedures and policies that outline proper measures to take when one of these emergencies is called.

Fire

In the event of a fire or suspected threat, follow the RACE mnemonic to guide the order of actions and the PASS mnemonic for use of a fire extinguisher, if indicated. The specific fire information is detailed under fire safety earlier in this chapter.

- In most facilities, when the fire alarm system is activated, some systems are automatically shut down (e.g., the oxygen flow system).
- Ensure fire doors are not blocked; many will close automatically when the alarm system is activated.

Severe thunderstorm/tornado

- Draw shades and close drapes to protect against shattering glass.
- Lower all beds to the lowest position and move beds away from the windows.
- Place blankets over all clients who are confined to beds.
- Close all doors.
- Relocate ambulatory clients into the hallways (away from windows) or other secure locations designated by the facility. Qs
- Do not use elevators.
- Turn on the severe weather channel to monitor severe weather warnings.

Bomb threat

- If a bomb-like device is located, do not touch it. Clear the area and isolate the device as much as possible by closing doors, for example.
- Notify the appropriate authorities and personnel (police, administrator, director of nursing).
- Cooperate with police and others: Assist with conducting a search as needed, provide copies of floor plans, have master keys available, and watch for and isolate suspicious objects (packages and boxes).
- Keep elevators available for authorities.
- Remain calm and alert and try not to alarm clients.

WHEN A PHONE CALL IS RECEIVED
- Extend the conversation as long as possible.
- Listen for distinguishing background noises (music, voices, traffic, airplanes).
- Note distinguishing voice characteristics of the caller.
- Ask where and when the bomb is set to explode.
- Note whether the caller is familiar with the physical arrangement of the facility.

Active shooter situation

These situations involve one or more persons trying to kill people in a confined area. Recommendations from the U.S. Department of Homeland Security on responding to an active shooter situation involve running, hiding, and fighting. Qs

- Running involves evacuation if there is a clear path of exit. This includes leaving without belongings and instructing others to follow but not waiting if they do not. It also includes keeping others from entering an area where the shooter might be.
- Hiding is the second option if it is not possible to evacuate the area. Key concepts include hiding out of view, locking or blocking the entry to the location, and remaining quiet and preventing noises (cell phones).
- Fighting involves taking action against the shooter if evacuating and hiding are not options. This should be done only if danger is imminent. This involves aggressive acts to stop or wound the shooter by throwing items or using weapons and yelling.
- General measures include calling 911 when safe, even if unable to talk; not attempting to move wounded people until the scene is safe; and remaining calm and quiet. If police enter the scene, keep hands visible and remain cooperative.

Active Learning Scenario

A nurse serving on a disaster preparedness committee is reviewing information about smallpox. Use the ATI Active Learning Template: Basic Concept to complete this item.

EXPECTED FINDINGS: List at least three manifestations.

NURSING CARE: List at least two treatment measures.

Active Learning Scenario Key

Using the ATI Active Learning Template: Basic Concept
EXPECTED FINDINGS
- High fever
- Fatigue
- Severe headache
- Rash
- Chills
- Vomiting
- Delirium

NURSING CARE
- Prevent dehydration.
- Provide skin care.
- Administer medications for pain and fever.
- Provide vaccination if within 3 days of exposure.
- Implement contact and airborne precautions.
- Administer antibiotics for secondary infections.

Ⓝ *NCLEX® Connection:*
Safety and Infection Control, Emergency Response Plan

Application Exercises

1. A nurse is planning safety interventions at a new clinic. Which of the following interventions should the nurse include?

   A. Have staff who will be performing x-rays wear dosimeters.

   B. Provide both latex and non-latex gloves for employees.

   C. Place sharps containers outside client rooms.

   D. Provide electrical tape for staff to repair frayed cords.

2. A nurse on an acute care unit is caring for a client after a total hip arthroplasty. The client is confused and repeatedly attempts to get out of bed. After determining that restraint application is indicated, which of the following actions should the nurse take? (Select all that apply.)

   A. Secure the restraint to a part of the bed frame that can raise and lower with bed controls.

   B. Obtain a prescription for restraints from the provider.

   C. Have a family member sign the consent for restraints.

   D. Tie the restraint to the side rail using a double knot.

   E. Ensure that only one finger can be inserted between the restraint and the client.

3. A nurse is reviewing the hospital's fire safety policies and procedures with newly hired assistive personnel. The nurse is describing what to do when there is a fire in a client's trash can. Which of the following instructions should the nurse include? (Select all that apply.)

   A. The first step is to pull the alarm.

   B. Use a Class C fire extinguisher to put out the fire.

   C. Instruct ambulatory clients to evacuate to a safe place.

   D. Pull the pin on the fire extinguisher prior to use.

   E. Close all doors.

4. A nurse is observing a newly licensed nurse and an assistive personnel (AP) pull a client up in bed using a drawsheet. Which of the following actions by the newly licensed nurse indicates an understanding of this technique?

   A. The nurse stands with both feet together.

   B. The nurse uses their body weight to counter the client's weight.

   C. The nurse's feet are facing inward, toward the center of the bed.

   D. The nurse rotates the waist while pulling the client upward.

Application Exercises Key

1. A. **CORRECT:** When generating solutions, the nurse should identify that radiation is a hazardous material. Provide dosimeters for staff to measure their cumulative radiation exposure.
   B. The nurse should use non-latex products, when possible, to reduce the risk for latex allergy development or reactions.
   C. The nurse should place sharps containers at the point of care to reduce the risk for needlestick injury.
   D. The nurse should instruct staff to remove equipment with frayed cords from the client care area and have someone certified repair the equipment.

   Ⓝ NCLEX® Connection: Safety and Infection Control, Safe Use of Equipment

2. A. **CORRECT:** When taking actions, the nurse should identify that restraints should be secured to a part of the bed frame that can raise or lower when the bed controls are used and according to facility policy and procedure.
   B. **CORRECT:** The nurse should obtain a prescription from the provider as soon as possible, typically within 1 hr. The nurse should identify that most agencies encourage informed consent for restraints.
   C. **CORRECT:** Instruct the family on the purpose of, alternatives to, and requirements for restraints.
   D. A quick-release knot must be used to secure the restraint. Do not secure restraints to the siderails of the bed.
   E. The distance between the restraint and the client should be two finger widths.

   Ⓝ NCLEX® Connection: Safety and Infection Control, Use of Restraints/Safety Devices

3. A. Know the RACE sequence: rescue the client, pull the alarm, confine the fire, and then extinguish the fire.
   B. The nurse should identify that class A fire extinguishers are used for paper, wood, and cloth.
   C. **CORRECT:** When taking actions, the nurse should identify that ambulatory clients can walk by themselves to a safe place.
   D. **CORRECT:** The fire extinguisher PASS sequence should be used: pull the pin, aim at the base of the fire, squeeze the lever, and sweep the fire extinguisher from side to side.
   E. **CORRECT:** The employee should close all doors to contain the fire. Also note that when a fire occurs in a client's room, the first step to take is to remove or evacuate the client from the room.

   Ⓝ NCLEX® Connection: Safety and Infection Control, Accident/Error/Injury Prevention

4. A. When pulling a client up in bed, spread both legs apart to create a wide base of support.
   B. **CORRECT:** When evaluating outcomes, the nurse should identify that the newly licensed nurse should use their body weight to counter the client's weight, which will make pulling easier.
   C. Both feet should point at the head of the bed instead of the center of the bed.
   D. Avoid rotating and twisting while moving clients to prevent injury.

   Ⓝ NCLEX® Connection: Management of Care, Assignment, Delegation and Supervision

References

Agency for Healthcare Research and Quality. (2022). *What is patient experience?* https://www.ahrq.gov/cahps/about-cahps/patient-experience/index.html

Alfahd, H., & Longo, J. (2021). "I'm here for you": Understanding the caring role of nurse preceptor in patient safety. *International Journal of Human Caring.* https://doi.org/10.20467/IJHC-2021-0018

American Hospital Association. (2022). *The patient care partnership: Understanding expectations, rights, and responsibilities.* https://www.aha.org/other-resources/patient-care-partnership

American Nurses Association. (2015). *American nurses' association code of ethics for nurses.* https://nursing.rutgers.edu/wp-content/uploads/2019/06/ANA-Code-of-Ethics-for-Nurses.pdf

American Nurses Association. (2016). *Nursing administration: Scope and standards of practice.* (2nd ed). ANA.

American Nurses Association. (2018). ANA position statement: Nursing advocacy for LGBTQ+ populations. *OJIN: The Online Journal of Issues in Nursing, 24*(1). https://doi.org/10.3912/OJIN.Vol24No01PoSCol02

American Nurses Association. (2019). *Guide for engagement with legislators.* https://www.nursingworld.org/~4a4e48/globalassets/practiceandpolicy/guide-for-engagement-with-legislators--2019.pdf

Cherry, B., & Jacob, S. R. (2019). *Contemporary nursing: Issues, trends, & management* (8th ed.). Elsevier.

Healthy Nurse Healthy Nation. (2022). *About HNHN.* https://www.healthynursehealthynation.org/about/about-hnhn/

Institute of Medicine (US) Committee on Quality of Health Care in America. (2016). *Crossing the quality chasm: A new health system for the 21st century.* https://www.ncbi.nlm.nih.gov/books/NBK222265/

Marquis, B. L. & Huston, C. J. (2021). *Leadership roles and management functions in nursing: theory and application* (10th ed.). Wolters Kluwer.

National Academy of Sciences Engineering Medicine. (2021). *The future of nursing 2020-2030: Charting a path to achieve health equity.* http://nap.nationalacademies.org/25982

National Council of State Boards of Nursing. (2019). *NCLEX-RN examination: Test plan for the National Council Licensure examination for registered nurses.* https://www.ncsbn.org/testplans.htm

National Council of State Boards of Nursing. (2022). *About the NLC.* https://www.nursecompact.com/about.htm

Nurse Licensure Compact. (n.d.). *Key provisions of the NLC.* https://www.ncsbn.org/public-files/NLC_Key_Provisions-FINAL.pdf

Picker. (2022). *The Picker principles of person-centered care.* https://picker.org/who-we-are/the-picker-principles-of-person-centred-care/

Potter, P. A., Perry, A. G., Stockert, P. A. & Hall, A.M. (2021). *Fundamentals of nursing* (10th ed.). Elsevier.

U.S. Bureau of Labor Statistics. (2018). *Occupational injuries and illnesses among registered nurses.* https://www.bls.gov/opub/mlr/2018/article/pdf/occupational-injuries-and-illnesses-among-registered-nurses.pdf

United States Census Bureau. (2019). *Living longer: Historical and projected gains to life expectancy, 1960-2020.* http://www.census.gov

United States Census Bureau. (2022). *About the topic of race.* https://www.census.gov/topics/population/race/about.html

World Health Organization. (2022). *Social determinants of health.* https://www.who.int/health-topics/social-determinants-of-health#tab=tab_1

STUDENT NAME _____

CONCEPT_____ REVIEW MODULE CHAPTER_____

Related Content

(E.G., DELEGATION,
LEVELS OF PREVENTION,
ADVANCE DIRECTIVES)

Underlying Principles

Nursing Interventions

WHO? WHEN? WHY? HOW?

STUDENT NAME _____

PROCEDURE NAME _____ REVIEW MODULE CHAPTER_____

Description of Procedure

Indications

Interpretation of Findings

Potential Complications

CONSIDERATIONS

Nursing Interventions (pre, intra, post)

Client Education

Nursing Interventions

Growth and Development

STUDENT NAME _____

DEVELOPMENTAL STAGE _____ REVIEW MODULE CHAPTER_____

EXPECTED GROWTH AND DEVELOPMENT

Physical Development	Cognitive Development	Psychosocial Development	Age-Appropriate Activities

Health Promotion

Immunizations	Health Screening	Nutrition	Injury Prevention

ACTIVE LEARNING TEMPLATE: *Medication*

STUDENT NAME _____

MEDICATION _____ REVIEW MODULE CHAPTER_____

CATEGORY CLASS_____

PURPOSE OF MEDICATION

Expected Pharmacological Action

Therapeutic Use

Complications

Medication Administration

Contraindications/Precautions

Nursing Interventions

Interactions

Client Education

Evaluation of Medication Effectiveness

STUDENT NAME _____

SKILL NAME_____ REVIEW MODULE CHAPTER_____

Description of Skill

Indications

CONSIDERATIONS

Nursing Interventions (pre, intra, post)

Outcomes/Evaluation

Client Education

Potential Complications

Nursing Interventions

ACTIVE LEARNING TEMPLATE: *System Disorder*

STUDENT NAME ______________________

DISORDER/DISEASE PROCESS ______________________ REVIEW MODULE CHAPTER ________

Alterations in Health (Diagnosis)

Pathophysiology Related to Client Problem

Health Promotion and Disease Prevention

ASSESSMENT

Risk Factors

Expected Findings

Laboratory Tests

Diagnostic Procedures

SAFETY CONSIDERATIONS

Complications

PATIENT-CENTERED CARE

Nursing Care

Medications

Client Education

Therapeutic Procedures

Interprofessional Care

STUDENT NAME _____

PROCEDURE NAME _____   REVIEW MODULE CHAPTER_____

Description of Procedure

Indications

CONSIDERATIONS

Nursing Interventions (pre, intra, post)

Outcomes/Evaluation

Client Education

Potential Complications

Nursing Interventions

STUDENT NAME _____

CONCEPT ANALYSIS_____

Defining Characteristics

Antecedents

(WHAT MUST OCCUR/BE IN PLACE FOR
CONCEPT TO EXIST/FUNCTION PROPERLY)

Negative Consequences

(RESULTS FROM IMPAIRED ANTECEDENT —
COMPLETE WITH FACULTY ASSISTANCE)

Related Concepts

(REVIEW LIST OF CONCEPTS AND IDENTIFY, WHICH
CAN BE AFFECTED BY THE STATUS OF THIS CONCEPT
— COMPLETE WITH FACULTY ASSISTANCE)

Exemplars